COMBAT

Twelve Years in the
U.S. Senate

COMBAT

Twelve Years in the U.S. Senate

WARREN B. RUDMAN

Random House

New York

Library of Congress Cataloging-in-Publication Data
Rudman, Warren B.
Combat : Twelve years in the U.S. Senate / Warren B. Rudman. — 1st ed.
p.   cm.
Includes index.
ISBN 0-679-44135-2
1. United States—Politics and government—1981–1989.   2. United
States—Politics and government—1989–1993.   3. United States.
Congress.   Senate—History—20th century.   4. Rudman, Warren B.
I. Title.
E876.R83   1996
320.973—dc20   95-49804

Manufactured in the United States of America on acid-free paper
24689753
First Edition

To my parents,
Edward and Theresa Rudman

ACKNOWLEDGMENTS

I want to thank a number of friends and associates who helped me produce this book.

Two wonderful women, Kathy Gowen and Marion Phelan, who worked with me in the Senate and continue with me now in private life, gave me the benefit of their recollections, helped with typing and transcriptions, and read and commented on the manuscript. Three talented men who served on my Senate staff were generous with their time as we summoned up past legislative battles: Bob Stevenson, my press secretary; Tom Polgar, my legislative director; and Bill Cowan, who advised me on intelligence matters. Brady Toensing was a tremendous help in assisting with the research.

I owe a special debt of gratitude to my dear friend Senator William Cohen of Maine. A gifted writer, Bill read the manuscript, chapter by chapter, and made suggestions that could only come from someone who shared a common experience. Two of America's finest lawyers were also generous with their memories and analysis: Arthur Liman and Mark Belnick, who were chief counsel and deputy chief counsel, respectively, to the select committee that investigated the Iran-Contra affair.

I thank my editor, Jason Epstein, whose enthusiasm, patient prodding and wise counsel contributed so much to the book. My deep appreciation also goes to Joy de Menil of Random House, who was so helpful in guiding me through the myriad details involved in publishing a book.

Finally, there is little I can say to express my gratitude to Patrick Anderson. An author of distinction, Pat assisted this fledgling writer and gave the book structure and whatever form and flair it may have. I am in his debt.

CONTENTS

Contents

COMBAT

Twelve Years in the
U.S. Senate

INTRODUCTION

A Lovely Visit
to the White House

An Arctic cold front had blown in overnight and was howling down Pennsylvania Avenue as Phil Gramm, my Senate colleague from Texas, and I drove from Capitol Hill to the White House. As we passed the great domed National Gallery of Art, I confessed I'd never visited it.

"Me neither," Phil drawled.

We were Hill dwellers, workaholics who rarely ventured downtown except when we were invited to the White House. My Washington world was bounded by my Senate office, the Capitol, my nearby apartment and the Monocle restaurant, where I sometimes dined with colleagues and friends. New Hampshire was my home; Capitol Hill was where I worked.

We passed homeless men huddled on the street corners, ragged reminders of the economic mess that Phil and I were trying to put right. That was why we were headed for the White House on this frigid morning of December 18, 1985, because along with Fritz Hollings of South Carolina we'd cosponsored the Gramm-Rudman-Hollings deficit-reduction bill that had just passed Congress and that Ronald Reagan was, reluctantly, honoring with a White House ceremony.

Phil and I cleared security, parked on the White House grounds and hurried shivering into the mansion. Once inside, we were in a different world, a world that was warm, serene and infinitely pleasing. Fires blazed in fireplaces as we made our way to the State Dining Room, where a gingerbread house, poinsettias, ivy and other decorations marked the holiday season.

As always, I was moved by the great portrait of Lincoln that hung above the mantel. If Congress had shown a fraction of his courage in meeting our economic challenge we wouldn't be in this mess.

Congressional colleagues and senior Reagan administration officials greeted Phil and me with handshakes and congratulations. They had come to honor the new Gramm-Rudman-Hollings law that was intended to end the annual budget deficits that were running $200 billion a year and threatened to wreck America's economy. Phil and I had conceived the law, and with the help of Fritz Hollings we'd rammed it through Congress in one remarkable three-month political offensive.

I should have been happy that morning, for this was the pinnacle of my political career. I was a first-term senator from a small New England state who had just won a historic legislative victory and more acclaim than many senators enjoy in a lifetime. In fact, as I accepted the compliments of my peers, I was wary, and I was angry.

Three months earlier, when we introduced our bill, the White House and congressional leaders had resisted—our radical scheme proposed to take away their power to spend without limit and without consequences—but our plan won such overwhelming public support that the politicians had no choice but to support it. Yet their priorities had not changed. They paid lip service to Gramm-Rudman-Hollings and its goal of a balanced budget, but three months of infighting had taught me how few of them really wanted deficit reduction if it interfered with their political ambitions. Our bill would inevitably mean less spending and probably higher taxes—the last things most politicians wanted to offer their constituents.

As more than a hundred guests waited for the president to arrive, the State Dining Room was aglow, not just with Christmas decorations and television lights but with the laughter and self-satisfied buzz of politicians who were exactly where they wanted to be, at the center of their universe. Many of the men around me dreamed of taking up residence in the White House—Jack Kemp, Bob Dole, Dick Cheney, Dick Gephardt and, of course, Phil Gramm—but until that blessed day arrived, visits like this were the next-best thing.

Phil, Fritz and I stood at the front of the room, greeting colleagues who'd helped pass our bill. The names Gramm, Rudman and Hollings may be forever linked by our legislation, but we were an unlikely trio. I was a lawyer and former prosecutor from New Hampshire—hard-nosed, I have been called, or even pugnacious. Phil, a brilliant, acerbic Georgia-born conservative turned Texan—and Democrat turned Republican—was possibly the least popular member of the Senate, which didn't bother him one bit. Fritz, the Democrat on our team, was a prickly, patrician South Carolinian who was a true deficit hawk but was never entirely sure that our legislation was the way to go. In time he would disown our bill entirely, causing Phil Gramm to quip, "Fritz not only wants a divorce, he wants to deny paternity!"

Cheers rocked the room as President Ronald Reagan marched in. As always, I was struck by his remarkable bearing, his ruddy complexion, his physical grace and the regal way he could disarm you with the twinkle in his eye, his Irish grin, that little nod of his head. Perhaps Reagan had never been a full-fledged star in Hollywood, but he had achieved historic stardom in politics. A year earlier he had carried forty-nine of the fifty states in winning reelection. Whatever his shortcomings as president, he towered above the political landscape.

When Reagan came to shake my hand, I thought to myself, I love this man, he is a wonderful, warm human being, and he's been good for the country. He may not like our legislation, he may not understand how dangerous the deficit really is, but he's a great leader, and now he must be persuaded to lead the fight against the deficit.

I believed then, and still do, that the deficit threatens our national survival. At that point, in December of 1985, with the passage of Gramm-Rudman-Hollings, Congress and the president had in theory put aside the madness of ever-increasing, trillion-dollar debt and pledged to move toward a balanced budget. But in truth many of my colleagues were addicted to deficit spending. I feared it would take more than pretty words—more, even, than an act of Congress—to cure their habit. Many conflicting interests filled the State Dining Room that morning, and I knew that for all this pomp and ceremony the deficit battle was far from won.

That was why we desperately needed the leadership that only Ronald Reagan could provide. Yet he had been ambivalent about our legislation. Reagan painted with a broad brush, cared little for details and relied heavily on his staff. During his first term few of those close to him dared confront him with the unpleasant truth that his huge tax cut and defense buildup, combined with his relatively minor spending cuts and refusal to consider new taxes, had not reduced the trillion-dollar debt he inherited but—amazingly and tragically—had doubled it.

That was the dirty little secret of the Reagan years: the Great Budget Balancer of the campaign trail had become the Great Deficit Spender of the Oval Office. Our legislation, no matter how you sliced it, was a stinging rebuke to the failure of Reaganomics.

I thought of two Reagan stalwarts who were not there that morning. David Stockman, the young Michigan congressman who had been Reagan's first budget director, had recently taken his talents to Wall Street—skipped town just in time, some would say. It was Stockman who in 1981 had used dubious reasoning and cooked-up numbers to convince Reagan, Congress and the nation that somehow, via the miracle of "supply-side economics," we could combine multibillion-dollar tax cuts with multibillion-dollar increases in defense spending and achieve a balanced budget.

It didn't add up—you had to take it on faith—and many of us had been skeptical. Howard Baker, the Senate majority leader, had called Reaganomics a "riverboat gamble." Later I told Howard that we'd not only lost the gamble but lost the boat. Yet Howard and I and majorities in both houses of Congress had supported Reagan's gamble, in part because of Stockman's super-salesmanship but mostly because we had seen no alternative to giving a newly elected, immensely popular president what he wanted.

Did I feel guilt for my complicity in this economic disaster? Yes, I did, and my crusade for Gramm-Rudman-Hollings was my way of atoning.

I was angry at advisers like Stockman, who I thought had acted out of personal ambition and political ideology to mislead Reagan and everyone else. I blamed Jack Kemp, too, but I thought he was sincere, a true believer in the supply-side dogma. If Stockman had been the chief financial officer of a Fortune 500 corporation, had misled his bosses as willfully as he misled Reagan and had produced a comparable disaster, he would have gone to prison, not Wall Street. I would gladly have prosecuted the case.

Cap Weinberger, the secretary of defense, was another no-show that morning—and no wonder. He hated our legislation and had urged the president to veto it. Weinberger feared, with good reason, that our legislation's automatic spending cuts, if invoked, would end the military buildup that had been the hallmark of the Reagan years.

Just eight days earlier, in a final, futile attack on Gramm-Rudman-Hollings, Weinberger had authorized his Pentagon spokesman to declare that its passage would send "a message of comfort to the Soviets."

As far as I was concerned, that came pretty close to accusing me and my colleagues of treason, and Cap Weinberger was well aware that I'd fought for my country in Korea, as well as for the Reagan military buildup in the Senate. It was just as well that Weinberger had skipped this ceremony. At the very least, I'd have told him exactly what I thought of his accusations, and I wouldn't have spoken in the Christmas spirit.

The president began his remarks, with Fritz, Phil, Bob Dole, Jack Kemp, Dan Rostenkowski, Dick Cheney, Connie Mack and me lined up behind him. I listened eagerly as Reagan spoke. What he said this morning mattered. Now was the time for the Great Communicator to rally America, to ring the bells for deficit reduction, to make it clear that this was the top priority of his three remaining years in office, even if it meant less defense spending and even higher taxes.

Instead, he started talking about tax reform.

"There's good news in the paper this morning," Reagan began with his famous grin. "Tax reform is alive and kicking."

The audience laughed. I didn't. I couldn't believe what I was hearing. Reagan's obsession with cutting taxes had helped double the deficit—and now he was plugging his ill-advised plan for even more tax breaks when he should have been speaking out for deficit reduction.

Eventually, he got around to our bill. "Now, Phil, Warren and Fritz, you who have given your names to Gramm-Rudman-Hollings, also deserve our congratulations. From now on, when the public hears the names Gramm, Rudman or Hollings, they'll think of deficit reduction."

No, I thought, not if you and your staff have your way, because you'll never let it work.

"We must move forward from here with all deliberate speed," the president continued, "to pass a tax reform bill that will spur economic growth, create jobs and give America's families the long overdue tax relief that they deserve."

I was furious. This ode to tax reform was the wrong speech at the wrong time. Reagan wove in a little lukewarm praise for Gramm-Rudman-Hollings, but his heart was not in it, and he soon returned to his favorite themes—his determination to veto any tax increases and to push on with his military buildup.

Perhaps I should have expected no better. This elegant White House ceremony was a kind of shotgun wedding. Eight days earlier, on December 10, after House and Senate conferees had agreed on the final version of Gramm-Rudman-Hollings, the president had issued a statement in support of the legislation, but with many reservations. "While this proposal is welcome," he said, "I am concerned that in the extreme it could have adverse effects on maintaining adequate levels of defense spending."

Two days later, the president signed our bill, in the privacy of his office, with no ceremony or media. He didn't sign it in the dead of night, but he might as well have. His statement spent less time praising our bill than it did discussing a possible constitutional challenge to it in court, one that we suspected he would not mind a bit.

The president's tortured comments on Gramm-Rudman-Hollings reflected the profound reservations he and his advisers felt for what we had done. In purely rhetorical terms, no man ever loved a balanced budget more than Ronald Reagan, but what he really wanted was lower taxes and more military spending.

After the White House took some heat from Congress and the media for its December 12 nonceremony, the president's men reluctantly scheduled this ambiguous gathering on the eighteenth. On the face of it, everyone was praising Gramm-Rudman-Hollings. In reality, the president and his advisers bitterly resented our meddling, many Democrats hoped to turn our law to their political advantage, and almost no one gave a damn about the deficit.

By the time the president finished his remarks I was seething. I hated this gilded hypocrisy. If Reagan disliked our bill so much, why hadn't he vetoed it? The president finished his statement, took no questions and made a quick exit. His guests were welcome to linger, and reporters were seeking interviews, but as soon as I could, I grabbed Phil and hustled us back into the bitter cold of the real world.

As we drove away from the White House the sometimes dour Phil was bubbling. "Oh, God, I love that man," he said. "Isn't he great?"

"Phil," I said, "doesn't it bother you that he talked about everything but our bill? Why did he keep talking about defense? There can't be any more defense increases unless we raise taxes—and he won't raise taxes. Why not tell the truth?"

"Aw hell, Warren, you don't go to the White House for a root canal," Phil said.

"Sometimes a root canal is what you need," I grumbled. "Listen, Phil, these people aren't on our side. They're going to look for ways around the law."

"Don't be such a pessimist," Phil said. "It'll work out."

"I don't think so," I argued. "We won't hit the reduction targets."

"If we don't, we'll come close."

"I'm not even sure we'll come close. You heard the president—he's not committed. Neither are the Democrats or a lot of our own people. They talk a good game but they'll look for ways to keep spending. They'll cook the numbers."

We lapsed into silence. Phil had heard enough of my gloomy predictions. I was sick of them too. I was by nature an optimist, an activist, someone who made things happen. But the president's halfhearted support for our legislation had left me angry and depressed.

Yet I was determined too. As we neared the Capitol, I vowed to do everything in my power to protect our legislation. I imagined myself as a pioneer father, surrounded by rampaging Indians who wanted to kidnap his baby, and I vowed to fight to the end to protect the little fellow. I knew how to play the inside game at the Senate, and I would go public too, give speeches, go on television, debate critics, do anything I could to keep public opinion focused on the deficit.

That's how it was to be a United States senator in 1985 who believed that our government must live within its means. I was outnumbered, outgunned by colleagues who were blindly, blithely spending America into ruin.

It wasn't how I'd expected to feel when I arrived in the Senate five years earlier, proud to be part of the Reagan revolution, bursting with plans for balancing the budget and changing the world. It wasn't what I'd expected at all.

CHAPTER ONE

ARRIVALS

From Ellis Island to the Senate

This book tells of my service in the United States Senate from 1981 until 1993, with particular focus on four events I was deeply involved in: the Gramm-Rudman balanced-budget law, the Iran-Contra hearings, the Ethics Committee investigation of the Keating Five and the nomination of my friend David Souter to the Supreme Court.

Three of these events embody the three responsibilities of the Senate that are set out in the Constitution: to legislate (Gramm-Rudman); to advise and consent on presidential nominations (the Souter nomination); and to enforce its own rules (the Keating Five investigation). A fourth responsibility, oversight over the executive branch, is not stated in the Constitution but has evolved over the past century, and is seen here in the Iran-Contra hearings.

As a moderate Republican, I often found myself in the middle, reaching out to both Democrats and conservative Republicans for coalitions and consensus, and never more than in these four episodes. I saw myself not only as a man in the middle but a man of the middle, trying to keep America moving forward in an increasingly bitter and partisan era. Few of my colleagues were fortunate enough to play such central roles in so many historic events of that era. I want to describe them not from the outside looking in, as journalists do, but from the inside, as a participant.

Originally I intended to focus exclusively on these four case histories, as examples of how today's Senate works—or fails to work. But I came to see that simply to tell those stories might not be enough. The reader would also want to know about this fellow Rudman. Who is he? Where did he get his opinions and values, his self-confidence and stubbornness? What made him such a combative legislator?

The story begins in the 1880s, when the teenager who became Abraham Rudman left his home in a village on the Russian-Polish border and made his way to America. He had only a few dollars in his pocket and spoke no English. His parents sent him halfway around the world because they feared the pogroms in Russia and the other dangers that made life miserable for poor Jews. At Ellis Island, my grandfather was given the name Rudman. We never knew what it had been before that. He was not a man to look back.

Abraham made his way to the Lower East Side, but soon he tired of tenements and sidewalks. One day he asked someone where he could find mountains and lakes and trees. This person told him he should get on the Boston train and ride it to the end of the line to a place called Maine.

My grandfather followed the advice, and in Maine he was befriended by a remarkable family named Wolman. He went to work on their farm north of Bangor and began to learn English. Soon he brought to America and married his distant cousin Dora, who came from Odessa. She was tall and fair, and five years younger than he.

A retired professor who lived on the farm taught Dora English. Soon she was reading classical literature, and both Abe and Dora spoke English like true Down-Easters. In time they bought a little hand-operated bottling machine and started bottling ginger ale in their home. They secured the franchise to bottle a popular carbonated drink called Moxie and moved to Portland, where my grandfather ran the Rudman Bottling Company. Then they moved to Boston, where he operated restaurants and other businesses.

Of Abe and Dora's five children, the oldest, my uncle Ben, went to the University of Maine and Tufts Medical School. The second, Morris, graduated from Harvard and Harvard Law. My uncle Sid also went to Harvard. My aunt Rita went to Wellesley.

My father went to work.

His name was Edward and he was born in 1897, the third of the four sons, and was considered by my grandfather to be the hardest-working, most serious of the boys. I remember him as a rugged, can-do man, about five-eight with broad shoulders and a big chest. While his older brothers went into law and medicine, my father followed his father into business—bottling, restaurants and similar ventures. Like his older brothers, he served in the army in the First World War.

After the war, in 1920 or so, my father read that the Canadian government was granting businessmen the timber rights to a hundred acres of land for every Canadian lumberjack they employed. He borrowed some money from his father, bought a portable sawmill, put it in the back of a truck, and drove to Magog, Quebec, where he hired a hundred lumberjacks and headed into the woods. He didn't speak a word of French, but somehow he and the lumberjacks built a sawmill and a log cabin. He stayed a year, made good money selling timber, then sold the sawmill and came home.

Soon he was building houses in Portland, living with his parents in Boston, and taking night courses in design and law. He was a voracious reader and had developed an interest in antiques. His many interests came together in the mid-1920s, when he bought a small company that reproduced antique furniture. He named it Old Colony Furniture. In 1928 my uncle Sid graduated from Harvard and my father made him his partner. Together, they ran Old Colony for nearly forty years.

In 1928 my grandfather was visiting friends when he met a young woman from New York. Her name was Theresa—Tess—and she was a Juilliard graduate who was teaching piano. Her family, the Levensons, had come to America from a village in Latvia and settled in the Bronx. Tess was a strikingly beautiful young woman, with black hair, blue eyes and a fair complexion. She's still beautiful today in her early nineties.

My grandfather was so impressed with Tess that he arranged for her to meet my father. They were married in 1929. I was born the next year, followed by my sisters, Carol and Jean.

In the mid-1930s my father decided to leave Boston and open a new plant in Nashua, New Hampshire. He borrowed about a hundred thousand dollars from a Yankee banker named George Thurber and converted an old mill near the Nashua River into his new factory, but two weeks before it was to open, the worst flood in New Hampshire history hit Nashua.

Everything was gone: lumber, tools, machinery, either ruined or swept down the river. None of it was insured. My father went to Thurber and said he was wiped out but if the banker would lend him more money, he'd rebuild and pay back every dime. Thurber approved a bank loan, and when that wasn't enough, added his own personal loan. In time my father paid him off, and Old Colony went on to achieve an international reputation for quality.

When the Second World War came, my uncle Sid, in his late thirties, became an officer in the army air corps. My uncle Ben, who had been an army doctor in the First World War, was commissioned a colonel in the medical corps. He worked all week in Boston with soldiers who'd been wounded in battle and often horribly maimed. On weekends he would flee to my parents' home in Nashua and take refuge in flowers. He would drive up in his 1939 LaSalle convertible, with a rumble seat I so admired, and immediately go to work in the garden. Sometimes, after the sun went down, he would keep on working by the headlights of his car.

During the war, Old Colony built furniture for the navy, as well as glider wings and parts, and even wooden bodies for army trucks. My father charged the army about half as much as other contractors, and at one meeting the others insisted that he charge more. He angrily refused. He hated the idea of making money from the war. His reward came when the army several times presented him with its "E"—for Excellence—award.

During the late 1930s my father with the help of some of his craftsmen built a beautiful Dutch Colonial home in a fine neighborhood in Nashua. When I was growing up, our house was filled with people and conversation. My uncles were often there, as well as my grandparents, and there was spirited conversation about books and music and current events. Every Sunday was a seminar on politics and history. My grandmother would cook a huge dinner, and everyone would sit around the table and talk about Father Coughlin, the anti-Semitic radio commentator, and Hitler and the war news and why Roosevelt didn't do this or that. My uncle Morris was an active Democrat. One of his enthusiasms was a young congressman named John Kennedy.

My father was a Republican, self-made and fiercely independent. Today we might call him a libertarian. He believed in the Constitution, in individual freedom and in minimal government intrusion in people's lives.

Our family was united by an intense love of America. We were proudly patriotic and deeply concerned about the anti-Semitism promoted by such bigots as Father Coughlin and Gerald L. K. Smith. By the late 1930s my family knew from Jewish newspapers that Jews were being rounded up and sent to camps in Germany. After the war we learned that scores of members of both my parents' families had perished in the German death camps.

As I reached my teens my father saw troubling signs of indolence in me. "You haven't had the benefit of poverty," he would say, even though I had worked weekends and after school in his factory throughout the war. By the time I turned fifteen I was a bit of a hell-raiser, at least by my father's standards. I liked to fish, play baseball and ride my bike, and thanks to school-yard encounters with anti-Semitism I was handy with my fists. My father thought I needed discipline and should go to a military school.

That sounded good to me. I wanted to see more of the world and gladly enrolled at the Valley Forge Military Academy in Wayne, Pennsylvania. I worked hard there, excelled in debate and boxing, and learned the military discipline and leadership that probably saved my life when I fought in Korea a few years later.

My next stop was Syracuse University, where I continued to box, raced stock cars on weekends, served in the ROTC and became engaged to a tall, brilliant young woman named Shirley Wahl, whom I met on the debate team. We were married soon after my graduation, not long before I shipped out for Korea. I'll talk about Korea a little later. Enough for now to say that I survived, and in 1954 was discharged from the army and returned to Nashua.

I was twenty-four, a college graduate, a combat veteran, a married man, and I had no idea what I wanted to do with my life. Soon I was in charge of production at Old Colony. It was a wonderful company, but it wasn't enough of a challenge. I began to think of law school. I was interested in public policy and knew from my college debates that I could argue well. Law seemed a logical step.

Still, I had a job, a wife, and children starting to arrive, and law school wasn't going to be easy. While I was in Korea, Shirley had worked as a biochemist in Philadelphia. After we settled in Nashua, she went back to college and earned master's degrees in chemistry and math. In the years ahead, Shirley taught math and computer science in both high school and college. Our children, Laura, Alan and Deborah, were born between 1953 and 1960.

I talked with my father's close friend and lawyer, Bill Green, about law school. Bill had attended Dartmouth and Harvard Law, and served as a marine officer in the South Pacific. Later he became New Hampshire's deputy attorney general, and might well have been attorney general had he not been Jewish. There wasn't a lot of overt anti-Semitism in New Hampshire, but no Jew had ever held a top statewide office.

With Bill Green's encouragement, and my father's blessing, I decided to go ahead with law school. The best night law school in the area was about forty-five miles away at Boston College, where I began classes in the fall of 1956. After a day's work at Old Colony, I would drive to Boston three or four nights a week.

When I received my law degree in 1960, at the age of thirty, I had offers from the leading New Hampshire firms, but my father still needed me at Old Colony, so for several years I worked mornings for him, then practiced law with a family friend, Morris Stein. After my father and my uncle Sid sold Old Colony and retired, in 1964, I practiced full time with Stein. I still had no particular goal in mind. I think a lot of people try too hard to plan their lives, and then are surprised when their lives refuse to follow the script.

In the early 1960s I built a Cape Cod–style house for us in Nashua. I was my own general contractor and did some of the work myself. By then Shirley was teaching and our children were in the Nashua public schools. Also in the sixties, both Shirley and I learned to fly, thanks to a college roommate of mine named Hans Einstein, a cousin of the great scientist. He had made the air force his career, and was eventually stationed near Nashua, where we renewed our friendship. Ever since then, flying has been one of the great joys of my life.

Another friend of mine in those days was Walter Peterson, the Republican speaker of the New Hampshire House of Representatives, whom I'd known since childhood. Walter had several times urged me to run for the legislature. I wasn't interested in running then, but I had gravitated naturally to the Republican Party. Not only did it reflect my own moderate political instincts, but New Hampshire was an overwhelmingly Republican state. With the exception of John Kennedy, the politicians I most admired had been Republicans, including Dwight Eisenhower and Nelson Rockefeller.

Late in 1967 Walter Peterson told me he was going to run for governor and wanted me to be his finance chairman. I protested that I knew little about politics. He said it didn't matter, because he wanted new blood and new ideas in his campaign.

Walter was a big, solid, soft-spoken Dane, a man of high principles and unquestioned integrity. He was a role model for me and largely responsible for my public career. Walter won a tough primary and then defeated a Democrat for the governorship. Walter was a moderate and was opposed by William Loeb's far-right *Manchester Union Leader,* the state's biggest newspaper, which had become notorious for its violent attacks on liberals and moderates who campaigned in the New Hampshire primary every four years. People often asked me what made Bill Loeb tick, but I never knew the answer. There must have been some great anger or frustration that drove him to use his power in such mean-spirited ways.

The biggest lesson I learned from Walter's campaign was that if you're going to run for high public office you'd better have a good reason. Too many people run out of pure ego or ambition. One of my complaints with Congress is that it's filled with people who've never held a real job. They go to law school, become assistant district attorneys, run for the state legislature, for Congress, and for the Senate, and there they are. What do they know about the real world?

After Walter's election, he asked me to head a task force that would recommend reforms in the state's tax structure. Our group produced a plan that changed the way New Hampshire taxed companies—essentially, to tax profits rather than assets—and paved the way for the state to move from producing shoes and textiles to the high-tech revolution of the seventies.

Walter made me his chief of staff, then in 1970 he appointed me attorney general—at thirty-nine, one of the youngest in the state's history—and the next year he named me to a full five-year term. I took over the office believing that it lacked the people, the organization and the professionalism needed by a state that was starting to grow rapidly. I put together a first-rate staff, headed by a brilliant young man named David Souter, who was working in our criminal division but soon became my deputy and close friend.

I was an activist attorney general. Besides trying many criminal cases myself, I expanded the size of our criminal division and established our first consumer-protection and environmental-protection divisions. I needed help to meet my goals. I was very aware that I was operating under the hostile scrutiny not only of Loeb's *Union Leader* but, after its candidate Meldrim Thomson defeated Walter Peterson in 1972, of the governor as well. Any mistakes we made would be magnified many times, so I needed people around me I could trust absolutely. David Souter became the person I most trusted and relied on.

David ran the office, under my direction. I was good at setting policy, trying cases, motivating the staff and directing investigations, but on matters of law I deferred to David's judgment. I had absolute trust in his understanding of the law and his good sense. Even then, he was a lawyer's lawyer, and I came to regard his as the finest legal mind I had ever known.

Those were busy and exciting years. With David's help, I recruited a staff of young, able, dedicated lawyers. We hired on the basis of talent alone, with no political or philosophical tests, and our staff became the envy of many of the state's law firms.

Not long after I took office, three of the "Chicago Seven"— antiwar activists David Dellinger, Abbie Hoffman and Jerry Rubin—accepted an invitation to speak at the University of New Hampshire. Conservatives, led by William Loeb, declared that they were coming to start a riot and should not be allowed to speak. That was a terrible idea. Legally, you can't enjoin speech without strong evidence that violence will ensue. Moreover, this was not long after the Kent State shootings, and I was afraid that if we banned the activists, rioting might break out on campus and create the very violence we sought to avoid.

Loeb denounced me, but he had to be careful of what he said, because I had a military record and he didn't. His ally, former governor Wesley Powell, called me "an apologist for filth and violence" and demanded my resignation. Eventually, the activists came and spoke. David and I were on the campus that night, along with a great many reporters and state police, but there was no riot. Life went on.

The Chicago Three might have been surprised to know how much sympathy I felt for their antiwar views. I watched the Vietnam war on television and felt tremendous concern for our young men. I thought it was the wrong war in the wrong place at the wrong time. It was a civil war, in a country that wanted to be unified, and I never believed that our corrupt allies in Saigon would be the winners. Too many people died because our politicians became trapped in their own rhetoric, unwilling to admit their mistakes, until our defeat was total.

Watergate unfolded during my years as attorney general, and I was stunned at the actions of the president and his associates. I had met Richard Nixon a few times when he came to New Hampshire. He was an awkward man, difficult to talk to, but I respected his intelligence and many of his policies, particularly in foreign affairs. Watergate left me totally disenchanted. Nixon let the country down badly. His resignation was entirely proper.

There were endless controversies when I was attorney general. Once, a group of truckers, protesting the high price of fuel during the 1974 oil crisis, tied up traffic in Concord. I saw this as a dumb publicity stunt and told their leader to move the trucks because they were endangering public safety. When he ignored me, I declared that I would call out the National Guard and have the trucks dumped in the river. That got the trucks moved.

"Warren," David Souter protested, "you don't have the authority to call up the National Guard."

"No, but they didn't know that," I told him.

Early in my term I prosecuted a doctor for performing abortions on University of New Hampshire women, but I dropped the case after the Supreme Court handed down its *Roe* v. *Wade* decision. I took a lot of heat from the *Union Leader,* but *Roe* v. *Wade* had made abortion legal. That didn't impress Bill Loeb, but I was sworn to uphold the law and the Supreme Court always impressed me.

Nor did I disagree personally with *Roe* v. *Wade.* A decision as personal and momentous as bearing a child is not for government to make. Later, when I was in the Senate, there were endless debates on when life begins. I considered that a theological, not a political, question, and I didn't intend to pass judgment on it.

During the early 1970s I brought obscenity charges against the owner of a theater in Grafton County for showing the popular porn movie *Deep Throat.* That fact later caused some people to question my commitment to the First Amendment right of free speech. I saw the issue differently. At that point, the Supreme Court had ruled that otherwise obscene material was acceptable if it contained redeeming social or literary value. I watched *Deep Throat* and didn't find anything redeeming. This wasn't *Lady Chatterley's Lover* or *Ulysses.* This was unalloyed pornography.

It's true that I was also offended by the fact that the theater was owned by the county attorney's family. I can't say that Grafton County was outraged by the film—the theater was packed every night—and I lost the case before a jury.

Perhaps I was too influenced by my personal distaste for the movie. I certainly wouldn't have challenged it a few years later, after new Supreme Court rulings liberalized obscenity law to the point that the offense barely exists. If the Supreme Court says that people have a right to watch trash, so be it.

Walter Peterson lost the Republican nomination for governor to the far-right Meldrim Thomson in 1972 because he honestly conceded that he might have to consider new taxes. I debated Thomson during the campaign and made my scorn for him abundantly clear. Still, when he won, I decided to continue as attorney general—I was an independent official—and we developed a decent working relationship.

In 1976 I returned to private life, joined Bill Green's firm and practiced mostly corporate law. When a proposal came along to permit casino gambling in New Hampshire, I formed something called the Citizens Alliance Against Casinos. Actually, I was the whole operation. David Souter, my successor as attorney general, also opposed legalized gambling, and together we defeated the proposal.

That fight brought me a good deal of publicity, on top of what I'd received as attorney general, and people urged me to run against Democratic Senator Tom McIntyre in 1978, but I liked Tom and had no wish to challenge him. He'd been a good senator and he was William Loeb's archenemy, which I admired. Instead, McIntyre was defeated by an unknown, ultraconservative airline pilot named Gordon Humphrey, who became the first New Hampshire candidate to make major use of Boston television.

In 1979 a lot of people were urging me to challenge our other senator, John Durkin, a first-term Democrat. Among them were two Republican senators I greatly admired, John Heinz of Pennsylvania and Howard Baker of Tennessee, who argued that

Durkin was an ultraliberal, controlled by organized labor, financed by out-of-state money, and out of touch with the voters of New Hampshire. I agreed.

I had support in all wings of the Republican Party, and among some Democrats too. Except for Loeb and a few other extremists, I had no problem with the state's conservatives. Most of them respected me for having been tough on crime as attorney general. Then and later, my political views upset a lot of people. I refused to fit in their pigeonholes. I'm a pragmatist, not an ideologue. I'm very conservative on fiscal issues, starting with the need for a balanced budget, and on the need for a strong defense and a strong foreign policy, but I'm more liberal on what are now called social issues, which I prefer to call human issues, including my pro-choice stand on abortion.

There'd also been talk of my running for governor, but I was more interested in national issues. My goal in running wasn't to satisfy personal ambition. I finally decided to make the race because I strongly disagreed with Durkin on three hugely important issues: national defense, foreign policy and fiscal policy.

I knew, from combat experience in Korea, what was required to fight a war, and I thought that during the Carter years our military forces had become woefully underfunded, underequipped, and undertrained—and that Durkin's Senate votes had contributed to that decline. I also thought the fast-rising federal deficit was going to eat us alive and that politicians like Durkin either didn't understand the danger or didn't care. And I thought that American foreign policy had to be much stronger than either Durkin or Carter advocated with regard to the Soviet Union, and to terrorists and the nations that supported them.

Durkin and I had a history, as they say. In 1974 he'd run against Republican Congressman Louis Wyman for an open Senate seat. The outcome came down to a handful of disputed ballots. As attorney general, I served on the commission that ruled on those ballots. At the outset, Durkin had led by ten votes, but we ruled Wyman the winner by four. Eventually the Democratic-controlled Senate ordered a new election, which Durkin won easily, but he blamed me for, as he saw it, stealing his initial, ten-vote victory.

Early in 1976 President Ford nominated me to be chairman of the Interstate Commerce Commission, but Durkin, serving on the Senate Commerce Committee, stalled my nomination. When I realized what was happening, I withdrew my name. In retrospect, opposing my nomination was the worst mistake Durkin ever made, because if I'd been serving on the ICC in Washington in the late 1970s, I probably wouldn't have run against him in 1980.

In September of 1979 I commissioned polls that showed my positive/negative rating was 78–9, compared with about 60–30 for most of the state's major political figures. I asked the pollster to see how the voters felt about out-of-state political action committees, or PACs, putting money in New Hampshire elections. The result was overwhelming. More than three quarters of the people resented out-of-state special interests intruding in our campaigns.

I agreed. I thought that big money, whether from the right or from the left, was corrupting our political system. Too often it was used for negative television advertising that misled the voters. Much of Durkin's money came from big labor and from liberal, out-of-state PACs. I wanted to turn that against him so that the more money he raised, the worse off he'd be. But I could do that only if I was clean on the issue. I told my friends I would run only if we could raise the money we needed in New Hampshire, plus whatever the Republican Senatorial Campaign Committee could give us. My friends said it could be done, and

I made a calculated decision to run without PAC money. To do so was both a matter of principle and an excellent campaign issue. It was there for the taking, but no one else had noticed it or been willing to take the risk of running without that sure source of funds.

First I had to win my party's nomination in an eleven-man primary. At the outset, the favorite was conservative former governor Wesley Powell. One of the long shots was John Sununu, a state legislator whom I admired. In a series of debates around the state, Sununu and I were widely viewed as the winners. As it turned out, Sununu finished second to me and Powell finished third. John immediately agreed to be my campaign manager in the general election. His support was important, because as a pro-life Catholic he could help me with Catholics who were troubled by my pro-choice stand.

I loved campaigning. I like people and I like issues, and they are what campaigns are all about. I'm not sure I'd enjoy running in California or New York, but in New Hampshire we practice retail politics. Candidates blanket the state, speaking to every civic club and community group they can find, walking the streets of the towns and villages, getting to know the voters one at a time.

I blasted Durkin as a big spender who cared too little about national defense and a balanced budget. There were clear-cut issues at stake. He supported the Equal Rights Amendment and I did not, because I believed that the Constitution already gave women equal rights. I favored the continued development of nuclear power and he thought it too dangerous. I opposed a "pro-life" constitutional amendment banning abortions and Durkin supported it. Ours was largely a clean campaign, focused on real issues.

My family supported my candidacy, although my father never thought much of politicians, and my mother thought it was silly to give up a wonderful law practice to go to Washington. Before it was over, both of them were out campaigning for me. So were Shirley, my daughter Deborah, who was a student at Bowdoin, and her sister, Laura, an artist who designed my campaign material.

My son, Alan, graduated from Dartmouth in June of 1979 and postponed entering law school so he could campaign with me. It was a great experience for a father and son. He was at my side all day, from the first breakfast meeting with voters to the last rally at night. Some nights we would get back home to Nashua, others we would share a hotel room somewhere. When I was low he would pick me up, and when I was too high he would knock me down.

It didn't hurt that Alan was a big, good-looking fellow—he'd been a terrific football player at Nashua High—and had a tremendous presence of his own. He worked a room with me not as an aide but as an equal. I noted that he made a major impact on some women voters.

My refusal to accept out-of-state PAC money was popular, but it also cost me a lot of money, and as the final weeks approached I urgently needed more money for television spots. Fortunately, on October 16, Gerald Ford came to Concord for the biggest fund-raising event New Hampshire had ever seen, a $100-a-plate dinner that netted about $160,000 for my campaign.

About ten days before the election, our polls showed Durkin with a slight lead. Moreover, we'd heard that he'd bought about three times as much TV time for the final days as we'd expected. We needed time to respond, perhaps a hundred thousand dollars' worth, but—despite the recent fund-raiser—we were broke. My advisers and I met in my living room. We didn't know where to raise that kind of money. Finally I said that we'd all worked hard and if I didn't take my best shot and lost this election I'd never forgive myself.

I had a house, a mortgage and less than ten thousand dollars in savings. But I was known in the town, practiced law, and had a good reputation and good health. So I called my banker and he gave me an unsecured loan of $100,000, which we used for an election-eve media blitz that matched Durkin's. That was what used to be called a character loan, much like the one another banker made to my father forty years earlier after the flood wiped out his new factory.

On election night, the voters of New Hampshire continued their habit of ticket-splitting. Ronald Reagan swamped Jimmy Carter by better than two to one. At the same time, Democratic Governor Hugh Gallen, to my delight, easily defeated a comeback attempt by Meldrim Thomson.

Meanwhile, I was in a horse race. I awaited the returns, with family and friends, in a suite on the third floor of the Ramada Inn in Concord. I chain-smoked as the numbers trickled in. At midnight I was ahead by fifteen thousand votes, and we wondered why Durkin hadn't conceded. A reporter called from his headquarters in Manchester and said the problem was that Durkin's wife and children were extremely upset and didn't want him to concede until defeat was a certainty.

I called Durkin and said it looked as if I had won, but if he didn't want to concede yet, I understood. I said I was going downstairs to thank my people and tell them that it appeared I'd won, but we could wait until morning to make it official.

At around 2:00 A.M. I took five or six of my staff people out for breakfast. After we ate, a friend named George Turner offered to drive me the thirty miles back to Nashua. As we drove along the turnpike in a heavy fog, I confessed to George that I still couldn't believe I'd won.

"Well, you have," he said.

It happened that we were passing a phone booth, and I asked him to pull over. I called Adolph Bernotas, a veteran AP reporter, who was still at his office, awaiting the late returns.

"Adolph?" I said. "Warren Rudman."

"Congratulations, Senator," he said.

I asked what the latest results were.

"Hey, you've won," he said, laughing.

"Give me the numbers," I insisted.

He read them to me—they were nearing the final 195,559–179,455 tally—and I thanked him and went back to the car, finally accepting that I had won.

There were heady days ahead as I barnstormed the state, thanking my supporters, and then flew to Washington to meet my new Republican colleagues, and yet I felt a certain disquiet. Not self-doubt, but trepidation. I thought of all the problems facing America and realized that now I would have a role in solving them—or making them worse. I thought of the modern senators I had admired—Harry Truman, Arthur Vandenberg, Robert Taft, Jacob Javits, Howard Baker, Barry Goldwater, Russell Long and Scoop Jackson—and wondered if I could live up to the standards they had set.

I'd been blessed with excellent preparation for the Senate. I had a wonderful family and a good education. In combat in Korea I'd learned a lot about myself and about other Americans from very different backgrounds. I'd helped run my dad's company, practiced law with a small firm, then had been attorney general and started to understand how government works. I had been a voracious reader of history all my life, and I thought I understood some of the challenges ahead, because others had faced them before me.

I knew I would confront hard issues and hard decisions. I knew that in politics it's often necessary to compromise—that's the nature of our system. Yet I also knew that on some issues I could not compromise. Not on abortion rights, nor on the separation of church and state, or the First Amendment, or civil rights or national defense. I was fifty years old, I knew who I was, and I was ready to give the Senate the best six years I had in me.

On the morning of January 3, 1981, the vast Senate chamber had a dark and foreboding look, yet the exuberance of the people gathered there for the swearing-in made it burst with light. I looked up at the gallery and saw Shirley and our children, and friends like David Souter, Tom Rath and Bill Green, but most of all I saw my parents. I saw the tears glistening in my father's eyes and I knew what he was thinking. A penniless Jewish immigrant had arrived at Ellis Island a hundred years before, and now his grandson was entering the United States Senate.

I was one of sixteen new Republican senators who had been swept in by the Reagan landslide and were taking the oath of office. Our party had captured the Senate for the first time in thirty years, and whatever our differences we were united by a tremendous sense of purpose. After the tragedy of Vietnam and Watergate, and the drift of the Carter years, we thought a new day had arrived. We thought we could change America.

To find myself a United States senator was overwhelming. Suddenly I was meeting men I'd admired from afar, men who were already part of history. That is not to say, however, that the Senate was exclusively populated by giants. One day, as I listened to a debate drone on, I thought of two letters Harry Truman wrote to his mother after he arrived in the Senate. In the first one he said, "Your boy Harry is surrounded by all these famous men and wondering what he's doing here." Then, a few months later, he wrote again and said, "Well, I've gotten to know some of these fellows, and now I'm wondering what *they're* doing here."

In time I saw that perhaps a third of the senators made the institution work. They were the players. They knew what they wanted and how to get it. Another third had some idea of what they wanted but not much idea how to proceed. The rest didn't have a clue. Perhaps they were great campaigners, or good at serving home-state interests, but they weren't legislators.

The least talented senators tended to rely heavily on their staffs. Far too often I saw staff-driven hearings and legislation— an aide had convinced a member that this or that issue would be good politics or good publicity. To confront one of these senators without an aide to whisper in his ear made it clear he didn't know if he was on foot or on horseback.

Still, the best senators were the most extraordinary people I've ever known—senators like Bob Dole, Sam Nunn and Pete Domenici, to name just a few. They worked long and hard, in the face of endless abuse, because they wanted to serve the nation. These days, when everyone is down on politicians, we often don't appreciate the great public servants we have, in both parties.

I was determined to be the best senator I could be. I've worked hard all my life, but only twice was I motivated to a supreme effort. Once was in Korea, when I feared for my life and the lives of my men. The second time was in the Senate, when I feared I might not make the most of this opportunity to contribute to a better world. I didn't intend, when I was an old man, to look back and think I'd failed.

I wanted no part of Washington social life and was soon turning down hundreds of invitations to parties. My idea of a good time had always been a quiet evening with a few friends—or with a good book—not a cocktail party with a bunch of strangers. I would go to a fund-raiser for a friend, but that was it. Nor did I have time for plays, movies or museums. The Senate, if you take it seriously, is all-consuming.

Washington is a seductive city. It's more than the parties. It's the way everyone treats you, from Cabinet members to head-waiters to strangers in airports. Even reporters, if they're not going after you, will flatter you. I saw a lot of people come to the Senate and forget who they were. It was easy to do. Sometimes I'd have to pull back and say, Wait a minute, Rudman, you're a lawyer from a small state and you'll go back there someday—don't get carried away by all this.

I took a small Capitol Hill apartment, just a few blocks from my office in the Dirksen Building. It was convenient and I couldn't have afforded anything more elaborate if I'd wanted it. I'd taken a cut in pay to come to Washington, from more than one hundred thousand dollars a year to about sixty thousand, and I was borrowing money to put my kids through college. Shirley came to Washington briefly, but wasn't happy there, and returned to New Hampshire. I returned home thirty-eight week-ends that first year, to see my family and keep in touch with my constituents. Weather permitting, I flew up in my own plane.

I put together a first-rate staff, most of whom stayed with me for a long time. One of my key choices was my press secretary, Bob Stevenson, who had covered my campaign for *Foster's Daily Democrat,* in Dover, an important paper in our state. Bob was only twenty-six, but he'd done an outstanding job on the campaign, and I wanted someone with a newspaper background. I thought there were too many press secretaries who were basically PR people who'd never been reporters.

I had never served in a legislature before, but I had worked with one as attorney general, and I knew that much of my success would depend on my personal relationships with my colleagues. I set out to forge the closest possible ties with the other senators. Each was different. What worked with one might not work with another. Learning my craft meant knowing my peers. I studied their records and their official biographies for clues to what made them tick. To be effective in the Senate, you have to multiply your vote by influencing others. Success depended on personal credibility—whether people respected your judgment, your fairness and your word.

During my first year I set out to meet every member on both sides of the aisle. Often I would arrive in the dining room early in the morning and see who was having breakfast alone. I'd say, "Can I join you?" and since few senators enjoy solitude I would usually be asked to sit down.

I'd say, "Tell me about that bill you introduced." In turn, I'd share my ideas. Most senators, if there's no strong home-state interest in a bill, are open to persuasion. Not on great matters of principle, perhaps, but on lesser issues that come along. As issues became more complex, senators became specialists, and everyone needed help sometimes.

One of the first senators I came to know was Howard Baker, our majority leader. I'd felt profound respect for his role in the Watergate hearings eight years before, when he put loyalty to the Constitution ahead of loyalty to Richard Nixon. Later I admired his courage in bucking party pressure to support President Carter on the Panama Canal treaties. Howard had been one of those who urged me to run for the Senate in 1978, and I'd supported his bid for the presidential nomination in 1980.

We became close friends—I was one of "Baker's dozen," moderates who worked with him to try to bring legislative order out of the prevailing partisan chaos. I thought Howard embodied the best in American politics. He combined brilliance, decency and a disarming, folksy Southern style that was highly effective. I loved expressions of his like "I ain't got a dog in that fight!" He had a wonderful sense of humor, and people genuinely liked him.

Howard kept us Republicans together, as well as anyone could have, mostly by quiet appeals to our loyalty, and that meant loyalty to him as much as to the president or the party. "Remember, we have a responsibility to govern," he reminded us, over and over. When I went against him, as I sometimes did, I always felt guilty about it, on a purely personal level, no matter how right I thought I was on the issue at hand.

Howard's great challenge in the early months of 1981 was to pass Reagan's economic program. It was based on the controversial supply-side economic theory, which held that we could have both a huge tax cut and huge increases in defense spending and still move toward a balanced budget, because the tax cuts would so stimulate the economy that the result would be more tax revenues rather than less.

Both Howard and I had serious doubts about this theory, but we swallowed hard and supported the Reagan plan, to our eventual regret. My regret inspired me, four years later, to cosponsor the Gramm-Rudman legislation, which attempted to undo the damage wreaked by Reaganomics.

During my first term in the Senate, aside from my growing concern about the deficit, I focused on two broad areas. First, I combined support of a strong national defense with a crusade against Pentagon waste. I also spoke out on domestic issues that ranged from protecting the First Amendment to supporting a woman's right to choose abortion to keeping the Legal Services Corporation alive in the face of the president's determination to dismantle it.

On domestic issues, I believed that if America was going to survive as a democracy, we truly had to promote opportunity for everyone. Somehow we had to bring our fast-growing, alienated, increasingly violent underclass into the middle class.

I agreed that many of the Great Society programs needed close scrutiny, but that didn't mean you threw out all programs for the poor. To deny people hope and opportunity was not conservative; it was shortsighted and stupid and would only lead to more misery, more violence and even civil disorder. Thus, I opposed some of the cuts Reagan proposed in social programs, including those in legal services, college loans and education for the handicapped.

I thought my beliefs were classically conservative. On balance, they put me near the middle of the political spectrum, a little to the right of center. I rarely had much doubt about how I would vote and I was always surprised at the indecision around me. I would ask colleagues, "What are your basic beliefs?" I didn't always get an answer.

Like most senators, I paid close attention to my home-state constituents. The first legislation I introduced, in April of 1981, the Small Business Innovation Research Act, was intended to stimulate economic growth in New Hampshire, although it would help other states as well.

Many studies had shown that small high-tech companies, like those that had grown up around Boston and in New Hampshire, produced a disproportionate number of successful innovations and created jobs at a higher rate than larger technology firms. But these companies often had a hard time raising seed money.

My bill proposed that federal agencies giving out more than $100 million in research grants each year be required to set aside 1 percent of their money for small businesses, with initial grants of fifty thousand dollars to test a proposal, then up to five hundred thousand to carry it forward until venture capital took over.

It was a modest proposal, but we soon encountered fierce resistance from three quarters. The big agencies that made research grants, such as Defense, Energy and NASA, were accustomed to funding the big universities, defense contractors and research labs, and they didn't want to bother with unknown entrepreneurs. The universities and others who were already getting the federal research money resisted as if the loss of 1 percent would destroy them. And some Reaganites in government argued that as a "philosophical" matter, small business should be left to fend for itself.

I lobbied my colleagues aggressively and was rewarded by a 90–0 vote in the Senate, but then my bill was blocked in the House. Finally I cut through the opposition with a personal appeal to the president, who expressed his strong support for SBIR. The opposition evaporated, the bill passed in 1982 and Reagan signed it in the Rose Garden that spring.

Another home-state concern was the high cost of home heating oil, for which some New England working families paid up to a third of their income. In the summer of 1981 Ted Kennedy and I teamed up to win some relief for these people. Despite opposition from the White House, we passed legislation that gave a tax credit of up to two hundred dollars for home-heating costs to families with incomes of less than twenty-five thousand dollars. It was little enough to do for people in terrible need.

Kennedy and I often worked together on issues of importance to New England. His personal life may have been a mess—he wasn't the only senator of which that could be said—but he was a skillful champion of the causes he believed in. I learned to admire people with deeply held views, even if they were much different from my own. I would see Ted working tirelessly for his causes, and think of all the tragedy he'd experienced, and I would admire him for being there when he could have been living a millionaire's life far from Capitol Hill.

I supported the Reagan administration about 80 percent of the time in my first year, but my convictions sometimes led me to oppose the president. In the spring of 1981 I began a twelve-year battle with the Reagan and Bush administrations to keep the Legal Services Corporation alive. Reagan had hated the LSC since he was governor of California. He believed, not without cause, that its lawyers pursued a liberal social agenda, especially when they went beyond helping individuals with specific grievances and began filing class-action suits against state and federal governments. Each year, starting in 1981, the Reagan budget would "zero out" LSC and I would put together a bipartisan coalition to restore the $300 million or so needed to keep the program going.

I'd dealt with LSC lawyers when I was attorney general. They could drive public officials crazy, but that wasn't the point. Equal justice under the law is a meaningless slogan if you can't afford a lawyer. Most of the LSC lawyers were young, idealistic and hardworking, and they were helping people who obviously needed help. LSC's critics argued that private lawyers, working pro bono, could take care of the poor, but that wasn't true. Law firms would never give their lawyers enough time to help all the people who needed help. I thought that providing legal services to the poor was profoundly conservative. What kind of country would this be if a third of our people had no access to justice? What is more radical than allowing the rich to wield overwhelming legal power against the poor?

I agreed that Legal Services had sometimes been too political, so our coalition put some restrictions on its political activity, and we kept Legal Services alive for twelve years, despite active White House opposition.

The National Rifle Association denounced me that fall because I refused to support its new firearms bill. The reason was that it contained a loophole that would have permitted felons to buy guns, and I couldn't support that. Eventually the NRA rewrote the bill.

Gun control had never been a major issue for me or my constituents. I owned guns and hunted and didn't consider myself either pro-gun or anti-gun. As attorney general I'd had no problem prosecuting people for illegal ownership or use of firearms. I opposed gun control not because I thought the Second Amendment gave individuals an unqualified right to bear arms. I don't think the Second Amendment does that at all. It clearly refers to militias, not individuals.

My opposition to gun control was pragmatic. New York has the toughest gun laws in the nation and what's the result? Honest people don't have guns and criminals do. I think people have a right to protect themselves. I was outraged to learn that I couldn't legally have a gun in Washington. Despite the law, I kept one in my office and one in my apartment, because there were plenty of armed criminals roaming the streets of Washington. Until someone figures out a way to disarm criminals, I won't support the disarming of law-abiding citizens.

In September, Fred Wertheimer, president of the "citizens' lobby" Common Cause, denounced me for having run as a critic of political action committees but then, once in office, not having done enough to oppose their influence. The real problem was that I hadn't cosponsored the Common Cause reform bill, which was poorly drafted and had no chance of passage. I thought that for him to criticize me, one of the few people in Congress who'd refused PAC money, was like criticizing Sergeant York for not killing enough Germans. I told my staff that henceforth Wertheimer and his colleagues were not welcome in my office. The "citizens' lobby" needed a lesson in how to deal with senators, or at least with this one.

Still, my first year in the Senate had only reinforced my belief that the overwhelming financial power of special interests was a threat to democracy. I later introduced a "20-30-50" plan that would have limited the amount of PAC money any Senate or House candidate could spend in one election to 20 percent of the total outlay. Another 30 percent could come from the candidate's political party, and at least half had to come from individuals. Realistically, we couldn't eliminate all PAC money, but I hoped we could limit it. That didn't happen. Senators need vast amounts of money to run for reelection, and PACs are the easiest way to raise it. Eventually there will have to be reform. The present system compromises good men and makes the public think everyone in Congress is on the take—which, I say emphatically, is not the case.

In 1981 I also resumed my long-running feud with my alma mater, Syracuse University. When I graduated, nearly three decades earlier, Syracuse had denied me my diploma because I refused to pay eighteen dollars for a college yearbook. My position was that when I enrolled no one had mentioned this fee. A year or so later, I'd written them again from Korea, still refusing to pay the fee, but thinking my parents might want the diploma if I was killed. They turned me down then and again when I returned home. But now that I was a senator they wrote to say there'd obviously been a mix-up and the diploma was in the mail. I refused to accept it. Then a group of university officials offered to pay a call on me to set things straight. I refused to see them. They offered to give me an honorary degree. I declined that too. If they wouldn't give me the diploma I'd earned, I damn sure didn't want one I hadn't earned. Maybe I was too stubborn. These weren't the same people who'd withheld my diploma in

1952. But I still thought that the way the university had treated me when I was a kid risking my life in Korea was an outrage. I wasn't ready to forgive and forget.

One of my most satisfying political fights was against the American Medical Association in the fall of 1982. The question was whether the Federal Trade Commission should continue to have the power to regulate doctors on such matters as certification, competition, advertising and the like. The doctors protested that they were already regulated by the states.

The issue arose after young doctors around the country began opening storefront clinics for poor people. The establishment doctors, who didn't like cut-rate competition, began bringing pressure on hospitals not to grant staff privileges to the storefront doctors.

It was a classic case of restraint of trade, an antitrust issue, and the FTC was ready to intervene when Jim McClure, a Republican senator from Idaho, introduced an amendment that would have stripped the FTC of power over doctors, lawyers and other professionals. It was, in effect, the AMA's amendment. I believed strongly in both antitrust laws and consumer protection and I decided to take them on.

McClure agreed to withdraw his amendment after I threatened a filibuster. That postponed the debate until the post-election, lame-duck session in December and gave me time to make my case. I buttonholed every member of the Senate, asking if they really wanted to vote against doctors who were trying to operate storefront clinics for poor people. I told Republicans that if we sided with the AMA, we were forgetting our own past, because the antitrust laws were the creation of progressive Republicans like Teddy Roosevelt.

Senators hated to confront this issue. The White House and consumer groups were on my side, but the AMA had money.

When the issue came to a vote in the House, all but 53 of the 403 Representatives who voted with the AMA had received money from its political action committee, part of the $1.7 million it had contributed to congressional candidates that year.

We offered a compromise. The FTC would keep jurisdiction over the medical profession's "trade practices" but not over "quality of care" issues. But the AMA rejected the compromise. They wanted an "all or nothing" Senate vote.

That was a mistake. The Senate wanted a way out. The AMA's refusal to compromise was greedy and arrogant. The final vote came at about six in the morning on December 16, after an all-night debate and intensive face-to-face lobbying of wavering colleagues by me and others.

As the night wore on I felt the tide running my way and indulged myself in some rhetorical flourishes.

"For the first time in twenty years, doctors are making house calls," I declared. "They've made house calls to the Dirksen Building and the Russell Building. They are so concerned about our health that the reception rooms are packed with them."

I accused the AMA of wanting to "perform a frontal lobotomy on the free enterprise system." I urged that we send the Gucci-shod doctors packing, down the Senate steps into their BMWs and Cadillacs and off into the night, while we cast a vote for the American people.

We won an easy 59–37 victory. The AMA hurt itself badly that night, with its refusal to compromise. Opposing them didn't cause me any problems. I neither wanted their money nor feared it. A few doctors from New Hampshire called, but when I explained about the storefront clinics they were satisfied.

The New Right's so-called social issues—opposition to abortion, gay rights, flag-burning and funding for the arts, along with support for prayer in schools—were increasingly on the

Senate agenda in my first term. A reporter once asked me my views on this "social agenda." "Do you have fifteen seconds?" I asked. "That's all it will take. I'm deeply committed to the right to choose, to the separation of church and state and to personal liberty. The conservative social agenda threatens them all."

I could have said much more. I was focused on two issues that involved our nation's survival—the deficit and national defense—and I thought the right-wing social agenda was largely a sideshow that had little to do with the real problems we faced.

I was of course pro-choice. I find abortion a lesser evil than forcing women to bring unwanted children into the world. The Supreme Court had spoken on abortion and I respected its ruling.

I opposed the constitutional amendment that would have permitted spoken "nondenominational" prayers in public schools. Clearly, any spoken prayer, imposed on all students, would violate the constitutional separation of church and state. As a compromise I was willing to support a moment of silence in which students could pray or not pray as they saw fit.

The Founding Fathers knew what evils a state-imposed religion had caused in England, and they intended to prevent one from being established in this country. It wasn't liberals who were "keeping God out of the schools," it was the Constitution. I therefore routinely voted against school-prayer legislation. For my troubles, Nackey Loeb, who had become publisher of the *Manchester Union Leader* upon her husband's death in 1981, accused me of driving the children of America into the arms of atheism.

Flag-burning was another issue that I saw as a matter of conscience. Jesse Helms was forever introducing legislation to make flag-burning a crime, and I always voted against him because flag-burning is a form of speech, protected by the First Amendment. I couldn't compromise on that. I couldn't say, "Okay, you can burn half the flag." If my constituents had disagreed with me—which by and large they didn't—I would have been willing to face the consequences. It helped that I had my military record to protect me from the charges of cowardice and treason that superpatriots like to hurl at their opponents.

Over the years I gave Jesse Helms a good deal of unsolicited legal advice. The National Endowment for the Arts sometimes awarded grants to artists whose work in my view was obscene and disgusting. Jesse, in response, kept proposing laws to protect America from art that offended those whose tastes, like Jesse's and mine, ran more to Norman Rockwell than Robert Mapplethorpe.

I would say, "Jesse, we can pass this law, but I promise you it'll be struck down by the courts." Sometimes he accepted my advice. I thought he and his staff had an imperfect understanding of the First Amendment.

Jesse and I served together for six years on the Ethics Committee and we were closely allied during the 1989–91 investigation of the Keating Five. I often disagreed with Jesse, sometimes violently, but I worked with him when I could, just as I did with liberals like Ted Kennedy when I thought they were right on an issue, or could be persuaded to be. As Howard Baker would say, even a blind hog gets an acorn once in a while. It's necessary, in the Senate, to compartmentalize your views of your colleagues. I disagreed with Jesse on, among other issues, abortion rights and the First Amendment, but we agreed on some issues, such as the need for a strong national defense. I was glad to have his support when I went after wasteful military spending, which became one of my preoccupations. When I took on the Pentagon I needed all the help I could get.

Throughout the Reagan years, I was both a strong supporter of the president's military buildup and one of the Pentagon's sharpest critics on waste and mismanagement. Some of my friends in the administration found this maddening. They would ask, in effect, "Are you with us or against us?" To me it was clear that I was never more "with" them than when I gave them hell for wasting billions on cost overruns and weapons systems that didn't work. Some of the Pentagon leaders could never grasp the simple fact that by wasting money they were not only discrediting themselves but undermining national security.

Soon after I arrived in the Senate, Ted Stevens of Alaska, who had been one of the legendary Flying Tigers of the Second World War, rewarded my service in Korea with a seat on his Defense Appropriations Committee, whereupon I set out to learn all I could about military issues.

I felt a duty, even a compulsion, to do everything I could to support our armed forces. Military readiness was not an abstract theory to me. As a young man, I had seen the reality of war, of weapons that worked or didn't work, of leaders who knew their jobs or didn't, and that experience inspired, three decades later, both my support of the Pentagon and my criticisms of it.

During my senior year at Syracuse, as a member of the ROTC, I knew I was headed for Korea, as were many of my friends. We knew we'd be there soon, because the mortality rate was high and there was a shortage of young infantry officers. We understood the dangers, but we had grown up with the patriotism of the Second World War. We believed this was aggression by a Communist nation against one of our allies. Despite our fears, most of our generation accepted unquestioningly that it was our obligation to serve our country in Korea.

The day after I graduated, early in June of 1952, a friend and I climbed into my 1941 Oldsmobile convertible and drove to

Fort Benning, Georgia, to enroll in infantry school. The commanding general was from the George S. Patton school of leadership. In his welcoming speech, he told us we would receive excellent training at Fort Benning and that most of us would soon be leading rifle platoons in Korea. Then he recited the casualty rates for small-unit leaders in Korea, which made it clear that many of us would soon be killed.

A few weeks after I arrived at Fort Benning, Shirley drove down and we were married on a Saturday afternoon in the base chapel. Our honeymoon lasted until five-thirty the next morning, when I had to return to duty. That was how it was in those days for a lot of young couples. Everyone knew the bride might soon be a widow.

I enjoyed basic training. I was in good physical shape, and I had a great head start because of my experience at Valley Forge. We spent much of our time at Benning learning about weapons and how to maneuver a rifle company, in night exercises, on forced marches and in live firing exercises. Next came leadership school at Fort Rucker, Alabama, where I was put in charge of physical training. Then, late in 1952, I boarded a troopship for the seventeen-day voyage to Japan. We spent a few days in Japan on a base that housed an army hospital. If we had any doubts about what lay ahead, the wounded men we saw there ended them. Finally we climbed onto a cargo ship for an overnight trip to Korea. We landed at Pusan and marched to a camp where we would stay in tents for a few nights. The camp was surrounded by thousands of Korean children begging for food. We gave them all we could, but we didn't make a dent in the misery around us.

About twenty-five miles north of Seoul, our forces and the Chinese faced each other, only a few hundred yards apart. It was there I met my company commander, a West Pointer, class of '51, named William Louisell, who later became a general and remains my friend. He assigned me to the third platoon of "K" company, third battalion of the 38th regiment of the Second Division. He said we were in a blocking position about half a mile behind the front line. In effect, he said, "Here's your platoon, here's your map, here's your top sergeant—welcome to Korea!"

I arrived in January, and a truce was finally declared in July. In the meantime there were heavy casualties and heavy fighting. Peace negotiations were in progress, and both sides wanted to show they had the will to keep fighting. Thousands of young men died to prove the point.

Soon after I arrived, Louisell said we were going to relieve the 3rd Infantry on line the next night. This was a night relief, a dangerous military exercise. One group is coming out, another is moving in, and if you're attacked there can be chaos. We were replacing nearly twenty thousand men along seven or eight miles of front.

That night we marched up Hill 468, almost straight up, and when we got to the top and looked down into a valley lit by flares, we saw the war. We had arrived. I found my counterpart and he said, "Okay, here's your bunker, Lieutenant," and then he left and we were in charge.

When the sun came up, we were looking down into Parachute Valley, just east of Pork Chop Hill. It was littered with thousands of parachutes that we used to drop flares. Facing us across the valley were the Chinese, from two hundred to six hundred yards away at various points. The valley between us had once been lush and green, but now was scorched by months of shelling.

That hill was my home, on and off, for six months. The Chinese were on a 700-foot hill and we were on a 468-foot hill. Both sides were dug into deep trenches, with sandbags and metal covers. You couldn't go out in the daytime; you'd be shot. We fought at night.

I lost count of how many night patrols I went on. Probably we saw combat on about every third patrol. These patrols were nightmares. You had no way of knowing when you might literally bump into the enemy—one man or a thousand.

I would lead the patrol, which included a noncommissioned officer as second in command, two Browning automatic-rifle operators, several riflemen, a radio operator and a medic. Maybe a dozen men in all.

The toughest job in war is leading small units in combat. It's face-to-face, kill or be killed. What I learned, leading night patrols, repelling attacks, engaging in close combat, is that no matter how desperate the situation, or how great my fear, I had to keep my composure, because my men were counting on me. At twenty-two, I was the "old man," three or four years older than the draftees I led. I had to lead by example. In some ways it's easier for the leader, because in combat you become preoccupied with your job and forget about yourself. But any man who tells you he's seen combat and not been afraid is either dishonest or very stupid.

In Korea, as in the Second World War, our army was truly representative of all strata of society. We had all kinds, black and white, rich and poor, graduate students and high school dropouts. Most of the men I commanded had backgrounds and attitudes very different from my own. I accepted authority and trusted our political institutions, but many of my men were highly skeptical of them. Yet no one debated the merits of the war, nor was anyone gung ho; we were fighting to survive. I never had any problems commanding my men, as long as they knew that I would do everything I asked them to do.

Our patrols had three purposes. Mainly we were a trip wire. There were twenty thousand Chinese just over the hill, and we were sent into the valley at night so that if they launched a surprise attack we would encounter them and warn our forces. In the process, of course, we would almost certainly be killed.

The second purpose was that every so often some brilliant intelligence officer would decide he needed a Chinese soldier from such-and-such a division to interrogate, so we'd be sent out to bring one back alive.

The third purpose was to attack the enemy, but mostly we just slipped through the darkness, wondering when we'd stumble onto an advancing Chinese regiment.

It was like a game, except that our lives were at stake. We would come down the hill, very quietly, perhaps a quarter of a mile down from the top of the ridge to the valley. We would patrol an area perhaps a thousand yards wide. Other platoons on either side of us were doing the same. We tried to go out on moonless nights; the last thing you wanted was moonlight. Sometimes, when the moon was full, our superiors would cancel the patrol, but if they didn't we usually had combat.

We went out wearing stocking caps, our faces darkened. We had no hooks to rattle or clang, and even our grenades were tied to us by cloth. Our weapons were cocked, ready to fire. If we left too early, before it was completely dark, the Chinese might see us and attack. But if we waited too long, they might get out first and trap us.

The Chinese were doing the same thing we were, and the question was who would ambush whom. We would walk ten yards or so and stop and listen. And smell, too, because the Chinese soldiers ate a lot of garlic. When we reached a predetermined point, I'd give a signal and the radioman would call in a code word to the company commander. If we were attacked or if he didn't hear from us, he would send out a rescue group. If we went out at eleven, we'd probably reach our destination around one in the morning, and we'd lie down in a diamond and check in with the company commander every ten minutes or so.

We'd stay maybe two hours in that position, then return, probably not the way we'd come, because the Chinese might have seen us come down and be lying in wait. They often attacked just as we thought we were safely back to our own lines. So we would return a different way, trying to avoid minefields. Most of the mines were ours, but no one was sure where they were.

Finally we'd reach the listening post in front of one of our platoons and give the password. Coming through the gate, we called it. There was never a better feeling in the world than coming through the gate and knowing I'd survived another patrol. As Winston Churchill once remarked, the most exhilarating experience in life is to be shot at and missed.

But many nights we ran into the Chinese or they ran into us. Men were killed by both hostile and friendly fire. We took casualties, reinforcements came down, and we carried our dead and wounded back.

Early in July, only a few weeks before the truce, the Chinese started shelling us at dusk. They hit us with five thousand rounds of artillery in an hour and a half. The Chinese had been taught by the Russians and were very good at shelling.

Then they attacked in force. Probably two regiments against our battalion, or five thousand of them to fifteen hundred of us. They came in waves and penetrated the rifle company to our left and killed some men I knew well. Artillery was going off, grenades were exploding, people were screaming, bugles were blowing and the Chinese soldiers were beating on pots and pans.

I couldn't get a view from my bunker, so two of my sergeants and I, like damn fools, got out and lay on the sandbags on top of the bunker. Louisell was nearby. He couldn't see, either, and wanted to know what the hell was going on. I was yelling into my radio for Louisell to have the air force drop flares. He was Blue Six and I kept yelling "Blue Six, give us some illumination." Finally he replied, "Light a match."

Air force cargo planes started dropping flares, and we saw thousands of Chinese moving toward us. We let loose with everything we had. We'd buried 55-gallon drums of napalm in the slope of the hill, each with a thermite grenade attached to a long wire that came back to our position. Each wire was tagged so we knew which drum it would set off. When the moment came we'd jerk the wire and the napalm would blow up and flow down the hill onto the Chinese. The battle—the Kumsong salient, to military historians—went on for hours. We used napalm and artillery and machine-gun fire, and we inflicted heavy losses on the enemy while our losses remained relatively light. When it finally ended I was shaking. Everyone was.

Another night that spring our patrol stumbled onto a Chinese platoon, perhaps forty or fifty men. Suddenly we and the Chinese were fighting with rifle butts and bayonets, and firing at close range. I shot a Chinese noncom, standing right in front of me, who was about to shoot me. I put a whole magazine into him.

We suffered three dead and three or four wounded. The next evening we went back to find out what we could about the Chinese we'd killed and bury them. The one I'd shot was seventeen or eighteen, with a corporal's two stripes. Probably a farm boy.

When the war ended at midnight on July 27, 1953, I was on Hill 468, elated to be there for the historic moment when the shooting stopped. In the morning we watched as thousands of Chinese came down into the valley to pick up the parachutes we'd used to drop flares. They would use the nylon to make into clothing. We waved at them and they waved back, men who until midnight had been trying to kill us.

I learned in Korea that war is a lousy idea. Some wars may be necessary, but history teaches that most are both avoidable and futile. There has to be a better way for nations to solve problems. In the case of Korea, I agreed with President Truman's decision to intervene, and believed we were there for a good purpose. But the truce negotiations stretched out far too long and a great many people died needlessly. I blamed the politicians for that.

Many years later I attended the opening ceremonies of the Korean War Memorial, and was moved by two inscriptions there. One was "Freedom is not free." The other said, "Our nation honors her sons and daughters who answered the call to defend a country they never knew and a people they never met."

The problem, then and always, was that the courage of those who fought was not matched by the wisdom of those whose duty it was to make peace.

When I ran for the Senate, twenty-eight years after I left Korea, the centerpiece of my campaign was that America's military might should be the greatest in the world. I viewed military power as a means to an end: a strong foreign policy that would promote democracy throughout the world. I was a young man when the Soviet leader Nikita Khrushchev declared at the United Nations, "We will bury you"—meaning Communism would bury capitalism—and I thought he was speaking literally. We had to stand up to the Soviets not only militarily but politically and economically, to show that ours was the system that would prevail.

Military supremacy means the best weapons, the best maintenance, the best leadership, the best training, the best morale. You don't send your troops into battle with anything less. Korea convinced me that force should be used sparingly, but when used, it should be overwhelming.

I believed that in the late 1970s the U.S. military had become dangerously weak. Partly that was due to the demoralization caused by our defeat in Vietnam. Beyond that, I thought that Congress and the Carter administration had made unwise reductions in the military budget.

Equipment was obsolete. Weapons systems didn't work. We weren't paying our troops well, and there was a serious drug problem in the ranks. We needed to upgrade our people as much as we did our equipment. I always supported better pay and living conditions for our troops, because I knew that no matter how good your equipment was it didn't matter if you didn't have top-notch, highly motivated people.

Ronald Reagan had campaigned on the promise of a stronger defense, and he intended to keep that promise. For his secretary of defense he chose Caspar (Cap) Weinberger, who'd been Nixon's budget director and was a true hawk on military affairs. I liked and respected Cap, but I thought he had become a captive of the Pentagon brass and was entirely uncritical of their more extreme spending schemes.

The generals were very impressive. They'd give you their top-secret intelligence reports, which always made the Russians look ten feet tall. If you took those reports literally, you couldn't sleep at night. Most of us were skeptical of those briefings. We knew that the Russians might have more tanks than we did, but half their tanks didn't run. Their military was in even worse shape than ours.

Cap Weinberger took those briefings literally, and he never met a weapons system he didn't like. He reminded me of Samuel Gompers, the founder of the American Federation of Labor, who, when asked what he wanted, always responded, "More."

The best secretary of defense I worked with was Dick Cheney, who was far more skeptical of the military than Weinberger and had a more sophisticated understanding of how Washington works.

It became obvious that the White House was giving the Pentagon more money than it could spend wisely. But the generals and admirals weren't about to refuse the money, so they dusted off all kinds of dubious projects that had been rejected in the past.

As early as May 20, 1981, when I made my "maiden speech"—a quaint phrase for an institution not famous for virgins—I focused on these concerns. Traditionally, a senator's first speech was a rite of passage, a statement of his priorities. Mine declared that while I believed in the military buildup, I also believed that reports of waste and fraud would undercut support for it.

The key paragraph in my speech spoke of the consensus that supported the Reagan military buildup:

> To assume that this consensus can be sustained indefinitely without changes in our military procurement practices is to indulge in fantasy. The public has condemned waste and profligacy in the administration of once-popular social programs. This should alert us to what will be an even more vehement outcry against the defense sector if we fail to develop a rational, cost-effective approach to meeting our national security requirements.

That speech anticipated my coming conflicts with the Pentagon over waste and cost overruns. Maybe they didn't take me seriously then, but in time they would.

In October of 1981 I became involved in the controversy over the president's proposed sale of AWACS (Airborne Warning and Control System) radar planes to Saudi Arabia for some $8.5 billion. The Jewish lobby strongly opposed the sale, which it viewed as a threat to Israel's security, and it looked as if the president faced a humiliating defeat in the Senate.

Reagan began an intense lobbying campaign in behalf of the sale, backed by the tireless efforts of Howard Baker. I became a key player in the battle because if I supported the sale it would be easier for other senators to buck the Jewish lobby.

I was under no pressure to support the AWACS sale. The White House assumed I would oppose it. But the more I studied the facts, the more I thought the controversy was ridiculous. This plane was no threat to Israel. It was defensive. Instead of weapons, it carried only a big radar disk. If war came, it would have taken the Israeli air force about fifteen minutes to blast all the AWACS out of the sky. I thought the sale didn't hurt Israel, probably helped stabilize the area, made money for the American companies that built the planes and improved our relations with the Saudis.

Howard Baker asked me to try to win over four wavering Republicans. That's what I call multiplying your vote. I was able to persuade the four and we won with fifty-two votes.

As a result, I took a lot of heat from AIPAC, the American-Israeli Political Action Committee. People called from all over the country, asking how I could do such a thing. I reminded them I was a senator first, serving the country's interest as I saw it, and Jewish second.

One zealot threatened to spend a quarter of a million dollars in New Hampshire to defeat me. I had to laugh. I told him that so much money from out of state, trying to defeat me for my AWACS vote, would probably up my margin of victory by 20 percent.

I would never have voted against Israel's interests, and I was deeply offended that anyone would accuse me of doing so. But from that time forward, when I spoke around the country, I'd meet people who'd say, "I'll never forgive that vote you cast for the Arabs!" There was no way to reason with them. It was visceral. The facts didn't matter.

The irony was that most people outside Washington didn't know I was Jewish, while a lot of people mistakenly thought my friend Bill Cohen, the senator from Maine, was, because of his name. In fact his father is Jewish, but Bill's mother is an Irish Protestant. Bill received mountains of anti-Semitic mail. He would say, "Rudman, you SOB, I'm going to take out an ad and tell people you're Jewish and they should write to you!"

I would say, "No, Bill, it's better for you to get the mail. You're much more secure politically than I am, and besides, you'd make a fine Jewish boy."

I hadn't been in Washington long before the military started courting me. Some mornings a car would pick me up and drive me to the Pentagon, where I would be taken to a comfortable dining room for breakfast with the secretary of the army and high-ranking generals. But my sympathies weren't necessarily with the generals. My priority was to protect the interests of combat troops.

The brass viewed me with suspicion. They were well aware of my military record and that I supported them on such major, controversial weapons systems as the B-1 bomber and the MX missile. But some of them couldn't understand why I would quibble about a few billion dollars here and there.

America's senior military officers are among the smartest, most highly motivated, most patriotic people I've ever known. And they are very good at carrying out their missions—Desert Storm was a reminder of that. Still, the military culture has its faults and blind spots, particularly in procurement.

A lot of military leaders believe that "If we didn't invent it, it can't be any good." They are skeptical of ideas or weapons that don't come from their own research teams or favorite contractors. Moreover, the military brass is reluctant to admit error. Once they've sunk billions in a weapons system, and are far over budget, they hunker down.

Whenever I criticized a weapons system I would quickly receive a call from a senior official who would politely invite me over for a briefing. The Pentagon had sensational briefers. They wielded charts and numbers and endless optimism to overwhelm you with their version of things. We in Congress had relatively meager research resources. Our best sources were lower-ranking military officers and civilian whistle-blowers who were appalled by waste and fraud and danger to the troops and would work with Congress at great risk to their careers.

To challenge the Pentagon you had to be a combination of sleuth, cynic, intellectual and street fighter. And a detective, too, digging out the messes that were hidden deep in their bureaucracy. Time after time I told military leaders that they'd be much better off, when they had a turkey on their hands, to simply tell Congress the truth, but that was a lesson they never learned.

The warnings I made in my maiden speech soon came true. Well-publicized cost overruns undermined the Reagan buildup. If Cap Weinberger had paid more attention to those of us who challenged him on Pentagon waste, he wouldn't have had to endure those Herblock cartoons that showed him wearing the infamous $600 toilet seat around his neck.

My first fight with the military came in the summer of 1982 over the Viper, a light shoulder-fired antitank weapon that had evolved from the bazookas of the Second World War. By then I'd met some colonels who were calling to give me the unhappy truth about the Viper.

Since 1976 we had spent about $250 million on the Viper, but it still wouldn't penetrate the armor of the latest Russian tanks, and its propellant had a limited shelf life. I imagined a soldier in a foxhole with a Russian tank rolling his way who's about to fire his Viper when he finds that the propellant went bad the month before.

During the Viper debate I told a *Newsweek* reporter, "If you're an infantryman in a foxhole and you fire at a Russian tank that's coming your way, you want to destroy him, not just piss him off."

That quotation was featured in the next issue of *Newsweek*, whereupon my mother called. She couldn't bring herself to quote me. She just said, "Did you use that word?"

"I probably did," I confessed.

"Warren," she said sadly, "what kind of parents will people think you had, talking like that in public?"

Fortunately, no one else complained, and I started using the story when I spoke to military groups. It always brought down the house.

In September I introduced an amendment to eliminate funding for the Viper, which was years behind schedule and millions of dollars over budget. By one account, its original estimate of $78 per weapon had grown to $1,400. My amendment passed, but the Viper wasn't that easy to kill. The Pentagon changed its name and kept on.

On February 23, 1983, Cap Weinberger came to testify on the administration's proposed defense budget. The secretary of defense is the absolute ruler of a vast empire. Generals scurry to do his bidding and armies march at his command. One of the few times mere mortals can gain his attention is when he is obliged to come before Congress to seek money. I decided to use the Viper to gain the secretary's attention.

I told Weinberger that the Viper—over cost, behind schedule and unable to meet the threat for which it was designed—was a microcosm of the Pentagon's procurement problems. I pointed out that the Viper had been criticized by at least four panels of defense experts, as well as by Congress. "Their advice was completely ignored," I declared. "For what do we pay these people if their advice is not to be heeded? Are your deputies so clairvoyant that they need only the general staff to pass on the merits of every weapons system? The fact is, the arrogance exhibited by those connected with Viper appears to be the norm. Do they take us for fools? Do they sit in their offices and decide which of them will be called upon to have his hand slapped at a congressional hearing while the military does as it pleases?

"All this," I reminded Weinberger, "for a weapon whose first purchased production round exploded in its launch tube."

Weinberger endured my lecture in silence, and when the time came to reply he grimly insisted that with a little more research the Viper saga might yet have a happy ending. But he'd gotten the message, and soon the Viper died a quiet death.

Next I went after the army's Sergeant York mobile antiaircraft gun, an even worse failure than the Viper. I called it the Sergeant Bilko. The Pentagon had spent nearly $2 billion on the Sergeant York and the program was years behind schedule. In September of 1984 the appropriations committee, at my urging, eliminated $484 million for its development from the fiscal 1985 military budget. The following August, Cap Weinberger formally killed the Sergeant York. I congratulated him on "closing the books on a textbook case of what's wrong with military procurement."

Why was the Pentagon so wrongheaded as to press ahead with obviously flawed weapons? The answer lies in the joys of spending an unlimited supply of other people's money. It makes you optimistic. There is always the hope that with a little more research, a little more time, a little more luck, your problems will miraculously be solved.

The issues aren't black and white. There will necessarily be failures when you are trying to develop sophisticated new systems. Sometimes there are remarkable successes. The question becomes when you must cut your losses. The Pentagon spends recklessly in part because it is so rarely called to account. Much stronger controls are needed, particularly in the post–Cold War era when major savings are possible.

The Reagan buildup had a logic that was rarely stated for public consumption. Many Republicans believed that if we carried out a major military expansion and the Russians tried to keep pace with us, we would spend them into bankruptcy. Our economy was stronger than theirs, and if it became a game of economic chicken they were going to lose. From that perspective, the president's stubborn insistence on his "Star Wars" missile defense system looks less crazy than a lot of people thought. We might never develop a "shield" against incoming nuclear missiles, but the Russians couldn't be sure of that.

In fact the Russian system did collapse, partly because it couldn't keep pace with our military spending. For all its excesses, the Reagan buildup worked. By the end of the 1980s, our military force was probably the best we'd ever had in terms of training, equipment and people.

My concern was not the military buildup but the administration's refusal to pay for it. Once I told Weinberger, "If it's a matter of national security, why not tell the American people that and ask them to pay for it? Don't you think they'd pay higher taxes for national survival?" But that logic was wasted on the Reagan administration, and the deficit kept on climbing.

In the spring of 1989 the government of Korea invited me to return to their country and, if I wished, to visit the battlefield where I had served thirty-six years before.

I was reluctant to go. I hadn't been back to Korea since I fought there. I lost a lot of good friends there and the memories of war were still painful. It was a closed chapter for me. Bob Dole once told me he felt the same way about returning to Italy, where he was so terribly wounded.

Still, there comes a time when you want to close the circle, to make sense of things if you can. Moreover, Ted Stevens said he would value my on-site evaluation of the political and military situation in Korea.

I made my return to the Demilitarized Zone accompanied by American and Korean military officials, and protected by a company of Korean army Rangers. Wearing combat gear, we returned to Hill 468, which I found a lot harder to climb at fifty-nine than I had at twenty-two. When we reached the top I was deeply moved to look out over the valley where my men and I had taken those night patrols so many years before.

We could see the North Koreans watching us from the hilltops across the valley, just as the Chinese had watched us during the war. I found my old bunker and trench lines. The timbers were rotting now. I could look over the valley and identify the positions we had taken and the places where we had fought. I walked down the hill to the place where my patrol was ambushed one night as we returned to our lines—"coming through the gate."

General Edward Burba, the ranking U.S. officer with me, asked me to tell the Koreans, through an interpreter, about the Chinese offensive that occurred not long before the July 1953 truce. About forty of us gathered on the knoll where my command post had been, and the others faced me in a semicircle. I described the initial confusion and then the flares that revealed thousands of Chinese coming our way. I drew in the sand and pointed to the places we'd fought, but my emotions overcame me and I had to stop.

As we descended the steep hill back into the valley that beautiful afternoon, I thought about the men who did not return from Korea. They will always be with me. No passage of time can ease the pain I feel when I think of friends who died in the flower of their youth.

While we were climbing those rugged hills, we came across a rusted U.S. Army helmet with a bullet hole in it. It was amazingly intact after so many years. Several months later, General Burba gave me the helmet with a plaque attached that commemorated my return to Korea. Although it brings back harsh memories, I keep it in my office to remind me of the bitter lessons of war and how they have shaped the way I have lived my life.

CHAPTER TWO

GRAMM-RUDMAN

A Bad Idea
Whose Time Has Come

All legislative Powers herein granted shall be vested in a
Congress of the United States, which shall consist of a
Senate and a House of Representatives.

THE CONSTITUTION OF THE UNITED STATES

As 1985 began, we Republicans were riding high. In November,
Ronald Reagan had won his triumphant "Morning in America"
reelection victory over Walter Mondale, sweeping 59 percent of
the vote and forty-nine of the fifty states. His landslide helped us
maintain a 53–47 majority in the Senate and gain fourteen seats
in the House.

Personally, I could look back on four good years in the Senate
and the prospect of more to come. All my polls showed that if I
ran again in 1986 I would win easily. As the newly appointed
chairman of the Ethics Committee I had achieved a leadership
role. Little that the Senate offered seemed beyond my grasp.

But I wasn't convinced I wanted a second term. I was frustrated by the president's ever-rising budget deficits, which I saw as a political betrayal and an economic disaster. One of the reasons I'd run for the Senate was to fight for economic sanity, and that meant fighting against the annual deficits that had grown larger since the mid-sixties. I'd run on the same ticket with Reagan, and we'd both pledged to balance the budget.

In 1981, during my first months in the Senate, one of my toughest decisions had been whether to support the new president's economic program, based on the supply-side economics theory developed by economist Arthur Laffer and pushed on Reagan by two Republican congressmen, Jack Kemp of New York and David Stockman, who had represented his native Michigan before becoming Reagan's budget director.

The supply-side scheme, which Reagan presented to Congress only four weeks after his inauguration, called for cutting taxes by 30 percent, increasing defense spending by three quarters of a trillion dollars, making domestic cuts of several hundred billion dollars (but not touching Social Security, Medicare and other "entitlements"), and still balancing the budget within three years. On the face of it, the theory made no sense—how did less revenue and huge defense increases balance the budget? But its zealous supporters shared the assumption—a leap of faith, really—that huge tax cuts would trigger such massive economic growth that we would wind up with more tax revenue, not less. Up to a point lower taxes *will* stimulate the economy. But clearly there is a point of diminishing returns—otherwise, why not eliminate all taxes?

As Reagan's 1980 rivals for the nomination, Howard Baker had called supply-side a "riverboat gamble" and George Bush ridiculed it as "voodoo economics." But now Bush was Reagan's vice president and Baker was the new Republican majority leader. Neither had any choice but to support the once scorned economic theory. When I shared my concerns with Baker during the Senate debate, he sighed and said we'd have to give supply-side a try; then, if it didn't work, we'd have to fix it.

In retrospect, the early months of 1981, as we debated the Reagan plan, were a turning point, comparable to Lyndon Johnson's escalation of the war in Vietnam early in 1965. In both cases, members of the president's own party shared grave doubts, but were confronted by a determined president who had just won an overwhelming victory and had widespread support in Congress and the nation.

Everyone was worried about the deficit, which in Carter's last year had risen to a then astounding $73 billion, even as the inflation rate reached double digits and interest rates were up to 21 percent. People were angry and frightened. The election seemed to have been a mandate for bold action, and Reagan had public opinion solidly behind him. Moreover, for all our doubts, we weren't sure his plan wouldn't work. It had many critics, but there were also respected economists who supported it.

We senators lacked crucial information as we considered our vote. We didn't know how far Reagan would go with his domestic budget cuts: a long way, as it turned out, but not far enough to offset his tax cuts and defense spending. Neither did we know how extreme his tax cuts would prove to be. The administration kept adding more corporate tax cuts to the package, and underestimating the loss to the Treasury. Eventually they added up to a revenue loss of $750 billion over five years.

Those of us who wanted a massive military buildup found another reason to support the Reagan plan. There were only two ways to finance the buildup. Either we raised taxes, which Reagan had vowed not to do, or we trusted in the supply-side theory to provide the needed revenue. It was a wonderfully seductive theory, because it promised so much and asked no pain or sacrifice in return.

In the end, the vast majority of Republicans, along with many Democrats, swallowed hard, hoped for the best and passed Reagan's plan. It didn't take long for us to find out how wrong we had been. Within a year supply-side clearly wasn't working, and by the end of Reagan's first term it had been a monumental disaster. Instead of balancing the budget, as promised, it had led to record deficits and an incredible doubling of the national debt.

For most of American history the federal government had gone into debt only during wars and depressions. Then, in the mid-1960s, Lyndon Johnson tried to pursue both the war in Vietnam and his ambitious domestic program without raising taxes. As a result, the deficit reached a record $25 billion in 1968, his last year in office. Even after the war ended, it kept climbing.

Most Americans assume the government should live within its means, and they responded with enthusiasm to Reagan's promises of a balanced budget. But what Reagan actually gave them was a deficit that rose to $128 billion in 1982, $208 billion in 1983, and $185 billion by 1984. Deficit spending, once an emergency measure, had become a way of life.

Given this sorry record, do I regret my vote? Of course I do. But I also believe that, given the pressures of the moment, we Republicans had little choice but to support our immensely popular president. We were impressed by the optimistic forecasts of David Stockman and other administration salesmen. It would have been extraordinary for a freshman Republican senator to vote against a popular Republican president in a Senate that had just gone Republican for the first time in a generation. We had our doubts, but we acted on the basis of the information at hand, spurred on by party loyalty and misguided optimism.

By 1985 I was disgusted. I agreed with Thomas Jefferson that for one generation to incur a public debt and pass it on to the next generation is a violation of natural and moral law. I felt betrayed by Reagan and his advisers.

In fairness, I think there is a larger dimension to our economic woes. I am impressed by Jeffrey Madrick's argument, in *The End of Affluence,* that our problem is the result of a sharp slowdown in economic growth from our historical average of about 3.4 percent a year since the Civil War to about 2.4 percent since 1973. Madrick says that the accumulated losses in goods and services due to slow growth in 1973–93 came to about $12 trillion. Without that decline, federal tax revenues would have been nearly $2.4 trillion more and the national debt could have been cut by more than half.

In that context, the ever-rising deficits of the 1970s and 1980s can be seen as the way we bridged the gap between the reality of economic decline and the rhetoric of the American dream. Rather than admit the jam we were in, we just kept borrowing.

The great unanswered question is whether this decline is temporary or, as Madrick warns, may be permanent and structural, the result of historic shifts in the world economy. Few politicians want to address the possibility that the ever-rising standard of living that Americans have counted on for more than a century has finally started to decline. For my part, I don't concede that we must accept that national loss. I have a lot of faith in America's resources, our technology and our people. But I also know that without strong political leadership we won't make the hard choices that deficit reduction demands, and unless we make those choices soon, all our resources won't be enough to save us.

By the early 1990s the annual interest payments on the national debt were nearing $300 billion. That was more than we were spending on defense and almost as much as we were spending on Social Security. These interest payments were as large as the annual deficits themselves, which means we were borrowing just to pay interest on past borrowing. We might as well take that money out and burn it. We get absolutely nothing for it. In theory, interest payments on an ever-rising national debt will eventually take all the money we have. But long before that comes to pass, financial markets will refuse us future credit, banks will fail, the government will stop meeting its obligations and the result can only be social and political chaos.

The solution is obvious. The government must pay its bills instead of borrowing. But that means spending less and/or taxing more—unpopular positions, which many politicians fear. Walter Mondale talked about tax increases in 1984 and carried one state out of fifty. Instead, throughout Reagan's first term, Congress kept right on spending money we didn't have, oblivious to the disaster waiting down the road.

For all these reasons, I wasn't sure I wanted to run again in 1986. Did I want six more years of this mess? I wasn't the only senator who was worried about the deficit, but I'm not sure anyone else was as obsessed as I was. I was proud to be a senator, but I was also ashamed to be part of an economic fraud.

I could go home to New Hampshire and be a lot happier. I loved the state and missed it. I missed my family and friends, and my parents. My kids were growing into interesting adults and I hated not seeing them more. I missed being able to wake up in the morning and take Olaf, my black Labrador, for a walk in the woods behind my home in Nashua. I missed the natural beauty of my state.

Too many people in Congress live in fear of losing their jobs, so they pander to the voters. I had the freedom that came from knowing I could live without the Senate. I could practice law in New Hampshire and live a far richer life. I loved the Senate and the opportunities it gave me to do good, as I saw it, but I was sick of the hypocrisy that had doubled the national debt in the four years I'd been there. I wanted to stay but not at the cost of my convictions.

The one hope I saw as 1985 began was a growing, bipartisan realization in the Senate that something had to be done about the deficit and that if the White House wouldn't lead, we would have to. I often shared my frustrations with Republican colleagues like Howard Baker, Bob Dole, Pete Domenici, Slade Gorton and Jack Danforth. I would say, "This is incredible. We're supposed to be the party of fiscal responsibility. Maybe the Democrats control the House, but you can't tell me that if we were serious about deficit reduction, with a president as popular as Reagan behind us, we couldn't do something about it."

I remember telling Pete Domenici, early in 1985, that if we didn't move on the deficit that year we were sowing the seeds of destruction of our own party. Pete agreed, and added that we'd probably get no help from the White House and face serious opposition in our own party. And yet, we agreed, we had to try.

During the mid-1980s I attended two White House meetings at which Republican senators told the president of their great concerns about the deficit. In the first of the meetings, in the Oval Office, I told Reagan that because of his immense popularity, because the people not only liked but loved him, he had the political power and moral authority to address this urgent issue. I said I was terribly disappointed that we Republicans not only had failed to reduce the deficit but were vastly increasing it.

Reagan replied amiably that he shared my concerns. Then his top domestic adviser, the stolid, doggedly loyal Ed Meese, angrily declared that the Democrats were to blame for the deficit, and that if everyone would just follow the White House game plan, everything would work out fine. You couldn't argue with someone like that. It was like throwing sand at the Sahara.

Meese's remarks stopped the deficit discussion cold, and we drifted into small talk. I gazed at Reagan, who could be so genial, so affable, who enlivened those meetings with hilarious and mostly unprintable stories of his Hollywood days, and thought, Here's the most beloved president of his time, a man with superb communications skills, a man who could truly lead the country, and what a tragedy it is that he's getting such terrible advice, because if he understood the problem he'd do something about it.

At the other meeting, in the Cabinet Room, we Republicans confronted Reagan with the billions we'd added to the deficit, and the grim projections for the coming years. When we finished, he turned to his budget director, David Stockman, and said in apparent amazement, "Wait a minute, this can't be true!"

Stockman calmly replied that if the White House plans and estimates worked out, our projections wouldn't materialize. He was clinging, despite overwhelming evidence to the contrary, to what he would later call his Rosy Scenario, which used wildly optimistic projections about inflation and the GNP to justify even more wildly inaccurate predictions of a balanced budget. Another of his tricks—revealed after he left the White House, wrote a book and blamed others for the disaster—was what he called the Magic Asterisk, which, when all else failed, he would use to denote unspecified future budget cuts that would lead to the dreamed-of balanced budget.

I blame Stockman for much of the budget disaster and for Reagan's failure to understand what was going on. People have asked me if Reagan didn't know from the beginning that supply-side was hokum but he pushed it nonetheless in order to lower taxes on the rich and boost the Pentagon budget. I don't believe that; I never doubted Reagan's sincerity.

It is important to understand that Reagan arrived in the White House with three passionately held beliefs: that taxes were too high, that government was too big and that the Russians might at any moment land at Cape Hatteras. Everything else flowed from those core beliefs.

Reagan held grand visions, was indifferent to details and relied on others to achieve his goals. That was particularly true for the budget, since his remarkable skills didn't include a mastery of economics. As a result, the very bright, ambitious, persuasive Stockman became a powerful adviser in the early months of 1981.

In his 1981 talks with journalist William Greider and his 1985 memoir *The Triumph of Politics,* Stockman shamelessly confessed to a record of budgetary deception and political cynicism that numbs the imagination. It wasn't just the Rosy Scenario and the Magic Asterisk. He told Greider that the real purpose of Reaganomics was "dropping the top (tax rate) from 70 percent to 50 percent—the rest of it is a secondary matter . . . a Trojan horse to bring down the top rate." He revealed supply-side economics to have been, in his mind, a hoax, a gussied-up version of the old "trickle-down economics" that assumes that if the government makes the rich richer, in time a few scraps of prosperity will trickle down to everyone else.

The best you can say of Stockman is that he was far over his head as an economic czar, but this is too kind. Whatever his confusions, he didn't hesitate to deceive Congress, the president and the public. His book makes clear his contempt not only for Congress, which he sees as a gang of ignorant, greedy fools, but for the president, who unwisely lifted him from obscurity. The real reason Reaganomics failed, he wrote, was that Reagan wasn't tough enough—didn't go far enough in cutting domestic spending—and therefore betrayed Stockman and the other supply-side true believers.

Yet however much I blame Stockman, along with Jack Kemp, Cap Weinberger, Jim Baker, Ed Meese and all the others around Reagan who put the president's popularity ahead of the nation's economic health, the fact remains that they were Reagan's creatures. He chose them and they gave him what he wanted. Some of us tried, but you couldn't get through to Reagan on the deficit, no matter how you battered him with facts and figures. The man inhabited his own reality. That was both his greatness and his failure as a political leader. His greatness was his ability to make Americans share his vision of reality, be it Morning in America, supply-side economics, Star Wars or the Evil Empire. His failure was that, at least in economic affairs, his reality was a delusion.

In the spring of 1985, however, the question was not how we'd gotten into the deficit mess but how, if at all, we might escape it. Though we assumed we'd get no help from the White House, Senate Republicans began to talk of proposing a fiscal 1986 budget (it would take effect on October 1, 1985) to include a serious plan to reduce the deficit. No one imagined our path would be easy. We were acutely aware of the tension between what was right economically and what was prudent politically. Serious budget reduction would have to include steps that would be hugely unpopular with millions of voters, such as tax increases and reductions in Social Security, Medicare and Medicaid spending.

In 1981 Stockman had proposed to reduce Social Security benefits for those people who choose to retire at age sixty-two, and in the next year's congressional elections the Democrats used that to convince many voters that "the Republicans will take away your Social Security." Now, in 1985, neither side was likely to forget that we Republicans had twenty-two Senate seats up in 1986 to the Democrats' twelve, and a net gain of only four seats would return the Senate to Democratic control. It was in this highly partisan context that a few of us set out to negotiate a budget that would bring down the deficit for fiscal 1986.

One of the key players in the budget debate was the new Republican majority leader, Bob Dole of Kansas, who was chosen after Howard Baker retired. I hated to see Howard leave, but I had to respect his decision that eighteen years was enough. Dole lacked Howard's easy Southern charm, but he was an outstanding leader. I knew how terrible his war wounds had been and how bravely he bore the pain they still caused him. Bob is an American hero, and I don't use the word lightly.

His sharp tongue had won him a reputation for partisanship, but the man I knew was always open, balanced and reasonable, someone who listened to all sides of an argument, who suffered fools patiently, and who cared about the poor and afflicted. I never knew him to use profanity and I saw him lose his temper only once. That was several years later when we Republicans were in the minority again. We were meeting in Bob's office on the second floor of the Capitol, with its gorgeous view down the Mall to the Washington Monument, when Malcolm Wallop of Wyoming unwisely suggested that Bob wasn't being tough enough toward the Democrats.

Bob didn't welcome the criticism, both because he prides himself on his leadership and because there were rumors of a conservative coup against him as majority leader. The conservatives didn't have the votes, but there still was talk.

Bob's face darkened as he glared at Wallop. "You don't seem happy with my leadership," he declared. "Maybe you could do better. Would you like to have an election right now?"

Wallop, stunned by Dole's anger, reddened and mumbled something conciliatory, and the moment passed. But Bob had bluntly reminded everyone that he had the votes to beat back

Wallop or any other challenger. That was the only time I saw him really angry. Dry, sometimes dark humor was more his style.

Even more than Dole, Pete Domenici of New Mexico, as chairman of the Budget Committee, was central to the anti-deficit crusade that spring. Pete, the son of Italian immigrants, had been mayor of Albuquerque before coming to the Senate, and in Washington he maintained a keen sense of grassroots reality. He is a serious, intense man, deeply committed to his work, a patriot and a fighter, and one of the best senators I know.

Some of us urged George Bush to consider Pete for his running mate in 1988. In addition to his outstanding record in the Senate and his popularity with the media, Pete was an Italian American, a moderate, a Catholic and a family man: in short, someone who would have brought a lot to the ticket. But Bush passed him over in favor of Dan Quayle, who was not the lightweight the media suggested, but lacked Pete's experience and solid record of accomplishment. Quayle had a lot to learn, but I ranked him near the middle of the Senate in terms of ability and effectiveness.

Pete Domenici, of course, I ranked in the top ten. I heard that Bush passed over Pete because he was willing to consider higher taxes and a cap on entitlements to reduce the deficit—extremely sensible positions—and because Barbara Bush didn't like the fact that Pete smoked cigarettes. That may or may not have been true, but it was a vice that I, as a smoker, could forgive—and one he eventually overcame.

Pete not only smoked but worried a lot, especially about the deficit, and I was delighted when he set to work on a 1986 budget resolution that would seriously confront it.

Clearly, such a budget would involve compromise. Liberals would have to accept more cuts in such domestic programs as the Job Corps, college loans and food stamps. Conservatives would have to live with a smaller defense budget. And both sides would have to accept politically explosive cuts in costly "entitlements," such as Social Security, Medicaid and Medicare, or at least in their annual cost-of-living adjustments, or COLAs, which increase payments in keeping with inflation. The COLAs were open-ended and they were killing us. To question them was to risk the wrath of millions of voters, but we had no choice. Entitlements were projected to grow from 47 percent of the budget in 1980 to 61 percent in 1997, and largely because of them our debt payment was expected to rise from 9 percent to 15.6 percent in that same period. Given the aging of the population, it was clear that we just didn't have the money to keep expanding payments to older Americans.

Deficit reduction required new revenues, but President Reagan was opposed to new taxes, and had promised to veto any that Congress sent him. If fifty-one senators voted a tax increase but we lacked the two thirds needed to override his veto, we would only have given the Democrats an issue that could defeat us.

The spring of 1985 was filled with intense negotiations, literally hundreds of meetings. The debate was more over politics than substance. Almost no one disagreed about what had to be done to lower the budget. The discussion was over the political risk and what help the president might provide.

Some senators felt relatively secure with their constituents. They felt strong enough to take political risks, because they could go home and give interviews and hold town meetings and win public support. But many of our colleagues lived in fear of an unpopular vote that might cost them their seats. The real question was whether the pain and sacrifice of budget reduction could become a popular enough cause to win majorities in both houses of Congress.

Finally Pete Domenici's committee produced a budget resolution that came before the Senate for a vote on the evening of Thursday, May 9, and was debated until the early-morning hours of May 10. The proposal sought bipartisan support by addressing all three major concerns:

—A one-year freeze on cost-of-living adjustments for Social Security and federal retirement benefits would save an estimated $30 billion. The freeze would have cost the average Social Security recipient only about seventeen dollars a month, but was politically significant because it dared to touch Social Security.

—The military budget, which had grown at an annual average of 8 percent since 1981, would increase only at the rate of inflation, not the inflation plus 3 percent the president insisted was essential to national security. If this passed, it meant Reagan's historic military buildup was finally over.

—More than a dozen domestic programs would be cut or eliminated, including economic development, the Job Corps, Amtrak, farm price supports and student loans. These cuts, although substantial, reflected the Senate Republicans' consensus that most domestic programs should be trimmed, but not eliminated entirely, as Reagan, Stockman, Meese and others wanted.

Overall, the package proposed to cut about $56 billion from a 1986 deficit projected at a record $230 billion. Over three years, it would cut nearly $300 billion. It was a reasoned, balanced, good-faith proposal, but intensely controversial. After years of giving people more and more benefits we finally proposed to give them a little less.

After several hours of intense debate, voting on the budget resolution began around one-thirty in the morning. We expected a largely party-line vote, but a handful of Republicans were wavering, and the outcome was by no means certain. Adding to the suspense, three senators were absent because of illness: the North Carolina Republican James East, Nebraska Democrat James Exon and California Republican Pete Wilson, who had entered the Bethesda Naval Hospital for an emergency appendectomy two days before.

Around two in the morning, with the opponents of the anti-deficit package ahead 49 to 48, Pete Wilson arrived at the Capitol by ambulance. Pete and I were good friends, and I hurried out to meet him as medical attendants wheeled him into the Capitol on a gurney, then helped him into a wheelchair before he entered the chamber.

"Are you okay, Pete?" I asked.

He managed a smile. He was weak and pale but game.

I followed him in. Two pages pushed open the double doors to the Senate chamber. The room was suddenly quiet.

"What is the question?" Pete asked, to laughter and applause. He raised his right arm and the clerk called out, "Mr. Wilson?"

Pete flashed a thumbs-up.

"Mr. Wilson, aye," the clerk intoned, and the chamber exploded.

Pete was rushed back to the hospital, but his vote had produced a 49–49 tie, permitting Vice President Bush to cast the deciding vote.

That meant we won, because the White House had reluctantly decided to support us. The president's men liked our proposed COLA cuts, hated our freeze on military spending, but thought politics demanded that they join the anti-deficit crusade. Our 50–49 majority included all but four Republicans (Al D'Amato of New York, Paula Hawkins of Florida, Charles Mathias of

Maryland and Arlen Specter of Pennsylvania) and one Democrat, Edward Zorinsky of Nebraska, whose crucial vote was rewarded when several hundred million dollars' worth of farm-related spending was restored to the budget.

We Republicans were proud of our dramatic victory. We thought it was a historic first step toward addressing runaway entitlement costs and, beyond that, toward taking on the deficit. Yet even as we celebrated we understood the political implications of looking "soft" on Social Security. Our votes were barely cast when a Democratic Party spokesman boasted, "We could cut our campaign TV ads right now!" In fact, a majority of Democrats had supported alternatives to the Domenici plan that included COLA cuts, but we never got that fact across to the public and we were again denounced as enemies of Social Security.

The Democratic-controlled House proceeded to pass a budget resolution that retained the COLAs and cut defense spending even more severely than we had. That was good partisan politics, but it contributed nothing to serious deficit reduction. The Democrats were clearly determined to use our votes for COLA cuts against us politically. Negotiations broke down until July, when an unexpected development changed everything.

On July 9 the president invited congressional leaders to the White House for cocktails. During the evening, Reagan and Democratic Speaker Tip O'Neill took a walk on the South Lawn of the White House, where they paused under a towering oak tree to cut a deal. After the meeting they announced a budget "framework" that eliminated the COLA cuts, O'Neill's major goal, and also gave Reagan what he most wanted, no new taxes and the Senate's higher level of defense spending.

The champion of America's conservatives and the old New Deal liberal had made a deal that gave each what he most wanted—and the deficit be damned. It was like the final scene in George Orwell's *Animal Farm*, when you can't tell the farmers from the pigs.

The Senate Republicans who had exposed themselves politically in behalf of deficit reduction were outraged by this betrayal. I told a reporter that I felt as if I'd flown a kamikaze mission. I didn't blame O'Neill. He did exactly what I would have expected him to do—protected Social Security and played partisan politics. It was Reagan who should have shown leadership but was too proud or stubborn or ill-advised to bend even a little. Many Senate Republicans had risked their careers to try to reduce his towering deficits, and his response was to disown us and make a deal with the Democrats.

Jack Kemp, one of the last supply-side true believers, was partly to blame, for he had urged Reagan to fight a tax increase at all costs, which, of course, was what Reagan wanted to hear. Insofar as he shared credit for the outcome, Kemp scored points against two of his rivals for the 1988 presidential nomination, Dole and Bush, both of whom had voted to cut COLAs in our 50–49 "victory" two months earlier. But politics aside, Kemp was dead wrong and he bore major responsibility for the collapse of deficit reform.

The deal with Tip O'Neill was a turning point for Reagan. He'd won his triumphant reelection eight months earlier. To have risked his political capital for deficit reduction would have been an act of high statesmanship. Instead, he clung to his popularity, his self-serving advisers and his rigid ideology, and both the nation's future and his place in history will suffer for it. It is true that the previous fall, in one of the campaign debates with Mondale, Reagan had boxed himself in by a promise not to touch Social Security; he should never have made the promise and, having made it, should have found a way around it in the interest of a balanced budget.

In late July the Senate passed a budget resolution that incorporated the Reagan-O'Neill deal. I denounced it on the Senate floor, speaking off the cuff, in one of the angriest speeches I ever made. I began by detailing the terrible damage that the budget deficits were causing our economy:

> It was in this context that the Senate on May 10 surprised the skeptics and passed a historic budget resolution calling for a $56 billion reduction in the federal deficit in fiscal 1986 alone and $295 billion in savings over the next three years.
>
> The Senate resolution accomplished this by making significant savings in the president's defense program, eliminating the automatic cost-of-living adjustments in most federal entitlement programs, cutting or eliminating a number of discretionary programs, and freezing most other discretionary programs at the fiscal 1985 level. The prospects on May 10 for meaningful action on the deficit appeared very bright. . . .

Nonetheless, I said, the Senate now had passed a budget that did little or nothing about the deficit. Why?

I said the blame for this failure rested with both parties:

> . . . the president and the majority leadership of the House of Representatives have agendas in which the budget deficit problem, notwithstanding their rhetoric, does not rank very high. The position of the House leadership is clear. The most important item on their budget agenda is to prevent any restriction on statutory automatic cost-of-living adjustments in any entitlement program, no matter how limited.

The Democrats were playing politics with Social Security, I charged, and were hell-bent on protecting every domestic program on the books, no matter how wasteful or inefficient they might be. But the Reagan administration was just as bad:

The administration is unwilling to consider any measure which will lead to a revenue increase. . . . It is determined to keep as much money flowing through the Defense Department as possible. . . . It is determined to avoid exercising any leadership on cost-of-living adjustments, an attitude similar to that of the House leadership on taxes. . . .

When it finally began to look like the Senate was making progress in conference with the House, the administration pulled the rug out from under negotiations.

Mr. President, I will conclude by simply saying this: After seven months of blood, sweat, and tears, we have come to this sorry state. I yield the floor.

As the August recess drew near, I was still angry, and before I went home I asked Tom Polgar, my brilliant thirty-one-year-old legislative director, to think about a way to control the deficit. I mentioned our New Hampshire law that mandates that whenever the state faces a deficit, a legislative committee must recommend enough cuts to the governor to balance the budget. Most states have some similar ban on budget deficits.

I asked Tom to think along those lines—something automatic, something mandatory, that could succeed where conventional means had failed. I didn't know exactly what I wanted—only that I was tired of all the double-talk and hypocrisy.

In August I traveled around New Hampshire, meeting with constituents in my offices in Manchester, Concord and Portsmouth, but finding time for my family, golf and visits with friends. About a week before Labor Day, Tom Polgar, down in Washington, read an AP story out of Texas that said Senator Phil Gramm was considering legislation that would provide for automatic spending cuts to bring down the deficits. Tom called and read me the story and I quickly called Gramm in Texas.

In effect, I said, "Phil, we're thinking along the same lines—do you want to work together?"

He said, "You bet I would, because you have a lot of friends on both sides of the aisle. I'm an economist, you're a lawyer, and we'd make a terrific team."

I called Tom back and told him to talk to Gramm's people and come up with a framework for us to consider when we returned to Washington.

Thus was born the controversial deficit-reduction plan that became known as Gramm-Rudman.

Phil Gramm, then in his first year in the Senate, was a lanky, balding, acerbic Georgia-born conservative who'd been an economics professor at Texas A&M before he was elected to Congress as a Democrat in 1978. In 1981 Gramm worked closely with House Republican leaders to pass the Gramm-Latta bill, which embodied the Reagan administration's plans for major cuts in domestic spending. House Democratic leaders were furious when they learned that after attending their strategy sessions, Phil shared what he'd learned with the Reagan forces.

Liar, spy, traitor, turncoat—those were some of the printable things Democrats called him. After the 1982 elections, they forced him off the Budget Committee, and he responded by resigning, switching parties and winning reelection to the House, then election to the Senate, as a Republican.

I didn't know Phil well at that time, but my impression was that he was politically astute, unconventional and sometimes ruthless. He had a gift for explaining economic theory in a way ordinary Americans could understand, and also a nasty talent for defining issues so that, politically speaking, it was almost impossible to oppose him.

Phil was not popular (he often said that was not his goal), but he was smart and dead serious. He was a true believer: the deficit had to be cut and he was going to cut it, one way or another.

Phil once told me how much he hated having to vote in the House to raise the debt ceiling to a trillion dollars. I, of course, had felt the same way in the Senate. He said that when the debt-ceiling vote arrived, Democratic Majority Leader Jim Wright declared that if your wife ran up bills, a gentleman would pay them, whereupon Phil jumped up and declared, "You might pay your wife's bills but the difference between what the majority leader is saying and the real world is that you and your wife and your children would sit down around the kitchen table, and you'd get out a butcher knife and cut up your credit cards and write a budget. What is happening here is that we're paying the bills but nobody is changing the way we spend!"

Phil then introduced an amendment to tie the debt-ceiling increase to a mandatory balanced budget. His plan was so popular that Jim Wright had to struggle to stop it from passing. Even that early proposal contained the concept of "sequestering" funds that would become central to Gramm-Rudman.

Phil's balanced-budget plan languished until 1985, when, with the debt approaching $2 trillion, he sensed another opportunity to act. We were thinking along the same lines and it made sense to join forces. He was better versed in economics than I, but I could reach out to Democrats who would never cooperate with Phil because they still resented his crossover to the Republicans.

After Labor Day, Phil and I and our staffs set to work and soon had a forty-page draft of the Balanced Budget and Emergency Deficit Reduction Act of 1985, as Gramm-Rudman was officially known. We also acquired a third cosponsor, the silver-haired, patrician Ernest (Fritz) Hollings of South Carolina. The bill then became Gramm-Rudman-Hollings, although most writers shortened it to Gramm-Rudman. Fritz always said that in South Carolina it was known as Hollings-Gramm-Rudman. We were happy to have a Democrat as a cosponsor. Fritz had long opposed deficits and advocated a value-added tax—in effect, a national sales tax—and he may have hoped that our threat of automatic spending cuts would push Congress toward a VAT.

In its original form, Gramm-Rudman directed the president and Congress to cut the deficit by $36 billion a year from fiscal 1987 to 1991, at which time we would have gone from annual deficits near $200 billion to a balanced budget. The president was required to withhold, or "sequester," across the board, portions of congressionally approved spending if the deficit was more than 10 percent over the specified level. It was this automatic sequestering of funds that gave the bill teeth.

Late in September we unveiled Gramm-Rudman to selected reporters over breakfast in a private room in the Capitol. Phil and I outlined our plan, discussed our legislative strategy and took questions. Most reporters saw our proposed automatic cuts as a good story but doubted that our bill would pass.

At 1:00 P.M. that day we held a news conference in a jam-packed Appropriations Committee hearing room to officially introduce the bill to the media. Before the session began, I learned that Fritz Hollings was having second thoughts about his role as a sponsor of the legislation. Fritz was taking heat from his fellow Democrats for joining forces with the turncoat Phil Gramm, and he was threatening to back out. I gave him a pep talk and didn't relax until I saw him walk in the door.

As the debate over Gramm-Rudman began, no one, including its authors, had any idea what would happen if its automatic budget cuts came into play. Automatic, across-the-board cuts were something new, and their impact was unpredictable. People could see in our legislation whatever they wanted to see; Phil Gramm said later, "The genius of Gramm-Rudman was that it was like truth inside a crystal; everybody saw it through a different facet."

Many of the bill's supporters, myself included, assumed that its doomsday machinery would never be used. We saw the legislation as a forcing mechanism. We thought the threat of automatic cuts would force Congress and the White House to compromise on a responsible budget. Automatic cuts would be, among other things, a shameful admission of political incompetence.

Many politicians saw Gramm-Rudman in purely political terms, as a way to wrap themselves in the flag of deficit-cutting. For Republicans it was a way to distance themselves from the Reagan deficits. For Democrats it was a way to shed the label of "big spenders." Some senators, in both parties, supported Gramm-Rudman because they calculated that its goals could never be reached by spending cuts alone, and therefore saw the legislation as a way to force Reagan to accept tax increases.

The White House agonized over Gramm-Rudman. How could Ronald Reagan oppose a plan to balance the budget? And yet the legislation, besides being a clear rebuke to the president's first-term economic failures, would almost certainly force him to choose between his defense buildup and the tax increases he so fiercely resisted. The president bitterly resented our legislation, and many of his advisers—Weinberger, Meese, Kemp—were urging him to veto it right up to the moment it reached his desk.

But even Reagan could not entirely ignore the political realities. In the 1930s musical *Dumbo,* Jimmy Durante walked onstage leading an elephant. When a policeman rushed up and demanded where he was going with the elephant, Durante asked innocently, "What elephant?"

By 1985, Ronald Reagan was innocently asking, "What deficit?"

The American people were starting to see the deficit as a political issue, and both parties wanted to blame the other for it. Many Republicans feared that the deficit would cost us the Senate and eagerly embraced Gramm-Rudman as political cover. That was fine. I didn't care why they voted for it, as long as it passed.

Amid much uncertainty about our proposal's consequences and prospects, Phil, Fritz and I divided up the Senate and began to buttonhole our colleagues. Phil took the conservative Republicans, I took the more moderate Republicans, and Hollings worked on the conservative Democrats.

The response was encouraging. When we unveiled the legislation on September 24, we had sixteen cosponsors, including such liberal Democrats as Chris Dodd and Paul Simon. Still uncertain of our prospects, but flexing our muscles a bit, we let it be known that we had twenty Republican senators who would join Democrats in blocking the debt-ceiling increase unless the Senate took up Gramm-Rudman. That was hardball, a warning to the White House and our Senate leadership that they must give us a vote or we'd shut down the government. Phil Gramm was delighted at the prospect: "Hell, if we shut down the government, folks might decide they don't want it opened back up. We'll declare victory and announce that at last our people are free!"

Our momentum kept growing. We had forty-one cosponsors by October 2, and were near fifty when Bob Dole placed it before the Senate the next day. Democrats like John Kerry of Massachusetts and David Boren of Oklahoma had come aboard. *The Washington Post* was using words like "groundswell" and "firestorm" to describe our support.

Our success was due in large part to a simple but highly effective legislative strategy. Congress was nearing a vote to raise the debt ceiling above $2 trillion. The debt-ceiling bill was going to pass. You could bet your life on it. An angry minority might stall it, and shut down the government for a few days in protest—that was a Senate tradition, each party embarrassing the other when it had the chance—but the final outcome was not in doubt.

Our strategy was to attach our balanced-budget amendment to the legislation that would raise the debt ceiling. It would pass, and our bill would pass with it.

That put Bob Dole on the spot. Although he was dedicated to deficit reduction—he had been brilliant and tireless in orchestrating our 50–49 victory in May—he was in the same position Howard Baker had been in 1981, when he was confronted with the supply-side economic program. A Republican majority leader can't buck a popular Republican president and keep his job. It was the majority leader's duty to keep the legislative trains running on time. In this case, the White House most decidedly didn't want to be embarrassed by a government shutdown that would only focus more attention on the already embarrassing bill to raise the debt ceiling to $2 trillion.

When Phil and I first told Bob of our plan, he tried to talk us out of it. "You've got a good idea there," he said. "We have to do something about the deficit, but we can't do it on this piece of legislation. The White House doesn't want it and I'd have to fight you."

But we were in a different position. Our obligation to the White House was less than our passion for deficit reduction.

"Bob, if you were in our place you'd do the same thing," I told him. "You know perfectly well that the only train that's going to leave the station and arrive at its destination is the debt-ceiling increase. There's no way Phil and I will ever get an honest debate and a vote on this unless we do it this way, and we're not backing off."

Bob, to his credit, didn't threaten us. He just made his case and said he'd try to beat us. But we weren't so easy to beat. The debt-ceiling legislation gave us a rare opportunity. If we'd introduced our bill on its own, it would most likely have died in committee. Attached to the debt-ceiling bill, it would have to be voted up or down. If it won a majority vote, it would reach the president's desk and be signed.

This strategy gave us a tremendous moral and political advantage. To vote for the debt increase and at the same time vote against a balanced budget would—we hoped—be seen as political suicide, and few of our colleagues were thus inclined. The debt-ceiling increase added an element to the equation that all politicians understood—fear.

The other key to Gramm-Rudman's success was that it captured the imagination of the American people in a way that is rare in politics. People were disturbed by the deficit—and its symbol, the $2 trillion national debt—and they understood that we were serious about ending it. Gramm-Rudman became the most talked-about, written-about legislation in years, and soon won widespread support. We saw that in talks with voters and in polls as well.

Even Tip O'Neill, who hated Gramm-Rudman for the spending cuts it would impose, was soon telling reporters that it would pass the House: "There's no stopping it," he admitted. "The mail is overwhelming."

When Gramm-Rudman was first introduced, the White House kept its distance. The Treasury Department, now headed by Jim Baker, saw it as unorthodox and messy; they wanted a "clean" debt-ceiling bill, not one complicated by our meat-ax approach to budgetary matters. At Defense, Cap Weinberger saw our automatic cuts as a threat to his military buildup.

Bob Dole initially underestimated our political strength. We heard from friends in the White House that Dole was telling them, "Don't worry, this thing isn't going to happen." Then, days later, he was saying, "My God, it's happening—they have fifty cosponsors!"

"At first the White House took a hands-off approach," Phil Gramm recalls. "I'm not sure how seriously they took us. Nobody understood the leverage we had. Nobody understood the power of the idea. Nobody understood our ability to get support from people they never thought would support us. So I think the right word for the leadership of both parties, and the White House, was shock. They were shocked that we very quickly went over fifty co-sponsors, and once we went over fifty we went over sixty."

At a White House breakfast on October 1, Dole took aside Reagan's new chief of staff, Don Regan—he and Jim Baker had traded jobs—and warned him that we might soon have the votes to pass Gramm-Rudman and the president had better get aboard.

On Friday, October 3, Reagan told reporters he was "in agreement" with the goals of Gramm-Rudman, but he stopped short of an endorsement. On Saturday he used his weekly radio address to endorse the bill, calling it "historic," but he added a "caveat," insisting that Congress give him military spending increases of 3 percent for the next two years. His uncertainties about Gramm-Rudman would increase in the weeks ahead.

We were glad to have Reagan's endorsement, but by then we had fifty-three votes and it was too late for the White House to have any serious role in shaping our proposal. The president was Ronnie-come-lately as far as we were concerned—we'd won this victory on our own.

When Bob Dole put the legislation before the Senate, it was as an amendment to the debt-ceiling increase. There would be no committee hearings. Dole said the Senate had to pass the bill immediately, because the government was due to run out of money the following Monday. He quipped that "The longer something hangs around here, the staler it gets. People start reading it."

Democrats objected bitterly to the lack of hearings or an opportunity to amend the bill. We responded that there wasn't time for debate—the time had come for a yes or no vote on balancing the budget.

In the face of Democratic threats of a filibuster, Dole scheduled rare Saturday and Sunday sessions that weekend. Thus, on Saturday, I found myself on the Senate floor, defending Gramm-Rudman before a group of skeptical Democrats.

Gary Hart argued at length that Gramm-Rudman would perpetuate Reaganomics by favoring domestic cuts over defense cuts. The White House, of course, feared just the opposite.

By then we had agreed that, for political reasons, Social Security would be excluded from the automatic cuts ("We can't drag that dead cat across the table again," Phil declared). For legal reasons, interest on the national debt and existing contractual obligations, including defense contracts, were also excluded.

During the debate that morning, I was asked to respond to a *Washington Post* editorial that criticized us for protecting Social Security. If cuts would fall on the poor, on farmers, on students, on veterans, on virtually every other group, should not the elderly also share in the sacrifice?

I said that I agreed entirely, and that as Gramm and I had originally written the bill Social Security would have been subject to our across-the-board cuts. But too many senators had warned that they could not support Gramm-Rudman if it touched Social Security. A bill that did so would have lost overwhelmingly. Social Security was off the table, period.

My most interesting exchanges were with George Mitchell of Maine, one of the senators I most respected. He had risen from humble beginnings to become a U.S. attorney in Maine, then a judge and finally a senator. Mitchell was a Democratic leader who could utter the most outrageous partisan statements and still sound as innocent as a choirboy. He was a man of such intelligence and civility that I could sharply disagree with him and yet remain his friend. I think he would have made a far more attractive presidential candidate than some of those the Democrats have put forward in recent years.

Mitchell was skeptical of Gramm-Rudman. He believed that the way to reduce the deficit was with a combination of tax increases and spending cuts, and he was vastly frustrated by the Reagan administration's refusal to consider even an increase on the cigarette tax, for example, or a minimum tax on corporations and wealthy individuals who paid no taxes at all.

Mitchell, baiting me, asked if Gramm-Rudman could include automatic tax increases as well as automatic spending cuts. I reminded him there was a constitutional problem there, in that tax increases must originate in the House. Then I added what he knew very well, that President Reagan had vowed to veto any tax increase, so that wasn't an option.

Soon our basic disagreement became clear: I believed that the automatic cuts would never happen and he feared they would.

I told Mitchell, "I am of the opinion that the mechanism that is called for in this will never be adopted. . . . I believe this is a mechanism which forces political compromise.

"I say to my friend from Maine, I doubt if the things that are set out here will ever happen. We will not have a $40 billion overage, followed by automatic cuts. That is not going to happen. There will be too much outcry in the country. Then we will say, 'Fine, you want it, you pay for it.' That is really the philosophy behind what we are trying to do."

Mitchell was not persuaded, for he feared Reagan would accept automatic spending cuts that would cripple domestic programs, and even reduce his military buildup, rather than agree to tax increases. To me, Gramm-Rudman's automatic cuts were an unacceptable alternative, one that reasonable people would reject, but Mitchell feared that Reagan and his advisers were not reasonable.

I believed the system would work and Mitchell believed it wouldn't. Time would prove him right.

That weekend session was a disaster for the Democrats. They were deluged with calls from people who accused them of trying to block a plan to balance the budget. At the same time the president, having reluctantly backed our plan, was presenting himself as its number one champion—the great deficit-maker was reborn as the dauntless deficit-fighter. The Democrats, to their dismay, saw Reagan escaping his record, stealing their issue and possibly dashing their dream of retaking the Senate.

On Wednesday the Senate passed Gramm-Rudman by an overwhelming 75 to 24. Twenty-seven Democrats, including such leading liberals as Ted Kennedy, joined all but four Republicans in supporting the bill.

The bill went next to the House, whose Democratic leaders saw Gramm-Rudman as unstoppable, and therefore set out to water it down as much as they could. They demanded that more and more domestic programs be exempted from cuts, even as conservatives fought to put more of the defense budget off limits.

The Democrats couldn't afford to appear to be opposing deficit reduction, but sometimes we thought they were trying to make the law so objectionable that Reagan would veto it—and, we feared, that might not take much.

One much debated issue concerned the legislation's "trigger" mechanism. Who or what would determine that Congress and the president had not met the law's deficit targets and that funds must therefore be sequestered?

We first proposed that the Office of Management and Budget be the trigger. But Democrats objected that OMB reported to the president and couldn't be trusted to be honest about the numbers. They had a point: under David Stockman, OMB had become notorious for underestimating deficits by tens of billions of dollars. Stockman was gone by then, but we feared that Stockmanism lived on.

As a compromise, the Democrats pushed for the General Accounting Office, which had links to both the executive and legislative branches. The president appointed its boss, the comptroller general, for a fifteen-year term, but Congress could fire him with a two-thirds vote of each house. That semiautonomy, plus GAO's reputation for independence, made it seem a reasonable compromise. Gramm-Rudman therefore provided that each year OMB and the Congressional Budget Office would submit separate estimates of what the deficit would be to GAO, which would then make its prediction. If GAO predicted a deficit of $10 billion more than the law's specified target for that year, and if there was no economic recession in view, the automatic cuts would be made.

We knew there might be constitutional questions. For the executive branch to delegate that power to GAO might violate the separation-of-powers doctrine. In fact, Gramm-Rudman was eventually challenged in court on those grounds, and Phil Gramm says that to this day he doesn't know if the Democrats insisted on GAO because they genuinely distrusted OMB or because they hoped the courts would invalidate the law. Or both.

I took the position that aside from OMB—which raised no separation-of-powers problem but did raise a conflict-of-interest problem—GAO was the best we could do, and we'd just have to take our chances in court. However, as a precaution, we wrote another trigger mechanism into the law, to take over if GAO was disapproved in court. Our fallback plan involved the House and Senate Budget committees in the decision to sequester funds.

Throughout the fall, administration officials kept calling to say, in so many words, "Warren, this can hurt the country, you've made your point, it's time to back off." Prominent among the callers were Don Regan, the chief of staff, and Jim Baker, the secretary of the treasury. Regan, at that point, had a reputation for belligerence, whereas the media portayed Jim Baker as suave and calmly persuasive. But in those calls they were just the opposite: Regan was easygoing and likable, and Baker would rant about loyalty to the president and the harm we were doing.

Despite the White House pressure, after his initial uncertainty Bob Dole never wavered in his support, nor did Pete Domenici or Bob Packwood (whose staunch support, as chairman of the House-Senate conference committee, was crucial), or Democrats like Russell Long and Lloyd Bentsen. The Democrats were never our problem. The problem was the Reagan administration, which hated our bill. Cap Weinberger acted as if we were handing the country over to the Russians. But we pushed on.

Phil and I maintained near-total unity during some very long and trying negotiations, although I did slip once. During a tense session with House negotiators, Gramm insisted on making a lengthy speech on constitutional law. That was my area—economics was his—and finally I slammed my fist down on the table and said, "Dammit, Phil, will you please shut up!"

I broke the tension by adding, "It's always a problem for a lawyer when his client wants to take over the case."

Still, I never doubted Phil's commitment to reform, and we trusted each other absolutely. We were going to win together or lose together; neither of us was going to cut any side deals. It reminded me of Korea: Phil was a good man to share a foxhole with.

With the House-Senate negotiations deadlocked, Gramm-Rudman was intensely debated across the land. For all its popular support, it met with plenty of hostility in the media. Gramm-Rudman was denounced far more for trying to reduce the deficit than Reaganomics had ever been criticized for creating the mess in the first place.

The New York Times called it "a fantasy" and "baloney" in the same editorial, and columnist Tom Wicker declared that the Gramm-Rudman cure was worse than the problem it addressed.

George Will announced on national television that "This is going to kill some naval aviators!" Why? Because, he explained, the navy would be forced to eliminate reenlistment bonuses. As a result, experienced pilots would leave the service and their replacements would crash. This foolishness most likely originated in Cap Weinberger's public relations office.

Will had a way of asking questions as if they were an indictment. Once, on *This Week with David Brinkley,* he said to me in effect, "Senator, you've always seemed like a reasonable fellow, but aren't you saying, in this legislation, that you've given up on your colleagues, given up on Congress's ability to do its job, and you want to put the whole thing on automatic pilot?"

"That's exactly right, Mr. Will," I replied. "Next question?"

Our critics tended to be purists who deplored Gramm-Rudman's meat-ax approach to budget-cutting. All that was needed, they would piously remind us, was for Congress to behave responsibly. The point, of course, was that Congress had repeatedly failed to behave responsibly, which was why we proposed drastic action. As Howard Baker might have said, sometimes you have to whack a mule with a two-by-four to get its attention.

While our adversaries were generous with their criticisms, our supporters were cautious with their praise.

The New Republic endorsed us with the headline A BAD IDEA WHOSE TIME HAS COME, a line they had borrowed from me.

Mortimer Zuckerman's editorial in *U.S. News & World Report* was headed "Gramm-Rudman—So Bad It's Good!"

William Safire wrote in *The New York Times,* "Is this sort of governing-by-formula a good way to run a country? No. Is it better than continuing to sink into deficit quicksand that would ruin the country? Yes."

The Washington Post, while endorsing Gramm-Rudman, called it "a clumsy way to legislate and, if not an abdication, at least an evasion of responsibility."

Many of our supporters paraphased Churchill's remark about democracy, that Gramm-Rudman was the worst way to deal with the deficit, except for all the others that have been tried.

By mid-November, with House and Senate conferees still at odds over what programs would be cut and by how much, we began to work on language to ensure that automatic cuts would be split fifty–fifty between domestic and defense spending. That had been our intent, but Democrats feared that Reagan would find some way to inflict heavier cuts on domestic programs. Their fears had deepened when Cap Weinberger declared that the president could not be bound by any "rigid formula" on defense, because of his obligations as commander in chief.

Annoyed, I told a reporter, "If the economy collapses because of these deficits, the Defense Department will face cuts not through the fat but through the bone."

In early December, with the fifty–fifty language agreed to, the negotiators exhausted, the public still demanding action and the government at the brink of a shutdown, both the House and the Senate passed Gramm-Rudman by substantial margins. In this, its final version, more than half the federal budget was exempt from cuts, including Social Security, interest on the national debt, Medicaid and Medicare, existing defense contracts, some veterans' benefits, food stamps and Aid to Families with Dependent Children.

The portion of the budget subject to cuts, some $265 billion out of a trillion dollars, included the remainder of defense, as well as science, energy, transportation, education, foreign aid, health, agriculture and the environment. If the automatic spending cuts ever went into effect, these programs would be disproportionately slashed.

The White House and the Pentagon were furious about possible cuts of about $6 billion from a $276 billion military budget. Cap Weinberger was still advocating a veto, and his Pentagon spokesman called Gramm-Rudman "a message of comfort to the Soviets."

I replied on the Senate floor:

How dare a spokesman for the secretary of defense state to the world press, as this one did yesterday, that supporting this bill gives comfort to the Soviets? The secretary of defense has been quoted on occasion as saying, every time we do something he does not like, that there is dancing in the streets of Moscow.

I suggest that our friends across the river ought to look at the dancing in the streets of Moscow when this government has to borrow $2.3 trillion; when America has become a debtor nation; when 40 percent of all the government's securities to finance the deficit in the last quarter were bought by foreign banks or foreign individuals. I wonder if there has been dancing in the streets of Moscow as they watched the American economy prepare to destroy itself.

It was the next day, December 12, that the president signed Gramm-Rudman in his office with no ceremony and no cameras. Then, a few days later, the White House held its Gramm-Rudman-Hollings ceremony in the State Dining Room, the one that left me so angry, because so many of the people present, starting with the president, cared so little about deficit reduction.

Still, barely three months after Phil Gramm and I joined forces, our radical plan to end the deficit was law. It was a remarkable political achievement, and it would be nice to end the story there.

But it was only the beginning. The assaults on Gramm-Rudman intensified in the months and years ahead.

The immediate challenge was cutting $11.7 billion from the 1986 budget, a partial cut to cover less than a full year. At this point, faced with automatic cuts, Congress should have written a sensible budget that combined spending cuts with a tax increase. Instead, exhausted by the yearlong budget battle, Congress let the automatic cuts take effect. The Democrats thought the cuts, insofar as they produced pain or chaos, worked to their political advantage, and we Republicans were too weary to protest. The president issued the sequestering order on February 1, and the cuts became effective March 1.

Though the $11.7 billion amounted to only about 4.3 percent of the amounts appropriated to the programs affected, I was sorry to see the sequestering occur, particularly after I'd predicted it would never happen, but at least we learned that the automatic cuts wouldn't bring down the republic. In most cases the reductions could be absorbed by attrition. But the public outcry was enormous. Phil Gramm and I were soon the two most vilified men in America. Everyone who suffered a real or imagined loss denounced us. The nuns in convent schools had their pupils writing us. My friends at the *Manchester Union Leader* accused me of turning old folks out into the cold. Every county selectman who couldn't build a new bridge blamed us.

This is a familiar ritual, called the Washington Monument Syndrome. Anytime Congress threatens to cut the Interior Depart-

99

ment budget, its officials announce they will have to suspend elevator service in the Washington Monument, whereupon thousands of tourists will have to trudge up the hundreds of steps to the top and many will surely drop dead on the way, all because of a heartless Congress.

The truth is that Gramm-Rudman never cut a dime from anyone's budget. All it did was put a limit on debt. The government remained free to spend all it pleased—as long as it had the money.

As we'd anticipated, Gramm-Rudman was challenged in the courts, in a suit brought by Representative Mike Synar, a Democrat from Oklahoma, and supported by the Reagan Justice Department.

On February 7 a federal court ruled that Gramm-Rudman violated the separation-of-powers doctrine, because the GAO had been given the executive-branch power to order spending cuts, although it was part of the legislative branch, in that Congress could fire the comptroller general. On July 7 the Supreme Court upheld that ruling.

At that point, the backup plan we had written into the law took effect. The GAO would still decide if automatic cuts were called for, but its recommendations would go to the House and Senate Budget committees, sitting as a joint committee, which would initiate legislation ordering the president to begin sequestration. That legislation would, of course, have to be voted on and approved by the House and Senate, and be subject to amendment.

That was the problem. The automatic cuts were no longer automatic. Our backup plan returned the hard budget decisions to the same Congress that had failed to make them before.

Nonetheless, Gramm-Rudman did hold down spending for three years, although Congress used various tricks to avoid full compliance. For fiscal 1987 automatic cuts were not called for because GAO said the deficit was not quite $10 billion over our target, and the law allowed that much leeway.

In the summer of 1987 the government again ran out of borrowing authority, and again needed to increase the debt ceiling, this time to $2.8 trillion. At that point, Phil and I introduced a new Gramm-Rudman. Once again the White House opposed us, but once again it was politically difficult for most members to vote against a budget-balancing bill. In September both the House and Senate easily passed Gramm-Rudman II. The new bill solved the constitutional problem by vesting the "trigger" authority in the Office of Management and Budget. I wasn't happy about this, because I still feared OMB's willingness to juggle the numbers for political purposes, but we wrote into the law exactly how OMB was to proceed and also gave the GAO a watchdog role.

Unfortunately, in order to pass Gramm-Rudman II we had to weaken it in two major ways. First, Congress moved the deadline for a balanced budget from 1991 to 1993. Next, the law provided that the automatic budget cuts for fiscal 1988 and 1989 could not exceed $23 billion and $36 billion, respectively.

Phil and I accepted those compromises because we had to. We no longer had the momentum we'd had in 1985. Ronald Reagan had worn Congress down. It seemed clear that he would veto any budget that included tax increases. Then the automatic cuts would begin, and many in Congress feared political, economic and bureaucratic chaos if that happened. Instead, Congress passed a two-year budget that eased Gramm-Rudman's provisions enough to avoid sequestering; in effect, we said, "Let's see who the next president will be." If either Dole or Bush was elected, it seemed likely that he'd be more rational on debt reduction than Reagan.

At that point, in the fall of 1987, with Gramm-Rudman II on the books, Congress and the president should have negotiated the relatively small $23 billion budget reduction needed to prevent the automatic cuts from taking place on November 20. Instead, they deadlocked. Reagan rejected the tax increase Democrats wanted. Democrats liked the idea of automatic cuts at Defense. With the two sides unwilling to compromise, sequestration seemed inevitable. Just then, an unexpected event reshaped the political landscape.

On October 19 the New York stock market fell by more than five hundred points. Other markets around the world fell in response, raising fears of worldwide chaos. Wall Street was quick to blame this disaster on the government's failure to balance the budget, even though the stock market had been rising steadily for years, hand in hand with the deficit.

Politicians were shaken by the stock-market crash and eager to demonstrate that they were fiscally responsible. Soon after the crash, Ronald Reagan's advisers, including Treasury Secretary James Baker, Chief of Staff Howard Baker, and Federal Reserve Chairman Alan Greenspan, persuaded a reluctant president to announce that he was willing to enter into an unprecedented "budget summit" with congressional leaders of both parties, and that he was at last willing to put tax increases on the table.

With the president finally showing signs of leadership, he and Congress reached a November 20 agreement for $33 billion in spending cuts and new taxes, well above the $23 billion demanded by Gramm-Rudman. The president's willingness to reverse himself, after seven years, and accept tax increases reflected a need to assert himself after a terrible year that had included the Iran-Contra hearings and the frustrations of dealing with the new Democratic majority in the Senate that had been elected in 1986.

The "budget summit" found it easier to make pronounce-
ments than to enforce them. It had no legal status and there was
soon disagreement on what the conferees had actually agreed on.
Inevitably, the real decisions were made in contentious House
and Senate committees in December. Congressional leaders who
attended the summit did not find it easy to deliver their rank and
file. In the House many Democrats thought their leaders had
given too much to Reagan, while conservative Republicans were
bitter that Reagan had robbed them of their status as the party
that always opposed new taxes.

The final agreement included a $9.1 billion fiscal 1988 tax
increase, aimed primarily at corporations and the rich. The average person's income taxes were untouched. The president's sig-
nature on the budget bill, on December 22, canceled the
Gramm-Rudman automatic cuts that had formally gone into
effect on November 20 but had been postponed pending the
outcome of the summit agreement.

This agreement was the high point of serious deficit-fighting
in the 1980s, and it was inspired far less by Gramm-Rudman
than by fears of another Wall Street crash and voter outrage. Still,
it proved that Congress and the president could reduce the
deficit if they wanted to.

The summit agreement also proved that Washington politicians, at both ends of Pennsylvania Avenue, have a healthy
respect for Wall Street. They can sometimes fool the public, but
they can rarely fool the stock market. In 1981 it had been a
basic article of supply-side doctrine that once the president
announced his tax cuts, the stock market would boom, thus setting off a miraculous economic revival. But that didn't happen.
Wall Street looked at "supply-side," ignored the optimistic
rhetoric and saw at once that it would lead to huge, inflationary
deficits.

Then, in 1989, automatic cuts were avoided because of OMB's calculation that the deficit would be less than $10 billion above the statutory target—a prediction that proved to be far off the mark. OMB played similar tricks in 1990. Unfortunately, the law provided no penalty for overly optimistic projections. These fellows didn't just cook the books—they microwaved them.

In May of 1990, with a $300 billion–plus deficit predicted for 1991, President Bush began a series of summit talks with congressional leaders. He insisted that higher taxes were on the table, despite his "Read my lips—no new taxes!" campaign pledge two years earlier. In fact, his proposals for fiscal 1991 already included $14 billion in new revenues from user fees and other devices. Bush by then was arguing that "no-new-taxes" had meant involuntary taxes—corporate and personal income taxes—but it was all right to increase taxes on discretionary items like cigarettes, whiskey and gasoline. His campaign pledge made it all but impossible for him to do what had to be done and be honest about it.

By October a deal had been struck by the White House and congressional leaders. Gramm-Rudman was postponed, then eventually junked, in favor of an agreement that supposedly set out an unalterable timetable for deficit reduction that would lead to a surplus in 1996. The unalterable timetable, needless to say, was soon forgotten.

Bush, like Reagan, failed to show courage on the deficit. Instead, he danced around the issue, and, in the end, had the worst of both worlds. He broke his "no new taxes" pledge and still didn't cut the deficit, which rose to $221 billion in 1990, $269 billion in 1991 and $290 billion in 1992. He would have had a stronger case for reelection if he'd confronted the deficit. He might still have lost to Bill Clinton, but at least he would have lost for a cause.

What did our legislation accomplish, besides making millions of people think my first name was Gramm?

In 1985 America was facing a record $220 billion deficit for fiscal 1986, and the Congressional Budget Office was warning of $300 billion deficits in the 1990s.

Gramm-Rudman helped change that trend. We cut the 1986 budget across the board by $11.7 billion. For three years we held the deficit to around $150 billion. The deficit dropped from 5.2 percent of our gross domestic product in 1986 to just 3 percent three years later. We were the only Western democracy whose expenditures declined in the 1980s. In fact, we reduced the rate of increase in government spending to the lowest level in thirty years. The budget restraint of the Gramm-Rudman years put a halt to Reagan's military buildup and contributed to a booming economy.

All this was good for the economy and good for America. Nonetheless, the Gramm-Rudman medicine was too strong for the Bush administration to swallow, so—hand in hand with a compliant Congress—they eagerly scrapped it and returned to the path of least resistance. Once they did, the deficit came roaring back, rising to nearly $300 billion in Bush's last year. In the end, Gramm-Rudman was defeated by politics as usual. The way it was undermined stands today as a textbook example of how politicians trick the American people into thinking they're acting on a problem when in fact they're ducking it.

But the story doesn't end there. Gramm-Rudman began a serious national debate on the deficit that was dramatically revived by the election results of 1994. Suddenly the call for a balanced budget was louder than ever. By the fall of 1995 President Clinton and Republican leaders in Congress were competing for public acceptance of rival balanced-budget proposals. If we ever do return to fiscal sanity—and I am optimistic that we will—I believe Gramm-Rudman will have paved the way for it.

In the last chapter of this book I'll take a closer look at the 1995 budget battles. For the moment, let me just look back and say that as 1986 arrived our initial success with Gramm-Rudman had banished my uncertainty about staying in the Senate. I was ready and willing to seek reelection—I thought we had achieved something historic. As a candidate, I had no problem selling our law to the people of New Hampshire. I ran on my record of having cut government spending fairly. I spoke all across the state, to farmers and the elderly and defense workers, defending cuts that hurt all those groups, and I won with 63 percent of the vote.

CHAPTER THREE

THE IRAN-CONTRA AFFAIR

The American People Have
the Constitution Right to Be Wrong

> The power of Congress to conduct investigations is
> inherent in the legislative process. That power is
> broad. . . . It includes surveys of defects in our social,
> economic or political system for the purpose of enabling
> the Congress to remedy them.
>
> U.S. SUPREME COURT
in Watkins v. United States, 1956

During the summer of 1985 I hired Bill Cowan to advise me on intelligence matters. Bill was a 1966 graduate of the Naval Academy who had served three and a half years as a marine officer in Vietnam, in combat and on special assignments, and later worked in top secret counterterrorist operations in Central America and the Middle East. He was physically and mentally tough, fearless and well connected in the shadowy world of covert operations. That fall Bill told me he was hearing reports that something strange was going on in Nicaragua. In 1984 Congress had passed the Boland Amendment, prohibiting further U.S. military support for the "Contra" rebels who were waging war against the leftist Sandinista government. But Bill was hearing rumors that large amounts of money and military supplies were still reaching the Contras and that a White House National Security aide named Oliver North was central to whatever was going on. Bill had known North in the marines, and he described him as a courageous officer, but a zealot, given to exaggeration and in need of close supervision. A cowboy, he called him. I asked Bill to keep checking, but for the time being we could learn no more.

On October 5, 1986, a C-123 aircraft carrying ammunition, uniforms and medicine for the Contras was shot down over Nicaragua. One crew member, Eugene Hasenfus, survived and was captured by the Sandinistas. Documents on board the airplane connected it to a charter airline in Miami with well-known CIA connections. Senior Reagan administration officials denied any U.S. involvement with the flight. Within days of the crash, both the FBI and the Customs Service began investigations to determine whether arms or combatants had been sent to Nicaragua in violation of the Neutrality Act. Both agencies soon received calls from Oliver North, of the White House National Security staff, assuring them the government had no involvement with the flight.

On November 3 *Al-Shiraa,* a Lebanese weekly, reported that the United States had secretly sold arms to Iran in hopes of winning the release of American hostages in Lebanon. At first the reports seemed incredible: few principles of U.S. policy had been more forcefully stated by the Reagan administration than its refusal to negotiate with terrorists or to sell arms to the government of the Ayatollah Khomeini of Iran.

Almost immediately the White House began a series of bumbling and unconvincing denials. President Reagan first sought to avoid comment on the ground that it might jeopardize the chances of gaining the hostages' release. In his first public statement, on November 6, he said that the reports of arms sales had "no foundation." A week later, on November 13, he conceded that the United States had sold arms, but branded as "utterly false" allegations that the sales were in return for release of the hostages.

At a November 19 news conference, Reagan denied that there was third-country involvement in the arms sales to Iran and asserted that all the weapons sold "could be put in one cargo plane." Twenty minutes later the White House issued a correction, admitting that Israel had been involved, and the "one plane" theory was also shown to be false.

On November 21 the president authorized his close friend Attorney General Ed Meese to conduct an inquiry into the arms sale. By then, Colonel North and his secretary, Fawn Hall, were busy altering and shredding documents relating to the arms sales and Contra-supply operation.

Despite the shredding, on November 22, Assistant Attorneys General William Bradford Reynolds and John Richardson discovered a memo in North's office which revealed that profits from the sale of arms to Iran had been used to support the Contras. When Reynolds reported this memo to Attorney General Ed Meese, Meese exclaimed "Oh, shit!" but took no immediate action to seal North's office, where the shredding continued.

Meese's investigation was at best incompetent. He didn't bother to take notes at some of his key interviews, and he did nothing to prevent the wholesale destruction of evidence. There is reason to doubt that he would have made public the memo had not two other Justice Department officials also known of it. However, on November 25, with the president at his side, Meese announced that proceeds of the arms sales to Iran had been used to support the Contras—a "diversion," Meese called it—at a time when U.S. military aid to them was prohibited by law. It was a stunning disclosure. Two highly controversial, perhaps illegal covert actions had been linked—the arms-for-hostages gambit in Iran and the arming of the Contras in Central America. In political terms one and one added up to a great deal more than two.

Although Meese insisted that the president had not known of the diversion, the November 25 admissions gave the impression of a White House spinning out of control.

I watched this fiasco unfold with anger and disbelief. All my experience as a prosecutor told me that something rotten was going on. It was clear that, with or without the president's knowledge, high government officials had been involved in transactions that were stupid, possibly criminal and perhaps unconstitutional. It was equally clear that the Democrats, who had just regained control of the Senate, would try to make the most of the scandal. It seemed unthinkable that as popular a president as Reagan could be impeached, but if he had knowingly defied the Constitution—by violating the Boland Amendment, illegally diverting government funds to third parties, or in some other fashion—impeachment could not be ruled out.

Around the time of Meese's news conference I called Senator Paul Laxalt of Nevada, one of Reagan's closest friends, and reached him on vacation in Bermuda.

"Paul," I said, "your friend is in trouble. He's getting bad advice. The story coming out doesn't ring true and there may be a cover-up. The media are in a frenzy and there's sure to be a congressional investigation. You'd better get back up here and tell your friend to get some people around him who know what they're doing."

On December 4 the incoming majority leader of the Senate, Bob Byrd of West Virginia, and the new minority leader, Bob Dole, announced that they would appoint a special, or "select," committee to investigate what was becoming known as the Iran-

Contra affair. Many senators soon were lobbying for a seat on the select committee. This would be the biggest investigation since Watergate, and as that televised drama had made national figures of Sam Ervin and Howard Baker, this one might also make reputations—or even identify a legislator with previously unnoticed presidential potential.

I was not among those seeking to serve. I wanted time to catch my breath after two years of the Gramm-Rudman fight, as well as my just completed reelection campaign. Also, I knew this could become a nasty, partisan affair. If you were a Republican and were committed to the truth, you might wind up at odds with your party and your president.

When our minority whip, Alan Simpson of Wyoming, asked if I'd be interested in serving on the select committee, I told him I wasn't seeking it but I'd serve if Bob Dole asked me to.

Dole and Byrd were like two opposing coaches, trying to field the strongest possible teams and keeping their plans very secret. On the evening of January 5 Dole called me at home in New Hampshire and asked if I would serve. I said I would, and he asked me to fly to Washington the next morning for the announcement.

Dole's office must have released the names that night, because when I arrived at the Boston airport I was greeted by reporters. Already, Iran-Contra was a raging story. A reporter asked me if I had a model as to how I should conduct myself.

"Yes, I do," I told him. "My model is Howard Baker in the Watergate investigation. And let me say something else—I consider myself an American first and a Republican second."

In Washington that morning, I learned that Dole had named me the ranking, or senior, Republican on the select committee. After we met with reporters, Dole and I went back to his office. In his usual matter-of-fact way, Dole remarked that the Democrats would do everything they could to use this scandal to cripple the president.

"Bob," I warned, "the fact that the Democrats are out to get the president is irrelevant if he and his people have done some of the things they're charged with. There may have been a cover-up. Some of this may even be unconstitutional. This is a disaster."

Dole took it all in stride. "Well," he said, "I guess you'll just have to find out."

The other Republicans picked for the select committee were my friend Bill Cohen of Maine, Orrin Hatch of Utah, Jim McClure of Idaho and Paul Trible of Virginia. We had all supported aid to the Contras. It was a good team. Dole planned to challenge Vice President Bush for the Republican nomination the next year, and the last thing he needed was any suggestion that he'd gone easy on the White House in this scandal. There was speculation that Dole hoped the committee's investigation would implicate his rival Bush, but as a practical matter, he could count on the Democrats to pursue the Bush connection without any prompting from him.

I particularly admired Bill Cohen for agreeing to serve. As a first-term congressman on the House Watergate committee he had been one of the first Republicans to vote for impeachment, even though he thought his vote might end his political career. That had taken courage, and it also took courage to expose himself to those pressures again.

The Democrats fielded an all-star team: Dan Inouye of Hawaii as chairman, along with George Mitchell of Maine, Sam Nunn of Georgia, Paul Sarbanes of Maryland, Howell Heflin of Alabama and David Boren of Oklahoma. Bob Byrd had shrewdly passed over his party's bomb throwers. If the Democrats went after the president, some of their most respected figures would be involved. Byrd's choice of Dan Inouye as chairman was brilliant.

Inouye wasn't flashy but there was not a more solid or respected man in the Senate. Perhaps Byrd anticipated that patriotism would become an issue during the hearings, because Inouye's missing right arm testified to his: he had lost it during combat in Italy during the Second World War. For his heroism he'd been awarded the Distinguished Service Cross, the nation's second-highest medal of valor.

Dan and I had served together on the Appropriations Committee. He was soft-spoken and thoughtful, a man of great dignity and inner strength, and I liked him immensely. A few days after the committee was announced he called me to his office and said he wanted to name me as vice chairman of the committee, with authority to conduct the hearings in his absence and to direct a unified staff. He said his service on the Senate Watergate committee had convinced him that if we didn't have a united committee we would spend more time fighting each other than seeking the truth.

It was a statesmanlike act. The Democrats, as the majority party, would have six members to the Republicans' five and would be free to dominate the hearing and set the agenda without us. But Inouye's goal was a bipartisanship that would lend credibility to our findings.

Our first job was to select a chief counsel. We wanted an experienced, nonpartisan lawyer whose integrity was beyond question. Many of America's finest lawyers were considered, but the leading contender soon became the fifty-four-year-old Arthur Liman, a partner in the New York firm of Paul, Weiss, Rifkind, Wharton & Garrison. (In the interest of full disclosure, I should say that after leaving the Senate, I joined Paul, Weiss, and now am proud to count Liman among my law partners.)

Liman had graduated first in his class at Yale Law. He had extensive courtroom experience, as both a prosecutor and a defense attorney, and was considered one of the top securities and white-collar-crime lawyers in America. He was a Democrat but did not have a partisan reputation. He had served as counsel to the state investigation of the 1971 Attica prison riots in New York, and in 1985 had supervised the investigation of charges that the New York City medical examiner's office had covered up police brutality. We were delighted when he agreed to serve as our counsel.

To avoid a polarized staff, Inouye and I agreed that each senator would select one lawyer, but these lawyers would report to Liman and must be acceptable to him. We assembled an extraordinary staff. For our deputies, we picked two extremely talented young lawyers: Mark Belnick, a partner at Paul, Weiss, and Paul Barbadoro, who had served on my staff before returning to practice in New Hampshire. Inouye arranged for Liman and the staff to share offices on the ninth floor of the Hart Senate Office Building.

With our staff in place, we confronted the huge amount of work that had to be done before hearings could begin.

In the early months of 1987 both the Senate Select Committee on Intelligence and the Reagan-appointed Tower Board, chaired by former senator John Tower, had held closed hearings and issued reports. Both were tough, particularly the Tower Board, which accused the president of losing control of his staff. It was to the Tower Board that Reagan gave three versions of whether he had authorized Israeli arms shipments to Iran: first he said he had, then that he had not, and finally that he couldn't remember.

Despite the earlier investigations, much remained unknown. Key witnesses had refused to testify. Little was learned about the origins or disposition of millions of dollars from the arms sales still held in Swiss bank accounts. No one knew how much money had gone to the Contras and how much remained.

The select committee had to answer those questions fast because our investigation was supposed to end on October 31. The leadership had given us that deadline so the investigation wouldn't continue into 1988, a presidential election year.

The president, on the face of it, was cooperating with our investigation. His early denials had been replaced by suggestions that honest mistakes had been made. On January 27, in his State of the Union Address, he said: "The goals were worthy. . . . But we did not achieve what we wished, and serious mistakes were made in trying to do so." In early March he added: "A few months ago, I told the American people I did not trade arms for hostages. My heart and my best intentions still tell me that's true, but the facts and the evidence tell me it's not." It was classic Reagan: poignant, disarming and more than a little mindboggling.

For our part, the committee had to concern itself not with the mysteries of the president's heart but with more mundane matters of fact. Thanks to Liman and our staff, we did a remarkable job of fact-gathering. It is not my purpose to set out here all the complexities of Iran-Contra, but I must summarize some basic facts that are needed to understand the case.

The scandal had its origin in two unrelated revolutions that occurred in 1979. In Nicaragua, the longtime dictator, General Anastasio Somoza Debayle, was overthrown by the leftist Sandinista rebels. In Iran, the pro-Western government of Shah Mohammed Reza Pahlavi was overthrown by Islamic fundamentalists led by the Ayatollah Khomeini, whose regime was rabidly anti-American.

The Carter administration had attempted a friendly policy toward the Sandinistas, hoping to coax them toward democracy, but Reagan loathed the revolutionary regime. Soon he had the CIA arming, clothing, feeding, training and supervising the

Contras, who nonetheless failed to win either popular support or military victories.

His policy became increasingly unpopular. Its opponents warned of "another Vietnam" if we persisted in military action. I supported aid to the Contras despite many objections from my constituents. I met often with wonderful, deeply concerned nuns who would plead with me not to support the Contras. They spoke movingly of the atrocities the Contras had inflicted on priests and nuns who worked with the poor in Nicaragua, as well as on their own people. Yet I continued to believe that we should oppose what amounted to a Communist government in Central America. Given the fact that the Nicaraguan people, when given a free election, voted the Sandinistas out, I think my position was a sound one.

However, the disclosure in the spring of 1984 that the CIA had secretly mined Nicaraguan harbors—and thereby risked blowing up Russian supply ships—caused an angry Congress to cut off funds for the Contras' military operations. This legislation, the Boland Amendment, became law on October 12, 1984.

There the matter might have ended, except for Reagan's emotional commitment to the Contras' anti-Communist mission. He ordered his staff to find ways for the Contras, in the words of former National Security Adviser Robert McFarlane, to keep "body and soul together."

The staff of the White House National Security Council (NSC) began a secret program to aid the Contras, and later expanded its operation to include the arms-for-hostages initiative in Iran. The man in charge of both operations was Colonel Oliver North, reporting to the White House national security adviser, first Robert McFarlane, then Admiral John Poindexter. All three men had graduated from the Naval Academy in the 1960s.

Denied money by Congress, the White House turned elsewhere to fund the Contras. Between June 1984 and the start of 1986 the president and his NSC staff secretly raised $34 million for the Contras from rightist regimes in such countries as Saudi Arabia and Brunei. Millions more were donated by wealthy Americans, who typically received a pep talk from North, followed by direct solicitations by conservative fund-raisers. This was what I later called "the old one-two punch." Major donors were sometimes granted brief audiences with the president. Even as these solicitations were in progress, administration officials were telling Congress that the administration was not "soliciting and/or encouraging third countries" to give money to the Contras because, as they conceded, that would violate the Boland Amendment.

At first the contributions were sent by their donors to bank accounts controlled by the Contras. But in July of 1985 North—fearful that the Contras were not managing their operation efficiently—took charge of the money. With the support of National Security Advisers McFarlane and Poindexter—and, according to North, of CIA Director William Casey—North channeled the money to the Contras and took a major role in managing their secret war.

At Casey's suggestion, North recruited Richard Secord, a retired air force major general, who set up the Swiss bank accounts where North henceforth deposited donations. Using these funds, and others later generated by the arms sales to Iran, Secord and his business associate, the Iranian-born Albert Hakim, created what they called the Enterprise, to carry out covert operations on behalf of the government of the United States and to earn millions of dollars in fees for themselves.

The Enterprise had its own airplanes, pilots, airfields, operatives, secret communications system and Swiss bank accounts.

For sixteen months, aided by the CIA, it operated as a secret arm of the White House, carrying out a covert war that Congress thought it had banned.

By law, covert operations must be approved in writing by the president and Congress must be informed. Neither was done. Thus the Enterprise was an evasion of the Constitution's most basic check on executive action, the power of Congress to deny funding. When rumors of the secret operation began to surface in the summer of 1985, McFarlane and Poindexter both lied to Congress about the program, as did North with their blessing.

That, in brief, was the status of the covert program to aid the Contras when one of its planes was shot down over Nicaragua and the operation began to unravel.

Amazingly, as if the Contra deception were not bad enough, it had been linked to a perhaps even greater outrage, the administration's secret arms sales to Iran.

It was an incredible policy. Only a few years earlier, Iran had humiliated the United States by seizing its embassy, taking American diplomats hostage, and calling for the death of President Carter. Moreover, the Iranians had supported anti-American terrorism that included taking three hostages in Beirut early in 1984, including William Buckley, the CIA station chief there, who was tortured to death. In public the United States had imposed an arms embargo on Iran and had spoken of them as they spoke of us: as evil incarnate.

And yet, a debate was begun on the question of arms sales to Iran within the National Security Council. By August 1985 such sales had been approved by the president. Why? In part because of the president's deep personal concern for the hostages and his hope that the arms deal might lead to their freedom. For some months, Reagan's staff had kept him isolated from the hostage families who sought to meet with him. But in June 1985 Reagan held the first of a series of meetings with the families, and, as his staff had anticipated, his very personal, emotional reaction to their suffering had a direct impact on his policies.

There were other pressures for the arms sales. Iran was at war with Soviet-backed Iraq and many policymakers considered Iran the lesser evil. The administration also claimed that it hoped the arms sales would strengthen "moderate" political elements in Iran, although no one was sure who those moderates might be.

The idea was that the United States would not sell arms directly to Iran, but would arrange for Israel to sell the arms and then would reimburse the Israelis. This ruse was intended to avoid both the legal and political consequences of an extremely unwise policy. The secretaries of state and defense, George Shultz and Cap Weinberger, when they heard of the plan, warned that such sales were contrary to oft-stated U.S. policy and would violate the Arms Export Control Act as well as the U.S. arms embargo against Iran. Weinberger exclaimed at one meeting, "We could all go to jail if we do this!" As a result, the two Cabinet secretaries were kept uninformed as the plan moved ahead.

With the president's approval, the Israelis shipped hundreds of TOW antitank missiles and HAWK antiaircraft missiles to Iran in August and September of 1985. Despite these shipments, only one American hostage, Reverend Benjamin Weir, was released, not all of them as had been promised. The Iranians took our arms, kept our hostages and assumed we were stupid enough to keep coming back for more. Unfortunately, we were.

By the end of 1985 Oliver North had realized that, whether or not the arms sales freed more hostages, they could generate huge sums of money to support the Contras. That, North later remarked, struck him as "a neat idea." He later testified that CIA Director Casey told him the diversions were part of a larger plan to finance an "off-the-shelf" covert capacity that could operate worldwide without congressional knowledge.

In February 1986 the United States, through the Enterprise, sold a thousand more TOW missiles to the Iranians. All of the remaining American hostages were supposed to be released, but none was. Still, the Enterprise made a $6 million profit on the deal; some of this went to the Contras and some of it stayed in the Swiss bank accounts.

In May 1986 the president agreed to ship parts for HAWK missiles to Iran but only if all the American hostages in Lebanon were freed. With the president's approval a mission headed by McFarlane, by then the former national security adviser, traveled to Tehran with the first shipment. This was an incredibly foolish move. McFarlane, who knew the most vital U.S. security secrets, went to Tehran under a false name with no guarantee of safe conduct. He was a private citizen who could have been taken prisoner and tortured by extremists.

That did not happen, but his mission ended in failure, with regard to the hostages. However, the HAWK parts changed hands and the Enterprise made another $8 million. By then the entire operation seemed less focused on arms for hostages than on arms for cash, with millions going to the Contras, the "off-the-shelf" operation, and into the pockets of various participants.

There was virtually no accounting for the profits from the arms deals. North claimed that he didn't know how Secord and Hakim spent the money they received. Our investigation revealed that of the $16.1 million profit from the sales of arms to Iran only about $3.8 million went to support the Contras. Overall, the Enterprise received around $45 million, from the arms sales as well as third-country gifts and donations from rich Americans. Of that, $16.5 million went to the Contras; $15.2 million was spent on the weapons that were sold to Iran; Secord, Hakim and their associates took $6.6 million in fees; almost $1 million went for other covert operations; $4.2 million was held in reserve for future operations; and $1.2 million remained in Swiss bank accounts.

A good deal of money came under North's personal control, and there was evidence that some went for his personal use, suggesting that his motives might have been mercenary as well as ideological. When we asked him if he didn't keep a record of the money he was given, he assured us that he had kept a ledger. When we asked for the ledger, he said that CIA Director Casey told him to destroy it and so he had. Casey by then was dead.

These were the core facts that we uncovered, and they raised many more questions, both legal and political.

The biggest questions were about the president's involvement in the far-flung Iran-Contra operation. Had laws been broken and had the president committed acts that might justify impeachment?

To have proclaimed one policy toward Iran and followed another was a major political embarrassment but was not illegal. Reagan admitted suggesting that his aides seek donations from other nations for the Contras, but said he did not know that the money went for weapons; few in Congress thought this amounted to a high crime or misdemeanor in constitutional terms. Reagan also admitted authorizing the arms-for-hostages swap, out of concern and compassion for the hostages, and said he had been advised by former attorney general William French Smith that he could export arms without violating the Arms Export Control Act; it was questionable advice, but the legal issues were probably too uncertain to lead to impeachment.

Those who argued for impeachment said that Reagan clearly had failed his constitutional mandate to see that the laws were faithfully executed and also might have violated the Boland

Amendment by authorizing funds to resupply the Contras. In a purely academic sense, either of those might have justified impeachment. But as a practical matter, Congress wasn't going to impeach as popular a president as Reagan unless there was a strong case involving gross misconduct. Seeing that the laws are faithfully executed was too subjective and nonspecific to meet that standard. As far as the Boland Amendment was concerned, the combination of the president's anti-Communist intentions and the uncertainty of the Boland Amendment, which had been revised several times, made it a poor basis for impeachment.

An unpopular president might have been impeached on those grounds, but a consensus emerged in Congress that Reagan was only at risk if it could be shown that he knew of the diversion of millions of dollars not only to the Contras but to shadowy international middlemen.

As I saw it, any profits from the sale of U.S. military property that was paid for by U.S. taxpayers belonged to the U.S. government. No one, from the president on down, had the right to give that money to anyone else, not to the Contras and certainly not to Secord and Hakim. And most particularly not to carry out actions that had been prohibited by Congress. Whoever authorized such a diversion might be guilty of a conspiracy to defraud the U.S. government, among other possible offenses. In my view, if Ronald Reagan had participated in such a scheme, he had violated the Constitution and was guilty of an impeachable offense.

On February 27, 1987, Don Regan was fired as White House chief of staff and replaced by Howard Baker. It was a smart move. Regan was no diplomat. Baker, by contrast, was widely admired and was the ideal person to serve as a buffer between the president and congressional investigators. Soon after Howard entered the White House, he invited Inouye and me to his office.

It was a cordial visit. We were all good friends. I was prepared to support Howard if he made a run for the Republican presidential nomination the next year.

Howard said he had been authorized by the president to say he and his staff would cooperate fully with our investigation. He said that the White House would waive any claims of executive privilege unless extraordinary circumstances arose. He also had a request. If any evidence emerged that suggested a serious problem for the president, Howard asked to be informed immediately. In effect, Howard was confessing that the White House might not know everything its underlings had done in this affair, or what they might say about the president. We agreed he would be informed at once if damaging evidence surfaced about the president. We couldn't have kept news like that secret even if we'd wanted to.

During the spring, the committee reached out in many directions for the truth about Iran-Contra. One question was whether the idea of diverting funds to the Contras from arms sales to Iran had originated with the Israelis—as the White House maintained—or in the White House, most likely with North. We heard from an American intelligence source that North had raised the diversion scheme with Israeli officials in New York late in 1985, but we had no confirmation for the report.

As it happened, Dan Inouye and I had met earlier that year with Prime Minister Yitzhak Shamir and other top Israeli officials, while they were visiting Washington, to seek their cooperation for our investigation. Our demands put them on the spot, because the Reagan administration had been strongly pro-Israel. But it was also true that Israel didn't have a better friend in the Senate than Dan Inouye, who was likely to continue in the Senate long after Reagan had left the White House. Shamir promised us his cooperation.

I was planning a trip to Israel that spring on defense-related matters, and Inouye and I agreed I would pursue the story about North. Before leaving, I obtained from a friend at the Israeli embassy the name of a high-ranking, recently retired official of Mossad, the Israeli intelligence agency. Upon arriving in Israel I met first with Prime Minister Shamir. I didn't mention my special mission to him, but I did to his staff, and told them the name of the man I was going to see.

I met with the retired intelligence officer—do Mossad officials ever really retire?—at his apartment in Tel Aviv. He was in his seventies, balding and rugged. After I explained what I wanted, he promised that I would hear from someone. He stressed that the information would be for our committee's internal use only. It was in Israel's interest to make it clear that the arms sales were North's idea, not theirs, but it was not in their interest to have the Reagan administration know they were giving us intelligence documents.

The next day I received a call at my room in the King David Hotel and was told to expect a visitor at nine that evening. At the appointed time my phone rang and a man who spoke English with an Israeli accent asked me to meet him in the lobby. The lobby of the King David is a scene from *Casablanca* or a cloak-and-dagger thriller. Emerging from the elevator, I saw twenty sinister-looking figures who might have been spies or worse. The man who approached me was conspicuous only by his normality—he was young, short, compact and all business. He led me to an alcove at the rear of the lobby, where he handed me an envelope, said, "I believe you will find this helpful," and vanished. The envelope contained a memo that an Israeli procurement official in New York had written after his December 6 meeting with North.

The meeting concerned the replenishment of Israeli TOW missiles. One of the Israeli officials had taken notes and filed them with Israeli intelligence. According to the notes, North told the Israelis that not only did the United States have no money to pay for the 504 TOW missiles it wanted to deliver to Iran, but that in the future the United States wanted to generate profits from these sales to finance the Contras.

It was an important piece of evidence, because it showed that the diversion scheme originated in the White House and was in place by early December of 1985. Later North testified that he couldn't recall the conversation. In keeping with our understanding with Mossad, our committee's report made use of this information but said nothing about its source.

The select committee did not attempt to question President Reagan, largely because of the legal issues raised by the constitutional separation of powers. We were, however, eager to gain access to the diaries he was known to have kept. We understood the intensely private and personal nature of a diary and yet we also viewed this as important evidence. After discussions with the White House, it was agreed that the White House counsel, Arthur B. Culvahouse, Jr., would review the president's handwritten diaries from January 1, 1984, through December 19, 1986, and would certify that he was making available to us all entries relevant to Iran-Contra. In return, the committee agreed not to publish or paraphrase the diaries without the president's consent. I knew Culvahouse and had no doubt that he could be trusted.

To minimize publicity, we sent the House and Senate chief counsels, rather than committee members, to the White House to examine the entries that Culvahouse produced. They contained no evidence that the president knew of illegal activities in relation to Iran-Contra, but they did make clear the president's intense concern for the fate of the hostages. That concern, although not a "smoking gun" by legal standards, was basic to understanding a policy that in so many ways was irrational.

By the time our public hearings began on May 5, a number of far-reaching decisions had been made. One, announced in March, was that we and our House counterpart would hold joint hearings. That move had been rejected back in January, but we were increasingly concerned that separate, competing hearings would be a two-ring circus and possibly a major embarrassment.

Yet there were also problems with joint hearings. One was logistical. We had eleven members and the House committee had fifteen. Had we anticipated joint hearings, we would have named smaller committees. As it was, we had an unwieldy twenty-six-member committee that guaranteed long, unfocused examinations of the witnesses.

Another problem was political. The House is a far more partisan institution than the Senate. The Senate doesn't play beanbag, but there is a good deal of bipartisan cooperation. By contrast, at that time, House Republicans were a seemingly permanent minority who, led by Newt Gingrich, increasingly resorted to guerrilla warfare to make their points.

The House committee was led by two excellent men—its chairman, Lee Hamilton of Indiana, and its ranking Republican, Dick Cheney of Wyoming—but it should be noted that Hamilton did not extend the vice chairmanship to Cheney, as Inouye did to me. Those of us on the Senate side who wanted a bipartisan investigation feared the worst when we joined forces with the House.

In fact, once the hearings began, the House committee was bitterly divided. For example, the Senate committee had one counsel, Liman, but the House had majority and minority counsels, and the Republican counsel often had to come to us for documents that his Democratic counterpart wouldn't share with him.

Another important decision had to do with granting limited, or "use," immunity to certain witnesses. The special counsel, Lawrence Walsh, was urging us not to grant immunity to such major figures as Poindexter and North, lest we cripple his efforts to bring criminal charges against them.

But North and Poindexter said they would not testify before us without immunity, and they had that Fifth Amendment right. George Mitchell and other Democrats opposed immunity. I recognized there were legal risks, but I thought we could grant immunity in such a way that Walsh's investigation would not suffer. If the choice was between giving the American people the fullest possible accounting of the Iran-Contra affair and deciding whether or not a hugely popular president might face impeachment or letting North, Poindexter or others escape what would probably be short prison terms, our priority must be to give America the truth. A scandal like Iran-Contra or Watergate can paralyze the White House. Getting this matter resolved was far more important than the legal fate of North, Poindexter and their associates.

That view prevailed, and the committee granted immunity to twenty-one witnesses, including North and Poindexter.

In April, Walsh had obtained guilty pleas from two minor figures in the scandal—conservative fund-raiser Carl Channell and his associate Richard Miller—who had raised more than $10 million for the Contras from wealthy American conservatives. They pleaded guilty to conspiracy to defraud the government by claiming the money they raised was tax-deductible. Both men named North as a co-conspirator, but he insisted he'd never directly asked anyone for money. Apparently that was true: North gave the pep talks, then Channell and his associates followed through.

At one point I told Walsh that we would defer immunity for North if he, Walsh, would bring an obstruction-of-justice charge against him for his admitted shredding of key government documents. If Walsh wanted a conviction against North, I thought he had him cold on the shredding. But Walsh refused, apparently because he wanted to bring a grander conspiracy case against North for violating the Boland Amendment.

For me, one of the most dramatic days of the investigation was Saturday, May 2, when John Poindexter came to Room 901 of the Hart Building to give his deposition under a grant of limited immunity. Our public hearings were to begin the next week. We had put off his deposition as long as we could, to give Walsh as much time as possible to build his case. The all-important question was whether Poindexter had informed the president of the diversion. His predecessor, McFarlane, had already sworn that he did not know of the diversion until mid-1986, after he had left the White House, and he had never discussed it with the president. But we did not know what Poindexter would say. If anyone's testimony might bring down the president, it would be his.

Poindexter was interviewed in a CIA-designed "safe" room we'd constructed in our offices. It was about six by eight feet, with fluorescent lighting—it looked like a frozen-food locker and was said to be impervious to bugging. We used it for top secret discussions, out of concern that someone might try to eavesdrop on us electronically. Tom Foley and I met Poindexter, his lawyer, and our counsels Arthur Liman and John Nields there at 9:00 A.M. Foley and I were there to grant official immunity to Poindexter from the House and Senate. Having done that, we departed, leaving Liman and Nields to question the former national security adviser.

We had promised Walsh that Poindexter's testimony would not be disclosed prior to his public testimony. Liman was to tell us nothing unless Poindexter testified that he'd informed the president of the diversion: if that happened we would have a bombshell on our hands.

We agreed that I would spend the day in my office, and if Poindexter incriminated the president, Liman would call me at once, whereupon I would summon Inouye, Hamilton and Cheney and we would meet to decide what action to take. Under our agreement with Baker, we probably would have notified the White House. At that point, with impeachment a real possibility, the investigation would have taken on a whole new dimension.

As I waited in my office I found the tension almost unbearable. I had expected Poindexter's deposition to take three or four hours, but by midafternoon there was still no word from Liman. I sat in my office, talking to my staff, trying to make the time pass. By five I had to restrain myself from going out and waiting outside the locked door of the safe room.

Rarely have I felt so torn. Intellectually, I had no doubt that if Reagan had known of the diversion he deserved to be impeached. But on a personal level I found that possibility agonizing. I thought that Reagan was a good man, who—despite the deficit, even despite Iran-Contra—had done much for the country and was loved by millions of Americans.

I thought he had suffered from bad advice, of course, but it was more than that. I thought that no matter how many times he was warned that certain actions were illegal, he never truly accepted the warnings. His heart did overrule his head on some decisions. I could understand that for Reagan the human plight of the hostages and their families was far more real than legal advice about the Boland Amendment or the Arms Export Control Act. He truly did inhabit a world of his own.

Secretary of State George Shultz later testified that at a December 7, 1985, meeting, Reagan brushed aside warnings that the arms sales might violate the Arms Export Control Act by declaring "the American people will never forgive me if I fail to get these hostages out over this legal question."

The hostages were Reagan's reality, not the law. I was agonized by my knowledge that the law must be obeyed, and yet if it was applied to Reagan on Iran-Contra it might tear the country apart.

I stewed and chain-smoked until Liman finally called at five-thirty. As I grabbed the phone my hand was shaking.

"Do you have news for me?" I demanded.

"No, Senator, no news," he replied. And that was that. Barring some unexpected revelation, our hearings were not going to lead to impeachment. Rarely in my life have I felt such relief.

My affection for Reagan never made me abandon the search for truth. Despite Poindexter's sworn testimony that he had not told the president of the diversion, I remained skeptical. One of Poindexter's top aides at the NSC was a naval officer who some on our committee thought, or hoped, could contradict Poindexter's denial. The officer had been questioned and had supported Poindexter's account, but some of us were not convinced. This led to a highly unorthodox interrogation in our safe room one day. Dan Inouye and I, along with Sam Nunn, who was both a member of the select committee and chairman of the Senate Armed Services Committee, confronted the officer. Nunn sternly reminded the man that his obligation was not to Poindexter but to his oath of office and to the Constitution. Once again, we asked him to tell us the truth.

The officer was a clean-cut man in his thirties, someone who gave every appearance of truthfulness. He continued to insist that he had no knowledge that Poindexter had told Reagan of the diversion, and that may well have been the truth. We had no evidence to the contrary. But this extraordinary session suggests our frustration as we sought the truth in a situation where documents had been destroyed and those involved told stories that often seemed incredible.

When public hearings began on May 5, we entered the second phase of our investigation. We had done an excellent job of fact-finding, but we can be faulted on the hearings themselves. Obsessed with the law and the facts, we did not anticipate the effect of television on the hearings. We failed to understand that they were less an intellectual or legal exercise than a piece of theater.

The witnesses who were trying to defend and justify the Iran-Contra events—and their lawyers—understood the show-biz aspect of the hearings far better than we did. They shamelessly wrapped themselves in the flag. They shaved the truth, made self-serving speeches, attacked Congress, replied to serious questions with wisecracks and skillfully diverted attention from their misdeeds. Their evasions were supported by some Republicans on the committee, particularly those from the House, who were there not as fact-finders but as unashamed defenders of the president.

As Bill Cohen and George Mitchell noted in *Men of Zeal,* their excellent book on Iran-Contra, even the size of our committee worked in the witnesses' favor. To fit the twenty-six members into the space available, a two-tier dais was constructed. It was an architectural gem but a political disaster. As Cohen and Mitchell wrote, "What none of us noticed was that we had transformed the hearing room into a mini-coliseum and that we appeared as the equivalent of Roman potentates turning thumbs up or down on the stoic Christians who would be dragged before us."

There was truth in this. The committee knew, as the hearings began, that there was no evidence that Reagan had known of the diversion, and thus there would be no serious call for impeachment. The nation would have to look elsewhere for high drama. They found it in the efforts of Richard Secord, Oliver North, Fawn Hall and others to portray themselves as underdog patriots standing up to a bullying and incompetent Congress.

Reagan flaunted his self-confidence, not long before the hearings began, when he joked with reporters, gangster-style, "There ain't no smoking gun."

The hearings began, as most hearings do, with interminable statements by the committee members. Still, anyone who paid attention heard the battle lines being drawn.

Chairman Inouye declared that "the story is one not of secret diplomacy, which Congress has always accepted, but secret policy making, which the Constitution has always rejected."

In my remarks, I called for an impartial investigation, but conceded at the outset that there was "sufficient evidence to establish that this is an inexcusable fiasco of the first order."

George Mitchell warned that "a democratic nation dependent on the rule of law and respect for that law cannot remain democratic if its government officials are not accountable to the law."

Bill Cohen declared that "if public officials are free to ignore the law, to stultify it, to twist or disfigure its meaning, in the name of superior motive or righteousness of cause, then we invite our undoing."

On the House side, Dick Cheney, a former White House chief of staff and later secretary of defense, and one of the most talented men in Washington, served notice of his sympathies when he said, "One important question to be asked is to what extent did the lack of a clear-cut policy [toward the Contras] by the Congress contribute to the events we will be exploring."

He had a point. The Boland Amendment had cut off military aid to the Contras, but it had not cut off "humanitarian" aid that was often vaguely defined. Congress had been ambivalent about the Contras, and our ambivalence would now be used to question our anti-Communism.

The first witness was Richard Secord—and the decision to start with him had not been unanimous. Secord's testimony about the Enterprise and its finances would be immensely complicated. Some had argued that we should first lay the groundwork with expert witnesses who could explain why covert actions can be a threat to democratic government. I was among those who feared that would be too dull, and we had to grab public attention at the outset. Our confrontation with Secord captured the nation's attention, but not quite as we had expected.

Secord, a former air force general, was a tough character and by no means repentant. As he saw it, he had been asked by the White House to perform a service, he had acted in good faith, and now he was a patriot being unjustly persecuted by the government he had served.

Secord was first questioned for two days by Nields, who was relatively friendly in directing the witness to lay out how he and his partner, Albert Hakim, had supplied arms to the Contras and the Iranians. Valuable information was put on the record, but in the process Secord was able to present himself in a positive light.

Arthur Liman questioned Secord next, and he was not friendly at all. He saw Secord as a mercenary who had profited at the expense of the American taxpayer. He battered the witness with questions about Swiss bank accounts and profit markups. A shaken Secord eventually admitted, among much else, that $8 million remained in the Swiss accounts, but he insisted it belonged to him and Hakim.

The American people might have been expected to be outraged by the millions of dollars that had wound up in Secord's bank accounts, but they seemed more outraged by Liman's tough questioning. Thousands of calls, telegrams and letters began flooding the committee's offices, protesting Liman and his manner. Arthur does not have the folksy style of a Sam Ervin or a Howard Baker. He looks like what he is—a tough, brilliant

New York lawyer—and that seemed to matter to millions of viewers more than the facts of the case.

Much of the criticism of Liman was of an ugly anti-Semitic nature. We had not anticipated that when we hired Liman—we only wanted the best person for the job—but, looking back, I'm not surprised.

When my turn came to question Secord, I was angry. Cohen and Mitchell wrote in their book, "There is always a sense about Rudman that he is about to enter combat. His throat thickens visibly and he barks questions in a fashion that instructs a witness not to play word games."

My goal was to make Secord admit that the profits from the arms sales belonged to the American taxpayers. He refused to concede that, probably because his lawyer had told him that he would be confessing to the crime of fraudulent conversion of U.S. property. Finally he said he would try to persuade Hakim to turn over the $8 million to start a fund to aid the Contras in the name of CIA Director William Casey, who had died a few days earlier, taking many secrets to his grave.

I thought that was preposterous and said so: "I must tell you that in my view, you or no one else has a right to send that money anywhere. That money belongs to the people of the United States and I will assure you that the Justice Department will make that claim."

Later, still angry, I told reporters I was sick of people who "wrap themselves in the flag and go around spitting on the Constitution." Perhaps many Americans shared my views, but those who called or wrote mostly denounced me, along with David Boren and Paul Trible, for joining forces with Liman.

Secord had fought back skillfully, but we had established that much government money had made its way into the pockets of people who had no business with it. Still, by the time Secord stepped down, we had begun to understand that, despite all the damning evidence we had assembled, we had a fight on our hands.

Contra leader Adolfo Calero was another formidable witness. He was a big white-haired businessman who had opposed the Somoza regime and been jailed by it, but had later fallen out with the Sandinistas. Calero was called because he had been a major recipient of North's aid. He gave the committee records that detailed some $34 million the Contras had received from various sources. Most of the money went to buy arms, but we were interested that $3 million had gone to purchase traveler's checks. In particular, we were curious about $90,000 in blank traveler's checks that Calero had given to North. To be blunt, this looked like a kickback, although Calero said North had told him he wanted to use the money to free the hostages in Lebanon.

The committee had documented that North had cashed some of the checks for what appeared to be personal use: to pay for his dry cleaning, for a $1,000 wedding gift, for groceries at a Giant Food store, for something—we weren't sure what—at a hosiery store, and for snow tires, among other uses.

When I pressed Calero, he insisted that these checks were legitimate "compensation," and he was sure North could explain all his purchases.

In some exasperation, I asked, with reference to the snow tires, "Mr. Calero, when was the last time it snowed in Managua?" That drew a laugh, as Calero conceded that snow was extremely rare in the Nicaraguan capital, but he completed his testimony appearing more of a patriot than a profiteer.

In early June the hearings were enlivened by the testimony of North's glamorous secretary, Fawn Hall. She had been granted immunity in hopes that she would shed light on North's activities, but she was determined to say as little as possible. We made that easy by treating her with extreme care. One rule that prose-cutors follow is that you never make a woman cry, and Hall often seemed on the brink of tears.

Even before her testimony began, Hall had shown that she was ready for a fight. When Senator Heflin unwisely commented that she had smuggled documents out of the Executive Office Build-ing in her brassiere, she quickly issued a statement accusing him of sexism. In fact she had smuggled documents out in her boots and inside her shirt, but her warning was clear: Watch your step, boys.

Our questioning of Hall centered on her role in helping North alter and shred Iran-Contra documents, and smuggle others out of their office after the shredding machine broke down.

On her second day of testimony, she portrayed herself as a loyal secretary who had "panicked" while in a "protective mode."

I asked her what she was trying to protect.

"I was protecting the initiative," she replied.

"From whom?"

"From everyone because I felt that I knew we were trying to get back the hostages and I knew we were dealing with Iranian moderates and if this is exposed, there would be people whose lives would be lost. And I also felt that if divulged—if this breaks out we are sitting up here talking about all kinds of things, we are revealing sources and revealing everything. In my opinion I don't think this is proper. . . . A lot of damage would be done if a lot of top secret, sensitive, classified material was exposed in public, so that the Soviets and everyone else could read it. That is how I felt."

"Ms. Hall, did you know it was White House personnel that was standing in the office barring people from leaving? You did know that?"

"I knew it was an NSC official, yes."

"It wasn't the KGB that was coming, Ms. Hall, it was the FBI."

Perhaps it was unwise to risk sarcasm with this articulate young woman, but I was annoyed that she had invoked the hostages and the Red menace to justify the destruction of evidence. Beyond that, humor was often the best way to make your points in the hearings.

Hall's most memorable comment came when House Majority Leader Tom Foley pressed her on whether she understood that it was wrong to alter and destroy sensitive government documents.

She replied, "I agree with you, sir, and at the time, as I stated before, I felt uneasy but sometimes, like I said before, I believed in Colonel North and there was a very solid and very valid reason he must have been doing this for and sometimes you have to go above the written law, I believe."

"*. . . sometimes you have to go above the written law . . .*"

There, finally, was an honest statement of what they all believed, from Fawn Hall to Oliver North to the president, that their moral and political certitude put them above the law, above the Congress, above the Constitution.

After Hall finished her testimony, the committee took a two-week break. On June 17 we received a letter from North's lawyer, Brendan Sullivan, warning that his client would refuse to testify unless we met certain demands as to when he would testify and what his testimony would cover. Many of the Democrats wanted to reject his demands and threaten North with contempt of Congress if he refused to testify.

Inouye, Liman and I argued that we could examine North effectively, even with these constraints, and we could not risk losing North and denying the American people a big part of the Iran-Contra story. During the committee's debate over the issue, George Mitchell made a motion that we reject North's demands, but dropped it out of respect for Inouye's and my efforts to forge a bipartisan coalition.

On the morning of July 7, Ollie North stood before us in his marine uniform, medals glistening, and swore to tell the truth, the whole truth, and nothing but the truth. I was outraged that he came in uniform—he never wore his uniform to work at the White House—to confess his sorry tale of shredding, lies and deception. Yet North was shrewd and his marine uniform was basic to his strategy of portraying himself as an anti-Communist, anti-terrorist patriot and Congress as an inept and craven obstacle to his lofty goals.

Bill Cowan had warned me that North was an actor, and might arrive in uniform, but it was not until I watched him take the oath that I focused on his potential as a witness. Angered as I was by North's posturing, I realized, from my courtroom experience, that the American people were going to love this guy.

There was much I disliked about North, but I never blamed him for the Iran-Contra fiasco. He was not a policymaker. It was his superiors, McFarlane and Poindexter, who authorized secret operations that they should have rejected as stupid and illegal, even if that meant standing up to the president. Clearly it was the president who had created the climate in which Iran-Contra could happen, whether or not he had detailed knowledge of the operation.

House Chief Counsel John Nields's first question was "Colonel North, were you involved in the use of the proceeds of sales of weapons to Iran for the purpose of assisting the Contras in Nicaragua?"

North invoked his Fifth Amendment right against self-incrimination. That was the moment when many thousands of those who have served in uniform exploded with rage. I am aware of the importance of the Fifth Amendment, but it remained a sorry spectacle to see it invoked by a uniformed marine officer who was sworn to defend his country and uphold its laws.

I was baffled that someone as image-conscious as North chose to invoke the Fifth Amendment before our panel. We would have permitted him, as we had other witnesses, to claim that right in private. I believe he did it because his lawyer wanted it absolutely clear that North had been granted immunity. Once he invoked the Fifth Amendment, Inouye officially stated that he had been granted immunity and could not refuse to answer, and the questioning began in earnest.

Our arrangement with the House was that our counsels and theirs would question witnesses alternately, and Nields drew the first shot at North. He could have treated North as a friendly witness, which in a sense he was, but instead he took a hard line. To an extent, that backfired, and Nields, like Liman before him, inspired a great many angry calls and letters. Once again, the problem was style. Nields's longish hair gave him something of a hippie look, and millions of Middle Americans—however unfairly—saw his exchanges with North as a contest between the kind of young man who'd fought in Vietnam and the kind who hadn't.

Nields quickly zeroed in on the secrecy that had surrounded North's operations, and the witness immediately began his counterattack. Had North lied to Congress? Yes, but he delivered a clever and self-serving speech—the first of many—that claimed he had lied in the interest of a higher cause:

I think it is very important for the American people to understand that this is a dangerous world; that we live at risk and that this nation is at risk in a dangerous world. And that they ought not to be led to believe, as a consequence of these hearings, that this nation cannot or should not conduct covert operations. By their very nature, covert operations or special activities are a lie. There is great deceit, deception practiced in the conduct of special operations. They are at essence a lie.

He insisted that in everything he did he had the approval of his superiors, McFarlane and Poindexter, and "I assumed that the president was aware of what I was doing."

North could not be shaken. He was a loyal, patriotic marine officer, following the orders of high-ranking White House officials, forced to choose between "lies and lives."

Had he accepted a $14,000 security fence for his home from Secord and Hakim and later backdated documents in an attempt to conceal the gift? Yes, North said, he had, but only because terrorist Abu Nidal, "the foremost assassin in the world today," had threatened his life and even the life of his twelve-year-old daughter.

Had he shredded documents? Yes, but only after CIA Director Casey had told him to "clean things up."

Had he used the traveler's checks the Contras gave him for personal expenses? Yes, but only as repayment for unspecified "out of pocket" expenses.

Had he lied to Congress? Yes, but only because Congress could not be trusted to keep a secret and he had lives to protect.

Had he ignored the Boland Amendment's ban on military aid to the Contras? Here North put forward an amazing argument, which the White House and some on the committee embraced: the Boland Amendment applied to intelligence agencies like the CIA but not to the NSC.

However shameless some of us found his replies, millions of Americans were impressed by the confident, boyish marine. Tom Shales, *The Washington Post*'s TV critic, wrote that North's performance was "a new classic in the annals of melodramatic political rhetoric," on a par with Richard Nixon's Checkers speech and Franklin Roosevelt's remarks about "my little dog Fala."

Shales wrote: "North stopped short only of taking out family photos of his wife and kiddies or getting down on one knee for a chorus of 'Swanee.' It was bravura, it was electric, it was vaguely deplorable, but it was fascinating to behold."

North's flag-waving struck home with many in the television audience. Soon congressional offices were receiving thousands of calls, telegrams and letters that supported North and denounced those on the committee who questioned his activities.

During our noon break one day, near the end of North's testimony, I learned how many of these messages were denouncing Chairman Inouye in the most contemptible ethnic terms.

I have made clear my admiration for Inouye's courage in combat. The day before North testified, I asked him a favor. Although Dan had been awarded the Distinguished Service Cross, he never wore it, although he sometimes wore the Good Conduct Medal. Once I asked Dan why he wore the medal that was so widely distributed, instead of one that was awarded to only a select few.

"Warren," he replied, "in those days, I was something of a hell-raiser. The actions for which I was given the DSC lasted only a few minutes and I was simply doing my duty. But for me to win the Good Conduct Medal took several years of hard work."

Knowing he was as modest as he was courageous, I said, "Danny, I want to ask a favor, as a matter of personal privilege. I've been told that North is coming in uniform. I want you to wear your DSC tomorrow. The cameras will show it and the reporters will say that none of North's medals are the equal of the one you earned."

He did as I asked, but his Distinguished Service Cross hadn't been enough to impress some of the bigots in the television audience, so when the hearing resumed that afternoon I asked to speak. I said that "something has occurred that has been so disturbing to me that I want to say what I'm going to say, probably over the chairman's objections." I said "ugly ethnic slurs" had been made against Senator Inouye, and added:

> The chairman was recommended for the Congressional Medal of Honor for assaulting two German machine gun nests in northern Italy, and then falling on the third one which was destroying his company, when he lost his arm which he left on that battlefield in Italy. He is one of the greatest men I have ever known, and the country ought to know the kind of leadership the Senate chairman exerts—and for all Americans to condemn the kind of ethnic slurs that have no place in America.

To his credit, North injected, "I fully agree, Mr. Rudman." But he and his advisers should have known that when people in public life start claiming all virtue and patriotism for themselves, divisions and hate are the inevitable result.

After a day or two of North's testimony, the committee members were well aware that "Olliemania" was sweeping the country. Some members began hailing him as a hero, and others who had previously been critical began pulling their punches. Not only did they praise North, but they began to criticize Liman and Nields for allegedly being too tough on the marine colonel. With a few exceptions, North had put the committee members on the defensive and was threatening to turn the hearings into a rout.

I saw no reason to give ground when I questioned North. I saw myself as a loyal Republican whose constituents expected him to seek the truth. Clearly North was riding a wave of popularity, but I thought the committee's cause was just and public opinion would in time move our way.

By then I realized that to debate North on the issues was a mistake. Those of us who challenged him would have to meet his speeches with speeches of our own, If he waved the flag for the Contras, we must wave it for the Constitution.

When my turn came, I said:

> Colonel North, you said about the Congress, "I suggest to you that it is the Congress which must accept the blame in the Nicaraguan freedom fighting matter, plain and simple. You are to blame because of the fickle, vacillating, unpredictable, on-again/off-again policy toward the resistance."
>
> You are entitled to your view, but I want to share some of my views with you. Under the latest Harris poll, in June, 74 percent to 22 percent of the people in this country opposed aid to the Contras. In April of '86 there was an astounding poll which I think refutes your idea that the American people somehow don't understand what's going on. That poll indicated that 56 percent of the American people were well aware of the threat which Nicaragua poses to its Latin American neighbors, that 50 percent of those polled believe it is in the long-term interest of the United States to eliminate Communism from Latin America—so far, so good—and then 62 percent of the same polling group say no aid to the Contras.
>
> As one who has with reluctance on occasion, but in the final analysis found there was no other solution, voted for that aid to the Contras—the people in this country just don't think that's a very good idea. And that is why this Congress has been "fickle and vacillating."
>
> I want to point out to you, Colonel North, that the Constitution starts with the words "We, the people." There is no way you can carry out a consistent policy if we, the people, disagree with it, because this Congress represents the people.
>
> The president of the United States, the greatest communicator probably we have seen in the White House in years, has tried for eight years to gain support for the Contras and failed; you have tried, and I think probably failed; and this relatively obscure senator from New Hampshire has tried with no success at all.
>
> The last thing I want to say to you, Colonel, is that the American people have a constitutional right to be wrong. And what

Ronald Reagan thinks or what Oliver North thinks or what anybody else thinks matters not a whit. There comes a point when the
views of the American people have to be heard.

My remark that the American people have a constitutional
right to be wrong was the most quoted comment I ever made,
and one of the best-known lines from the hearings, along with
Fawn Hall's remark about going above the written law and the
assertion by Brendan Sullivan, North's lawyer, when he was
asked to be silent, that "I am not a potted plant!"

Afterward I wondered how many people realized that I spoke
in irony, since I believed the American people were by definition
right and it was North and the White House who were dead
wrong.

Given North's success in using television to present himself as
a hero and to put the committee on the defensive, I've often
been asked if we made a mistake in letting the hearings be televised. The answer is no, absolutely not. The Senate Intelligence
Committee and the Tower Board had previously held closed
hearings and then filed reports. That was fine, given their mandates and traditions, but our job was to get the truth about Iran-
Contra to the American people. That meant open hearings and
television.

North, like Reagan himself, was effective in using television to
make his case. That may mean that we on the committee should
have done a better job of questioning him, but it is no argument
against public hearings. We got the truth out to millions of
Americans, only a fraction of whom wrote or called in support of
North. If you believe in democracy, you have to believe that it is
always right to let the people hear as many competing voices as
possible. They will occasionally be misled by scoundrels, but in
the long run they will do what is best.

After North's testimony, the hearings continued for three more weeks. Perhaps the most significant of the remaining witnesses were Secretary of State George Shultz and Admiral John Poindexter.

Shultz's appearance before the committee, on July 23, was, as Cohen and Mitchell put it in their book, as welcome as a Saint Bernard at an avalanche. Shultz had warned the president and his advisers against the arms-for-hostages scheme, and when he finally learned what was happening, he insisted that the president tell the truth to the American people. One of the highlights of his testimony was his declaration that "trust is the coin of the realm." Democratic government is not possible without trust between the branches of government and between the government and the people. There were those who argued that Shultz should have known what was going on around him, and should have resigned, but all the evidence was that he had been kept in the dark and did all he could under difficult circumstances. He was, as I declared at the end of his testimony, one of the few heroes of the Iran-Contra affair.

Poindexter's testimony stood in dramatic contrast to Shultz's. Puffing stolidly on his pipe, the admiral repeated what he had said in closed testimony, that he had never told Reagan about the diversion of funds to the Contras and the middlemen. He said he had pursued the scheme under the president's general policy of helping the Contras, and he was confident that if he had asked Reagan's approval of the diversion he would have gotten it. But, he insisted, he never asked. "The buck stops here with me," he declared, in an amazing reversal of Harry Truman's declaration that the hard decisions come to the president's desk.

Many observers doubted Poindexter's testimony. If he lied before, they said, why wouldn't he lie again? Not to inform Reagan of something so important went against Poindexter's reputation as a perfect staff man who always kept his superiors informed of everything. His critics noted that the highly intelligent admiral suffered a remarkable lapse of memory during the hearings, claiming 184 times that he couldn't remember the events about which he was asked.

To the president's defenders, Poindexter was a hero, whether or not he was telling the truth. Not long after his testimony he entered the Army-Navy club for lunch and was greeted with a standing ovation. I cannot see anything heroic in his actions. Even if he didn't tell the president of the diversion, he served him poorly with a reckless and secretive policy. North was at least motivated by ideological zeal. Poindexter, as far as I could see, was motivated by nothing grander than careerism.

Those who thought Poindexter lied to protect the president also doubted Reagan's insistence that he had not known of the diversion. Many of the Senate Democrats felt that way, and I understood their skepticism, but the fact remained that you couldn't impeach a president without evidence, and there was not a scrap of evidence, developed either by us or by the independent counsel, to show that the president had known of the diversion or that Poindexter had told him of it.

That is not to say the president was blameless.

When the hearings concluded, in early August, the committee was faced with the task of writing its report—two reports, actually, one for a majority of the committee and another for the minority.

There was no great suspense about where the members would come down. That had been made clear by the positions they took during the hearings.

The majority report was signed by all the House and Senate Democrats and three Republican senators, Bill Cohen, Paul Trible and myself. The minority report was signed by two Republican senators, Jim McClure and Orrin Hatch, and all six of the House Republicans.

Thus it was Cohen, Trible and I who kept the committee from splitting along partisan lines. To that extent, Inouye's call for nonpartisanship succeeded. To Cohen, Trible and me, it was not a question of partisanship but of making an honest judgment on the evidence. Our support was important in that the White House could hardly claim to be the victim of a partisan witch-hunt if three out of five Republican senators had joined the Democrats in criticizing the president.

I had a hand in writing the majority report, and if I had any special impact, it was in causing the report to stress, more than the Democrats might otherwise have done, that there was no evidence that the president knew of the diversion.

The majority report was a sweeping indictment of the president's policies and the activities of his underlings. It began by stating:

> The Iran initiative succeeded only in replacing three American hostages with another three, arming Iran with 2,004 TOWs, and more than two hundred vital spare parts for HAWK missile batteries, improperly generating funds for the Contras and other covert activities, producing profits for the Hakim-Secord Enterprise that in fact belonged to U.S. taxpayers, leading certain NSC and CIA personnel to deceive representatives of their own government, undermining U.S. credibility in the eyes of the world, damaging relations between the Executive and Congress, and engaging the President in one of the worst credibility crises of any administration in U.S. history. . . .
>
> The common ingredients of the Iran and Contra policies were secrecy, deception, and disdain for the law. A small group of senior officials believed that they alone knew what was right. They viewed knowledge of their actions by others in the Government as a threat. They told neither the Secretary of State, the

Congress, nor the American people of their actions. When exposure was threatened, they destroyed official documents and lied to Cabinet officials, to the public, and to elected representatives in Congress. They testified that they even withheld key facts from the President.

The report went on to say that the "ultimate responsibility" for Iran-Contra rested with the president, that he had failed "to take care that the law reigned supreme," and that if he didn't know what his national security staff was doing, "he should have."

The report said that the White House decision to give secret aid to the Contras was an "evasion" of Congress's power to appropriate funds for government programs and had violated the letter and the spirit of the Boland Amendment.

The minority report called the majority report "hysterical" and said the administration had made mistakes but broken no laws. It declared that there was overwhelming evidence that the president had not known about the diversion and said Congress had overstepped its constitutional powers when it tried to cut off aid to the Contras.

I thought the minority report was a disgrace. It refused to concede that Iran-Contra had raised serious constitutional questions, and instead viewed the whole affair as a continuation of the six-year-old partisan debate over policy toward Nicaragua.

At the press conference in November, when the reports were released, I was asked what I thought of the minority report. I said, "I'm reminded of Adlai Stevenson's great remark: 'This particular report is one in which the editors separated the wheat from the chaff, and unfortunately it printed the chaff.' It is a pathetic report."

The committee had the authority to recommend legislation to deal with the Iran-Contra abuses, and we did seek to increase the president's obligation to keep Congress informed of covert actions. But the problem in this sad affair was not the law, it was ignorant, ambitious, zealous men who held the law in contempt. The need was not new laws but a new commitment to constitutional government.

We needed a president who understood that he had both a legal and a moral duty to take care that the laws were faithfully executed. We needed government officials who understood that they must observe the law even when they disagree with it. We needed officials who respected the role of Congress in foreign policy and saw Congress as a partner, not as an adversary. These recommendations are not remarkable. They embody the principles on which this country is based. What was remarkable was that they were so shamelessly violated in the Iran-Contra affair. Congress cannot legislate good judgment, honesty or a respect for law. We could only hope that our hearings reminded the Reagan administration and others to follow of their importance.

After the drama of our televised hearings, the aftermath of Iran-Contra was largely anticlimactic.

As I had promised Secord, the Justice Department filed suit to recover the several million dollars he and his partner still had in Swiss banks. But as I write this eight years later, the money is still frozen in those banks and the case is still before the courts.

Our investigation might have been a disaster for Vice President Bush if we had shown that he was involved in Iran-Contra—the result might have been President Dole or President Dukakis the next year—but although Bush had attended several meetings on the Iran initiative, none of the participants could recall his views. In this case, ignorance was bliss, and an untainted Bush proceeded to the presidency.

The independent counsel continued his investigation for six years after our committee completed its work, yet he uncovered no significant evidence that we had not found out in ten months, nor did he reach any conclusions that differed from ours. Had we not granted immunity to North, Poindexter and others, it would have been years before America learned the facts of Iran-Contra, and public discontent would have been entirely justified.

On March 16, 1988, a federal grand jury returned criminal indictments against North, Poindexter, Secord and Hakim. The twenty-three counts in the indictment included conspiracy to defraud the United States, theft of government property, obstruction of justice, wire fraud, false statements, and destruction and removal of documents. One of the charges against North related to his having converted to his personal use at least $4,300 of the more than $90,000 in traveler's checks he had been given by Adolfo Calero. Robert McFarlane had previously pleaded guilty to four misdemeanor counts of withholding information from Congress and agreed to testify against the others.

North and Poindexter were convicted on numerous counts, but their convictions were overturned on the grounds that the immunity we granted them had tainted the special prosecutor's case. I disagreed with the court's decision, but I had always believed that whether or not they went to jail was far less important than getting their testimony before the public, and I have no regrets about that outcome.

North emerged as a hero of the far right, and in 1994 he ran for the Senate against Chuck Robb. Virginia is a conservative state, 1994 was an exceptionally good year to run as a Republican, and Robb had been hurt by his admission that he had dallied with a young beauty queen. Nonetheless, North lost. At present he is contributing to political enlightenment as the host of a radio talk show. When people call in to disagree with him, he cuts them off with the sound of a toilet flushing. When North appeared before our committee in 1987, and aroused such popular enthusiasm, he seemed to some the proverbial man on horseback who might become a political menace. Today, he seems not a menace but a minor irritant, a zealot who has found his level.

Ronald Reagan was embarrassed and politically damaged by the scandal, yet he left office almost as popular as when he arrived. The American people seemed willing to forgive him almost anything. However much they might question his policies, they continued to love him.

I think the greatest importance of the Iran-Contra hearings was in educating the public about the Constitution and the differing roles of the president and Congress. Perhaps we also educated not only Reagan and his staff but other presidents and staffs who will follow them. Recent presidents have too often fallen victim to obsessions that harmed them and others: Johnson and Vietnam, Nixon and his "enemies," Reagan and the hostages and the Contras. Presidents and those around them need reminding that they are not all-powerful. Perhaps, after Reagan's great 1984 reelection victory, he and his more zealous followers thought they had a mandate to do anything. It is truly amazing that they thought an operation as big and bizarre as Iran-Contra could be kept secret. Perhaps the exposure of their covert foreign policy will discourage other presidents and their men from attempting another such adventure anytime soon.

If our system of government is to work, everyone involved must respect the rule of law. In our two biggest recent scandals, Presidents Nixon and Reagan failed to inspire in their staffs a respect for the law. As a result, Nixon was forced to resign and Reagan was sharply rebuked. The system worked in both cases. The Constitution may not be as beguiling as presidential rhetoric or as dramatic as the histrionics of a dashing young marine officer, but it is based on enduring truths and politicians challenge it at their peril.

CHAPTER FOUR

THE NOMINATION OF
DAVID HACKETT SOUTER

What Have I Done to
My Best Friend?

He shall nominate, and by and with the Advice and Consent of the Senate, shall appoint Ambassadors, other public Ministers and Counsels, Judges of the supreme court. . . .

THE CONSTITUTION OF THE UNITED STATES

Finally, Mr. Chairman, I must say it is remarkable that there are some people here in Washington who view a man who has a single-minded dedication to his chosen profession, the law, and possesses great qualities of humility, graciousness, frugality, charity, reverence to his faith and to his family is somehow regarded as an anomaly and somehow out of touch with life. I believe that most Americans see these as endearing and desirable qualities, all too often sacrificed in the frenetic pace of modern life.

I was angry and showed it as I spoke these words to conclude my introduction of David Souter to the Senate Judiciary Committee on September 13, 1990. I was angry not with my fellow senators but with those reporters who for seven weeks had written about

152

David in a way that I found irresponsible. Without a trace of evidence, major publications had felt it necessary to raise the "question" of his possible homosexuality, despite abundant evidence to the contrary. Beyond that, reporters in search of lively copy had described this warm, kind, witty, dedicated man, whom I considered my closest friend, as some sort of oddball, simply because he had never married and had dedicated his life to the law.

I knew how much this pained David. A few nights earlier he had protested that he wouldn't have accepted the nomination if he had known that his privacy would be invaded in this outrageous way. Perhaps more than anyone else, I knew what a loss that would have been to the country.

As I closed my remarks and David prepared to confront skeptical Democrats on the committee, I thought back twenty years to my first day as attorney general of New Hampshire. That was the first time I actually met David, although we'd said hello a few times when I was the governor's legal counsel. David was ten years younger than I, a slight, soft-spoken man who projected an air of immense self-confidence. I'd already heard that he would be the star of my new staff, and later that day, after I read his personnel file, I thought, Good Lord, what a gem we have here!

David's family had been in New England since prerevolutionary times. He was born in Melrose, Massachusetts, on September 17, 1939, and in 1950 the Souters moved to the village of East Weare, New Hampshire, a few miles west of Concord, where his father worked in a bank. In 1957 David graduated from Concord High, where he was named "most likely to succeed." He was known in those days by his middle name, Hackett. He proceeded to Harvard, where he wrote his senior thesis on one of his heroes, Justice Oliver Wendell Holmes. Then he went to Oxford on a Rhodes Scholarship, and finally to Harvard Law. He practiced law for two years with a leading Concord firm, but he was drawn to public service and left to become an assistant attorney general.

His résumé was the kind you expect from a Supreme Court clerk, or a young hotshot with one of the top Boston or New York firms. But David had turned down the big-city jobs to return to the rambling, book-filled farmhouse where he'd grown up and to work in his adopted state.

In my first weeks as attorney general, I brought my assistants in one at a time for a get-acquainted chat. When David's turn came, I asked what his goals were, where he was headed. He said he didn't know. In the meantime, he was working in our Criminal Division and was clearly the most talented person on my staff. He spoke in an utterly concise and direct way. His writings were crisp, and his logic was always well supported by case law.

As it happened, the deputy I had inherited, Bill Cann, wanted to be a judge, and I was able to arrange his appointment by Governor Peterson, who also agreed that David would be my new deputy. That was the beginning of a friendship that still continues. I have worked with many wonderful people, but my friendship with David remains the most rewarding, exciting, fulfilling experience of my professional life. If my six years as attorney general were in many ways more satisfying than my two terms in the Senate, it was largely because of David. He was like a very special younger brother.

People usually separate their professional and personal relationships. David and I, at the office, had a relationship that was both personal and professional. We worked together closely, for long hours under great pressure, often talking ten or fifteen times a day. We came to share a deep affection, we made each other laugh, and we had complementary talents that kept the office on track no matter how hectic things became.

Soon we were joined by Tom Rath, who later became David's deputy attorney general and went on to become attorney general himself. Tom liked to joke that his job was "to go to lunch with Warren and explain what David was saying." Sometimes it wasn't a joke.

David and I saw each other socially, but not as much as we would have liked, because neither of us had much time for a social life. Not long after David became my deputy, I invited him to join me and my family for dinner. It was a beautiful summer evening and we cooked steaks in the backyard and ate on the porch. David spent much of the evening getting to know our children, particularly Deborah, the youngest, who was about eleven. It was a long evening and the kids stayed up late, and all fell under David's spell. David was particularly fond of Deborah. When she was elected to Phi Beta Kappa he was as proud as I was; later, he attended her wedding and she came to the White House ceremony when he was sworn in as a member of the Supreme Court.

It was the same with Tom Rath's kids and the children of David's other friends. They found David fascinating because he could communicate with them on their own level. David has an enchanting quality about him. He's a wonderful storyteller with a gift for drawing people out. Children idolized him.

It was because I knew David in that way, knew his decency and warmth and humanity, that I was so troubled when, after his nomination to the Supreme Court, the media portrayed him as eccentric. If David Souter is odd, our society is in big trouble.

It's true that David was always utterly and entirely himself. He did what seemed right to him, not what fashion dictated or the world expected.

That did, sometimes, set him apart from the rest of us.

David's favorite lunch was yogurt or cottage cheese and an apple. The whole apple, core and all. One day someone showed him an article that claimed that apple seeds were poisonous. After this, David stopped eating apple cores. At least we thought he did. When a writer raised the matter years later, David good-naturedly insisted that he'd learned that apple seeds were dangerous only in large quantities, so his apple-eating habits had remained unchanged.

In those days, our top state officials were given personalized license plates. Mine was "Attorney General 1" and David's was "Attorney General 2." One day David picked me up at the airport in his battered fifteen-year-old Chevrolet. One door wouldn't open from the inside. The car was dirty and rusty and missing chrome, a wreck. I hated to ride in it. I didn't think it was safe. To David, of course, a car was just a machine that took him to work and back, and he saw no reason to spend money on a new car when he could use it for books and records instead.

That day, as we drove in from the airport, we stopped at a light and some guy began razzing us. It was along the lines of "You've got to be kidding, Mac! You're the attorney general and you're driving that piece of junk!"

David didn't care, but I saw an opportunity. When we got moving again, I said, "David, I'm going to take you to a Volkswagen dealer who'll sell you a nice clean used Rabbit."

He went peaceably, and bought a Rabbit, which he drove until it, too, was falling apart. He stuck with Volkswagens, however, and when he was nominated to the Supreme Court in 1990 he was driving a 1987 Golf. He's still driving it.

David never married. The law was his mistress. He dated various women, some seriously, but I think he was happiest when he was reading his lawbooks, or the works of literature and history that filled his old farmhouse, with its sagging porch, peeling paint and ill-tended lawn. Reading and listening to classical music were his passions, along with hiking and mountain climbing, often in New Hampshire's Presidential Range. His favorite night out was to drive to Boston with a friend or two for the symphony, with a stop at Goodspeed's rare-book store.

David was modest, scholarly and reticent, but no hermit. He was immensely popular. He had a wonderful sense of humor. Sometimes he would send his friends thank-you notes written in Latin. When one of his law clerks used a four-letter word, he left a bar of soap on her desk. At parties he could be prevailed upon to do his imitations, including a wicked one of Meldrim Thomson, the right-wing governor we both served for a time.

One snowy morning, early in 1975, I asked David into my office. My term as attorney general was ending, and I assured him that if he was interested I would do everything I could to persuade Governor Thomson to appoint him in my place. Once again I asked him what he wanted to do with his life. I thought he might eventually want to teach law. Once again he said he wasn't sure.

I said, "David, there are very few people I think should be a judge, because I believe that under our system of law judges are so incredibly important. They hold people's lives and fortunes in their hands. They should not only be intelligent, but should have compassion, should understand the human condition. And I think you should be a judge."

I was not surprised when he replied that he didn't know if he'd be a good judge.

"You ought to think seriously about it," I insisted. "If you'll let me, I'll be your champion. Maybe you can replace me as attorney general and maybe some governor will put you on the bench after that. I want to see you go as far as you can go. You could be an extraordinary teacher, but I think the judiciary is the ideal place for your talents."

In light of what happened fifteen years later, it was an extraordinary scene. We were two obscure lawyers in a small New

England state, but I truly believed he was capable of outstanding service, even greatness. I had it in the back of my mind that I'd get into politics, and then maybe I could nudge his judicial career along.

At my urging, Governor Meldrim Thomson did agree to make David my successor when I left office early in 1976.

David compiled a splendid record as attorney general. Several times he was obliged to advocate controversial positions taken by the ultraconservative and somewhat erratic governor who had appointed him, such as Thomson's decision to lower the state and American flags over state buildings on Good Friday. But David became known as a tough prosecutor, and a champion of the environment, consumer protection and victims' rights.

I continued to think he should be a judge, and in time David began thinking along the same lines.

In New Hampshire we have two state courts, the superior court, or trial court, which has thirty-plus judges, and the five-person supreme court. In 1977 there was an opening on the supreme court, and several of us urged Governor Thomson to appoint David. Eventually, David and Tom Rath went to see the governor. While they were talking, Thomson left the room to take a phone call, and when he returned he told David—seemingly in some distress—that he couldn't put him on the supreme court, but that he'd gladly appoint him to the superior court. David declined the offer and continued as attorney general. Tom Rath is convinced that the call was from William Loeb, vetoing David's appointment to the supreme court.

Early in 1978 there was another opening on the supreme court, but again Thomson offered David a place on the superior court, adding that if he had a few years' experience there it would be easier to promote him to the supreme court. David at first declined the offer, but that night I urged him to accept it. It was a calculated risk, but I assumed that he would be so outstanding on the superior court that some future governor would promote him to the supreme court. There were no guarantees, but it seemed worth the gamble. David accepted my advice, took the appointment and was replaced as attorney general by Tom Rath.

David had more free time as a superior court judge than he did as attorney general, and he was able to serve as a trustee and for six years as president of Concord Hospital. It was a demanding job but one he loved. In this he was influenced by his aunt Harriet Bartlett, a pioneer in medical social work. Later, when David was nominated to the U.S. Supreme Court, amid widespread speculation about his position on abortion, only a few people noted that he'd helped set policy for a hospital where abortions were performed.

Most important, at the age of forty, David was on the bench, and I continued to believe that was only the first step.

After I won the Republican nomination for the Senate in 1980, the runner-up, John Sununu, gave me his all-out support in the general election. Two years later John decided to run for governor and asked my help. I gladly agreed to be the honorary chairman of his campaign.

The incumbent Democrat, Hugh Gallen, was a decent man and a good governor. In 1980, while I was beating Durkin, he had trounced Meldrim Thomson, for which I shed no tears. But John ran a superb campaign, aided by my organization and my help with fund-raising.

On election night, I watched the returns with John, his parents and his wife and their many children in his suite at the New Hampshire Highway Hotel, a big rambling place in Corcord that's gone now. At first he and his family were nervous, because he was trailing, but I knew that he was holding his own in places he should have lost, and I assured him that he was the next governor. He wasn't convinced until television proclaimed him a winner, then bedlam broke out. His parents—Lebanese immigrants—were crying, and everyone was cheering and hugging and kissing. John threw his arm around me and said he'd never forget what I'd done for him.

"Warren, anything you want in this state, you've got," he declared.

I laughed. "John, you shouldn't have said that," I said, "because there is something I want."

He asked what it was.

"Sometime soon, you'll have a vacancy on the New Hampshire Supreme Court," I told him, "and I want your nominee to be David Souter. He's an extraordinarily able man and he'll distinguish himself on the court."

At that point John didn't know David, but he said, "Warren, it's done." And when an opening came up in mid-1983, he kept his word.

David moved up to the supreme court and soon was recognized as its intellectual leader. In mid-1986, when the chief justice retired, I urged Sununu, who was still governor, to name David to replace him, but he followed tradition and promoted a more senior justice.

David was disappointed. The challenge of being an associate justice was wearing thin. Once again he was uncertain about his future. He even considered leaving the court. The irony is that if John Sununu had made him chief justice of our state supreme court, David might never have reached the United States Supreme Court, because he probably wouldn't have given up the chief justiceship for promotion to the federal circuit court of appeals, which led in time to Washington.

The U.S. Court of Appeals for the First Circuit traditionally has one judge from New Hampshire. At that time he was Hugh

Bownes, a fine judge who'd been appointed by Lyndon Johnson. In 1987 I heard that Bownes was considering the semi-retirement status the federal system permits, but was hesitating because he feared that President Reagan would appoint a right-winger to replace him. I went to Howard Baker, the White House chief of staff, and confirmed that if Bownes stepped down, David would be named to the First Circuit.

Then I took a deep breath, because this was a delicate matter, and one winter day I went to see Bownes at his chambers in Concord. I told him that if he had any inclination to retire, he had my absolute assurance that he would have a worthy replacement.

He laughed and said, "I assume you mean David Souter."

I assured him I did, because I knew he thought highly of David.

But Bownes wasn't ready to step down.

In 1988, Judge Robert Bork's nomination to the Supreme Court was defeated, largely by Democratic senators who portrayed him as a racist, sexist, right-wing ideologue who would vote to overturn *Roe* v. *Wade,* the milestone 1973 decision legalizing abortion. I respected Bork's intellect and supported his nomination, but clearly he was burdened by a combative personality and a huge backlog of writings that his enemies could mine for controversy.

After Bork's defeat, President Reagan nominated a judge who was forced to withdraw after it became known that he'd smoked marijuana. At that point in this comedy of errors, I called Howard Baker and said, "I've got the man you need, sitting on the New Hampshire Supreme Court."

The White House people talked to David and were impressed, but Attorney General Ed Meese held out for his fellow Californian Anthony Kennedy.

Early in 1990 Hugh Bownes did step down. By then John Sununu, having helped George Bush win the 1988 New Hampshire primary, was White House chief of staff. I quickly spoke to Sununu, Attorney General Dick Thornburgh and President Bush, and they agreed that David should be nominated for the First Circuit. David was unanimously confirmed by the Senate. The oath of office was administered to him on May 25 by First Circuit Court Chief Judge Stephen Breyer, who would later join him on the Supreme Court. He hadn't had time to participate in any decisions when the word came on Friday, July 20, that Justice William Brennan was retiring from the Supreme Court.

My press secretary, Bob Stevenson, called me in New Hampshire with the news. I immediately called Sununu and told him we had a chance to do something important for America. The next day I spoke to the president, and told him, "Mr. President, you've just appointed this man to the First Circuit Court of Appeals and he can easily be confirmed for the Supreme Court. I can guarantee you that he has no skeletons in his closet, and he's one of the most extraordinary human beings I've ever known." The president thanked me but was noncommittal.

I called David and told him what I'd done.

His response, as it often was, was to chide me. He said he appreciated all I'd done for him, but that the First Circuit was his greatest dream fulfilled. "They aren't going to appoint me to the Supreme Court," he said. "I don't know the president or anybody important."

"I take that personally, David—you know me," I reminded him, and we both laughed. I told him he would probably be hearing from Boyden Gray, the White House counsel.

David called back to say that the White House had tracked him down in his chambers—where, as usual, he was working on Saturday afternoon—and asked him to fly to Washington on Sunday for a Monday meeting with the president. We had a pretty intense discussion. His attitude, at least at first, was "What have you done to me now?" He said, in effect, that he didn't want to go through this exercise, that there were other candidates who were better known and more politically connected, and it just wasn't going to happen.

I said, "David, you don't know that. You've always trusted my political judgment, and I'm telling you that you're the perfect candidate because, first, you're superbly qualified; second, you don't have any skeletons; and, third, you don't have a long record the opposition can beat you with."

David remained skeptical. He was happy to have reached the First Circuit, and he'd been through this before, when his name was floated at the time of the Kennedy appointment. He resented having his hopes raised and ending up an also-ran.

He called a second time to ask if it was possible to fly directly from Manchester to Washington on Sunday. I assured him it was, and lest he miss the plane, I insisted on driving him to the airport.

That night David called again. "I've been thinking about this," he said, "and I don't want to go to Washington if anyone is going to ask me how I stand on abortion or *Roe* v. *Wade*. I won't take a litmus test. I'll discuss judicial philosophy with them, but I won't go down there and be compromised. I won't discuss how I might rule in future cases. They ought to know that beforehand. It might save us all a lot of time."

I told him that wouldn't happen, but he wanted a stronger assurance. So I called Sununu and said, "John, I'm just being an honest broker here, but the fact is that there's no sense in this if you plan on quizzing him about abortion."

John told me that absolutely wouldn't happen, and I reported that back to David, who agreed to go and meet the president.

The next day, Sunday, David met me in Manchester so we could talk before his 6:00 P.M. flight to Washington. We drove to an ice cream parlor called Friendly's, where I had a milk shake and he had iced tea.

He was still saying that this was an honor but he would never be the nominee. I said, "David, when you meet with the president, just be yourself."

"I don't know how to be anything else," he replied.

When I dropped him at the airport he was carrying an ancient, battered suitcase that his ancestors might have brought over on the *Mayflower*. He got out of the car, then turned to me with a pained expression.

"What's the matter?" I asked.

David pulled out his wallet. "Warren, I've only got three dollars," he said.

I gave him a hundred dollars in cash. "I ought to pin a tag on you," I told him. "You know, one that says, 'Please take this boy off the plane in Washington.' "

It was reported Monday morning that the president had narrowed his list of possible nominees to five. The other four were Solicitor General Kenneth Starr and three federal appeals court judges: Edith Jones of Texas, a conservative who was known as Jim Baker's candidate; Lawrence Silberman, who had joined in a ruling that overturned one of Oliver North's Iran-Contra convictions; and Clarence Thomas, former chairman of the Equal Employment Opportunity Commission.

I thought David rated very well in this field, and not only because of his exceptional personal qualities. We all knew that the shadow of the abortion controversy hung over this nomination. No issue since the Vietnam war had so bitterly divided the nation. It was unlikely that any lawyer or judge, however distinguished, could be confirmed for the Supreme Court if he or she was clearly either pro-life or pro-choice.

How had our politics come to this? Why had abortion, a common medical procedure that the Supreme Court had ruled legal seventeen years earlier, come to dominate our politics?

The answer lies in the rise of the evangelicals. There have always been backwoods preachers in America denouncing the wicked ways of city dwellers and the rich. But something had changed by the 1980s. One milestone may have been Richard Nixon's skill in rallying his Silent Majority against opponents of the war in Vietnam. The war passed, but not before such figures as Jerry Falwell, Pat Robertson and Jesse Helms had seen the possibilities of using television to rally religious conservatives who felt threatened by a fast-changing society.

These people were also upset by teenage sex, drugs, homosexuality, the ban on school prayer and the sexually candid books and movies and TV shows that invaded their very homes. But of all these outrages the worst was abortion, the cold-blooded murder—as they saw it—of a helpless unborn child. During my Senate years, I learned it was pointless to meet with anti-abortion groups, because they couldn't discuss the issue objectively. If you disagreed with them you were a baby-killer. When an issue arouses that much raw emotion, there will always be politicians eager to exploit it.

Amid such passions, it was unthinkable that George Bush would appoint a pro-choice nominee. To do so could have split the Republican Party and cost him his renomination. Similarly, a pro-life nominee would almost certainly have been defeated in the Senate, either by majority vote or a filibuster.

The last thing George Bush—or the Senate, or the nation— needed was a bitter fight over abortion. Yet we faced the possibility that Justice Brennan's departure would leave the Court split 4 to 4 on a repeal of *Roe* v. *Wade*. With Brennan gone, there were only three firm votes for *Roe,* with four justices hostile to it, and a fifth, Sandra Day O'Connor, whose position was unclear but who had voted to let states impose major restrictions on abortion. That had been the result a year before in *Webster* v. *Reproductive Health Services.* In the aftermath of *Webster,* several states had enacted restrictions that effectively blocked abortions for many women. Those laws had been challenged in the courts, and one of them—the *Casey* case from Pennsylvania—was likely to reach the Supreme Court in the next year or two.

At that point, pro-life advocates hoped—and pro-choice forces feared—the Court might use *Casey* to repeal *Roe,* if either O'Connor or Justice Brennan's replacement provided the fifth anti-abortion vote.

Thus, Bush's first Supreme Court nomination was potentially explosive. Even leaving aside its impact on the 1992 presidential campaign, the 1990 congressional elections were at hand, and Bush didn't want the Democrats using his nominee to convince the women of America that the Republicans were about to take away their right to choose. Within hours of Brennan's resignation, the battle lines were drawn.

Kate Michelman, executive director of the National Abortion Rights Action League, said that unless Bush's nominee pledged "unequivocal support" for *Roe,* abortion-rights activists would launch a national campaign against the nominee equal to the one that brought down Bork. Meanwhile, conservative leaders warned the president that after he had backed away from his no-new-taxes pledge, invited gays and lesbians to a White House ceremony, and granted trade status to China, the choice of an anti-abortion Supreme Court nominee was his last chance to redeem himself with the conservatives he needed for renomination.

I suspected that the president was less concerned with how his nominee eventually voted on *Roe* than that he or she be nominated without a fight. Earlier in his career Bush had been pro-choice, then he embraced the pro-life cause when he attached himself to Ronald Reagan, but I doubted that his original feelings had changed. His priority was to find a nominee who could be confirmed without harming his party's congressional prospects that year or his own in 1992.

On the New Hampshire Supreme Court, David had dealt mostly with criminal cases, zoning disputes, utility rate increases and the like. His more than two hundred written opinions demonstrated his first-rate legal mind but said nothing at all on abortion. Since he had no public record on abortion, David could legitimately claim that he would approach the issue with an open mind. He could also argue that it was improper for him to discuss the *Roe* decision, since *Casey* or other challenges were headed for the court. He was an ideal candidate if he could avoid being pinned down on *Roe*.

For my part, I didn't know how David felt about abortion, nor did I want to know. When *Roe* v. *Wade* was announced, we were not two academics at leisure to debate it, we were two prosecutors who adjusted our policies to comply with it. It was not a subject we ever had occasion to discuss. I was glad of that, once he was nominated. If I had known his view, and been asked what it was, my choices would have been to refuse to comment, to lie (which I would never have done to my Senate colleagues), or to tell the truth and perhaps torpedo his nomination. It was best not to know.

However, knowing David's mind rather well, I had my suspicions. My guess was that he probably thought, as I did, that *Roe* had been wrongly decided, as a matter of constitutional law. The Court had based the legality of abortion on a "right of privacy" that many of us could not locate in the Constitution. Intellectually, that right of privacy was a very big leap. The Court had, I thought, made the right decision for the wrong reason.

I suspected that David shared this view, but that because of his belief in stare decisis (the Latin term for judicial respect for precedent) he would never vote to overturn the decision, knowing what turmoil that would cause in our society.

One of the ironies of the debate over David's nomination was that he was often described as "Sununu's candidate," because John had named him to the New Hampshire Supreme Court. Sununu encouraged this, telling conservatives that David was "okay" and thus hinting that he shared John's anti-abortion views. But how could Sununu have known? I was David's best friend and I didn't know.

I suspected that John, whom I viewed as more of a pragmatist than an ideologue, shared the president's hope for a trouble-free confirmation, and was glad to help it along with a wink and a nod.

As long as David said nothing on the issue, and his silence gave hope to those on both sides of the debate, neither side had the emotional ammunition to launch an effective campaign against him. Partisans could only complain, as columnist George Will did, that Bush was asking the country to buy "a pig in a poke." That was inelegant but true. Only a pig in a poke had much chance of passing the Senate.

On the Monday morning that David went to the White House, I was in New York meeting with *Time* magazine's editorial board. When they asked me who I thought would be the Supreme Court nominee, I advised them to put their money on the man from the Granite State. They were skeptical, but later thought me quite a prophet.

David spent Sunday night at the home of an assistant attorney general, then was taken to the White House on Monday morn-

ing. He met first with Boyden Gray and other White House officials, then was taken up to the president—Mrs. Bush joined
them later. They discussed David's view of the judiciary, without
getting into specifics. As I had expected, David and the president hit it off extremely well. They came from similar backgrounds: Yankee, white Anglo-Saxon Protestant families that
believed in the old values of hard work, integrity and public service. The president was impressed by David's intelligence, mod-
esty and sense of duty, and he was shrewd enough to anticipate
that the Senate and the nation would be impressed by those
qualities too.

Bush proceeded to announce his decision at a news conference
that very afternoon. Speed was essential to the president's strategy. He wanted his nominee confirmed and ready to serve when
the Supreme Court convened in October—and before the elections in November. He also wanted to seize the initiative, to control events before the pro-life and pro-choice camps could define
the debate. Less than seventy-two hours passed between Brennan's resignation and David's nomination—a remarkable example of presidential decision-making. On an incredibly important,
potentially explosive decision, George Bush didn't blink—and
his judgment could not have been better.

In the seven weeks until David's confirmation hearings in September, ideologues on both sides were frantically trying to determine if he was a liberal or a conservative. What they could not
grasp was that David was neither; he was simply a decent, scholarly, compassionate man who had dedicated his life to the American system of justice, and would be guided by his conscience,
not ideology, in his service on the Court.

When I landed at National Airport that afternoon, I had a
message to hurry to my Senate office, because David's nomination was about to be announced.

After the White House news conference, David was in shock. The president looked at him and said, "You look like you could use a drink," and took him upstairs. While they were relaxing, the president picked up the phone and called David's mother in her New Hampshire nursing home. "Mrs. Souter, I've just nominated your son to the Supreme Court," he told the astonished woman.

Later a White House car brought David to my office. It was bedlam there. We went into my office and embraced and we both wept. I was so proud and happy for him, truly overwhelmed.

David had planned to spend only one night in Washington, but now he needed to be there for the rest of the week, to begin planning with me and others for his confirmation, so I suggested that he stay with me.

"You bet I'll stay with you," said David, who was not one to squander money on a hotel if a friend had a guest room handy.

When it was time for dinner, we walked over to the Monocle, one of the Hill's old-line gathering spots, always filled with politicians, congressional aides, reporters and lobbyists. When David and I entered, the room fell silent. These people had seen the news and I sensed the whispers of "Is that who we think it is with Rudman?"

Soon enough, they'd be saying, "Who's that with Souter?"

Our dinner was punctuated by a long line of politicians coming by to meet the nominee. Finally we left and went to my apartment on Harbour Square, overlooking the Potomac in Southwest Washington. Neither of us is much of a drinker, but we had one or two that night, as we sat in my living room and talked. I stressed that he must not express an opinion on abortion or *Roe,* one way or another. To me, that was a political imperative. To David it was also a moral imperative—he could not be compromised by indicating how he would vote on an issue that was sure to come before the Court soon.

I told David that I intended to drop everything and take him around to meet as many as possible of the senators who would pass on his nomination. I knew that the best argument for David Souter was David Souter, and I wanted my colleagues to know him as I did. The White House was officially in charge of getting him confirmed, but this was an unprecedented situation—a Supreme Court nominee whose best friend was a senator—and they deferred to me. I had a lot of friends in the Senate and few real enemies. This was my turf and I took charge.

In the next two weeks David and I visited eight or ten senators a day, and David talked to all but one or two of the ninety-nine besides myself who would vote on him. Usually I sat in, although some said they'd rather meet one-on-one with David. All the visits were cordial, but not many senators were committing themselves. We assumed most Republicans were with us, but pro-choice Democrats were extremely uneasy about this little-known judge who was being called "the stealth nominee," after the fighter plane that supposedly can slip in under enemy radar.

If pro-life Republicans voted for David, and he turned out to be pro-choice, they could at least blame the president for nominating him. But if a pro-choice Democrat voted to confirm David, and he proved to be anti-abortion, that senator would have to face not only his own conscience but outraged pro-choice women.

Our first visit was to Bob Dole. The two men exchanged pleasantries, but Dole wasn't looking for a substantive discussion. I had already discussed David with Bob at length; we were close and he trusted my judgment. As Republican leader, Dole would be responsible for getting the nomination through, and he wasn't much interested in discussing the finer points of the law. Barring some unexpected disaster, his support was not in doubt.

COMBAT

Next we went to see Strom Thurmond, the ranking Republican on the Judiciary Committee. Strom has been a controversial figure for half a century, but even his enemies admit he's a remarkable human being, a walking history book.

He was in his eighties, but he greeted David with the enthusiasm and firm handshake of a man in his twenties. "How are ya, Jedge?" he demanded in his thick South Carolina accent. His office was filled with pictures and plaques and flags. David talked a little about his life, then Strom reached impatiently into his desk and pulled out a bound volume of the Constitution.

"Jedge," he declared, "you're gonna be confirmed and you're gonna serve on the Supreme Court, and just make sure that whatever you do is in this book!"

David still has that copy of the Constitution in his office at the Supreme Court.

One of our next visits was to Joe Biden, the chairman of the Judiciary Committee. Joe and I had worked together on crime legislation over the years and developed a friendship and trust that overcame partisan differences.

Joe was young, smart, ambitious, disorganized and bursting with energy and enthusiasm. For all his remarkable success, I knew that his life had often been one of hardship and tragedy. He came from a modest family background and as a boy had to overcome a painful stutter. In 1972, at age twenty-nine, he had upset an incumbent Republican senator by three thousand votes. Then, six weeks after his victory, his wife and infant daughter were killed when a truck hit their car. After that unspeakable tragedy, Joe wanted to quit the Senate, to devote himself to his surviving children, but finally he took the oath of office and it was a good thing for the country that he did.

Earlier that year Joe had come to me for a favor. He was running for reelection, and he'd heard that his Republican opponent was preparing TV ads that questioned his integrity. He expected the spots to play off the fact that Joe had dropped out of the 1988 presidential campaign because of charges that he'd plagiarized a speech by the British Labour Party leader Neil Kinnock. As I understood it, he'd attributed the Kinnock quote in many campaign speeches, then neglected to attribute it a time or two, and that led to a media attack on him.

I considered Joe Biden an honorable man, and I was glad to grant his favor, which was that I make a TV spot in which I spoke of our work together and my regard for his integrity. Bill Cohen also made a tape, but as it turned out Joe never had to use them.

My friendship with Joe paved the way for David's meeting with him, but Joe was still in a bind. He was a Catholic who had straddled the abortion issue, but as a liberal he counted women's groups among his strongest supporters, and the last thing he wanted was to approve a Supreme Court justice who might cast the vote that overturned *Roe* v. *Wade*. Nevertheless, he couldn't have treated David more fairly. They talked for an hour about constitutional law and specific Supreme Court cases, then Joe introduced the staff people David would be dealing with and gave him a good idea of what lay ahead, both as to procedure and substantive concerns. He also agreed to prompt hearings, starting on September 13. No Republican nominee could have been better treated by a Democratic committee chairman than David was treated by Joe Biden, even though Joe's vote remained in doubt to the very end.

One of our courtesy calls was on Dan Inouye, the Democratic senator from Hawaii. Dan was another of the senators, like Bob Dole, John Chafee, Bob Kerrey and John McCain, with whom I felt a special bond because we had served our country in combat. Perhaps our bond had deepened after I defended him against racist slurs during the Iran-Contra hearings three years earlier.

When David and I arrived in his office, Dan greeted us warmly. His office is decorated with wonderful Hawaiian artifacts, including a totem pole, and features a marvelous aquarium. Dan greeted us with that deep voice of his, shook hands with his left hand, and invited us to sit down. Before we could speak, he said, "Judge, I'm going to vote for your confirmation. I'll vote for you because there is no man I trust more than your friend Warren Rudman. If Warren says you'll be a good Supreme Court Justice, that's good enough for me."

I also took David to meet Bob Kerrey of Nebraska. I listened as they had a spirited discussion about the role of a Supreme Court justice—the old debate about making the law versus interpreting it. Kerrey was younger than I, and only in his second year in the Senate, but I greatly respected him. While serving in Vietnam in 1969, Kerrey had led a navy SEAL team on a mission to an enemy-held island. During the attack he suffered massive injuries from a grenade that exploded at his feet, but despite his wounds he continued to direct his men in what became a successful mission. For his bravery, he was awarded the Congressional Medal of Honor, our country's highest award for valor in combat.

Once, Bob and I were on the Senate floor when the two sides began bickering over some petty matter. As the rhetoric escalated, Bob and I looked at each other and smiled. For some reason, we walked around the back of the chamber, I from the Republican side and he from the Democratic, and met in the middle.

"What are you smiling about?" he asked.

"The way these guys carry on, you'd think this was important," I said. I laughed and added, "After all, Bob, nobody is shooting real bullets."

David and I were making our Senate rounds amid growing media frenzy. When we arrived at the Senate each morning we would be met by dozens of reporters and photographers who followed us from appointment to appointment. Once, to be polite, I invited the media into my office. There were so many of them we had to rotate them in and out. Yet we had absolutely nothing to say except Good morning, how are you, isn't it a fine day?

I should have understood that the media attention was ominous. This wry, scholarly, mild-mannered outsider was too good to be true—the journalistic instinct soon would be to debunk him.

By the end of the first week David needed a trip home, and we were delighted when the president sent word that he was flying to Kennebunkport and wanted us to join him on Air Force One.

We met the president and his party at Andrews Air Force Base and joined him and Mrs. Bush in their compartment for the hour-and-ten-minute flight to Pease Air Force Base in Portsmouth, New Hampshire. We had coffee and the president quizzed me about some upcoming votes in the Senate and in particular about David's prospects.

I told him things were looking fine. By then my concern wasn't so much the Senate as the media, which I thought were shameless in their coverage of David. But I didn't share that concern with the president, and when we landed I was delighted to see the huge crowd that had come to give David a hero's welcome.

The president stepped out first. David told me, "You go ahead," and gave me a little push to follow the president, but I said, "Like hell—you go out there and I'll come with Barbara." This was David's moment. He joined the president and the crowd went wild. Finally Bush looked back and said, "Warren, where are you?" and pulled me out onto the ramp. I was so proud of David. He'd left the state five days before as an obscure federal court judge and now he was returning on Air Force One as the most talked about jurist in the world.

We had urged David to say as little as possible to the media. As we left the airport, reporters asked him how it felt to be home.

"Damn good," declared David, who was emerging as the most laconic man in American public life since Cal Coolidge.

Pressed for more, David grinned and said, "I have two words to say: Hi and good-bye."

We returned to Washington the next week to complete our courtesy calls, then the Congress entered its August recess, whereupon five of us went to Tom Rath's condo on Newfound Lake in central New Hampshire to prepare for the hearings. We rented an extra condo to house the overflow, laid in plenty of food and beer, and settled down for two intense days of brainstorming. In addition to Tom, David and me, the others were Fred McClure, the White House counsel, and A. B. Culvahouse, who had served as legal counsel to President Reagan.

We had two previous confirmations to guide us. Bork's, in 1988, had been bitterly confrontational and had ended in disaster. It was followed by Anthony Kennedy's, which had been relatively uneventful and led to easy confirmation. We had videotapes of both hearings, but mostly we watched Kennedy's. We were confident that David's hearings, given his personality and record, would resemble Kennedy's much more than Bork's.

We would watch as a senator asked Kennedy a question, then stop the tape and ask David for his answer. Often we argued vehemently about the answers he should give. We grilled David more relentlessly than the Judiciary Committee did a month later.

But ultimately we couldn't coach David. He was going to make his own decisions. However, since he'd never bothered to watch any previous televised hearings, we could at least show him the pitfalls and the possibilities that the forum presented. For example, he needed to remember that in Washington the fact that you're asked Question A doesn't rule out giving Answer B, if that suits your purposes. Presidents and senators do it every day.

Later, we returned to Washington, where David holed up in an office in the Executive Office Building, next to the White House, studying Supreme Court cases. We also held mock hearings, in the EOB's Indian Treaty Room, where Boyden Gray, Bill Kristol of the vice president's staff, and Justice Department lawyers and I grilled the nominee. Another person who worked closely with us was Ken Duberstein, who'd been Reagan's chief of congressional relations and now was back in private life.

As the hearings drew near, I was confident that David could hold his own before the senators and avoid being pinned down on the abortion issue. But this war was also being fought in the media, and that was the worst of the ordeal.

From the outset, much of the media assumed that there had to be something wrong with David and they would fearlessly dig it out.

Soon after David was nominated, while we were still in Washington, reporters and television crews arrived at his isolated farmhouse and began peering in windows and climbing on the roof, trying to see inside. Some used floodlights to film the books in the library. They went to local video stores to see what videotapes he was renting. Presumably they were hoping he watched porn, but the exercise was pointless since David didn't own a VCR—he only reluctantly owned a TV. Reporters even invaded the nursing home where David's mother lived and represented themselves as doctors to try to gain access to Mrs. Souter. Eventually, the state police had to protect David's home from intruders.

A *Washington Post* reporter called me and said she and a colleague were going to New Hampshire to learn everything they could about David. The message I got was that she was looking for scandal. She asked for my help and I gave her the names of plenty of people who knew David. A couple of weeks later she called and said it was amazing but they couldn't find anyone who would say anything bad about David.

Neither could anyone else, but that didn't stop them from trying.

The media leveled two main charges against David: that he was gay and, when that fizzled out, that he was a recluse, an oddball, and by implication someone who lacked the understanding of ordinary Americans needed on the Supreme Court.

The gay issue arose simply because David was fifty years old and had never married. There was absolutely nothing to support such speculation. Tom Rath and I had known him for many years and we knew better. The conservative John Sununu had appointed him to the state supreme court. Neighbors who'd known him since childhood laughed at the allegations, and women he had been involved with were not hard to find.

Yet reporters from leading publications felt obliged to raise this "issue." In years past, I believe, such media-inspired speculation would not have been deemed fit to print. But American journalism had changed. In the 1950s, its standards of taste were set by *The New York Times*; by 1990 they seemed to be set by supermarket tabloids.

Time's August 6 cover story on David raised the issue twice, first with a vague assertion about unnamed "activists" who were looking into his record: "Some wondered if the 50-year-old lifelong bachelor might be gay. (Friends assured them he is not.)"

Warming to the subject, *Time* continued:

Souter had barely left the podium in the press room of the White House before Republican Party officials were raising "the 50-year-old bachelor thing," which was widely interpreted as a way of introducing speculation that Souter is homosexual.

Were unnamed "Republican Party officials" really raising this "thing," or were unnamed editors trying to spice up a cover story?

Time proceeded to name two women David had dated and mentioned a third without naming her. But why raise such an issue gratuitously and then knock it down? Why raise it at all? If someone is homosexual, that's his or her business, but if someone is not, he shouldn't be accused of homosexuality simply to titillate newspaper and magazine readers. These charges were being made about a man who'd been nominated to the Supreme Court. To print sheer gossip that might have such tremendous political implications—not to mention its impact on David Souter's feelings—without a shred of evidence strikes me as the height of irresponsibility.

Even after the charge was discredited, many papers continued with murky reflections about unmarried men, closet gays, changing social mores and the like. *The Washington Post*'s ultra-hip Style section began a story as follows:

> He's a bookworm who looks like Pat Paulsen. He wears extremely bad ties. David Souter is not your standard hunka hunka burning love. News that the 51-year-old judge had never married set off a flurry of speculation that the Supreme Court might be getting its first gay justice. When reporters unearthed three former girlfriends, it appeared instead that he is simply a scholarly workaholic too busy for romance.

What can you say about writing like that? That it's colorful? It's contemptible. Why does a major newspaper print such garbage?

David liked women and women liked him. In time, several of these women stepped forward to praise him. Ellanor Stengel

Fink, who dated David for several years while she was a student at Wheaton and he was in law school, described him to *The Washington Post* as "tremendously fair-minded . . . wonderful to be with intellectually . . . a friendly, warm person and extremely considerate . . . an individualist . . . real class."

In my experience, precious few men win that kind of tribute from the women in their lives, past or present.

When the gay stories played out, lazy reporters fell back on the idea that David was simply peculiar.

Time, in its September 3 issue, carried a Q&A with me. One exchange went like this:

> Q. Souter comes across to much of the public as rather weird.
> A. Weird? He has lots of friends. He has a very active social life. He lives on a farm a few miles from the capital of our state. I hardly think you have to come out of the Upper East Side to qualify for a seat on the Supreme Court.

Time next raised the horrid prospect that David might prefer books to people, never considering that he might like both. A *Washington Post* writer, in a fit of invention, described David as a combination of E.T., Calvin Coolidge with Richard Nixon's five o'clock shadow, and "an oddly fearless substitute teacher coming into a tough class on a rainy day."

If you know the person involved, particularly if he is David Souter, writing like this is maddening. It had nothing at all to do with the David I knew and admired, nor was it designed to please a man who treasured his privacy as passionately as David did.

Not long before the hearings were to begin, we heard from friends in the media that a gay newspaper in New York was poised to publish an article that would "expose" David's secret life. In fact the story never appeared, and if it had, it would have been either someone's fantasy or a deliberate lie. By then I had concluded that some elements of the media are more irresponsible than I'd ever thought possible, and I'd never been optimistic on the subject. I was sufficiently concerned that I went to Joe Biden and told him what might happen and that it was absolute fiction. Joe assured me that he understood. He clearly wanted to confront David on the issues, not on gossip, but I was only half joking when I said that Tom Rath and I could give him the names of several women who could testify to David's heterosexuality. Joe laughed off my offer.

The entire exercise was a chilling reminder that in today's political and journalistic climate anyone (however obscure) can accuse anyone else (however honorable) of just about anything and have a decent shot at making news.

David and I weren't bursting with joy when we returned to my Harbour Square apartment the night we heard reports of the possible "outing." I ate a sandwich and David fixed a salad. He was unusually quiet, and finally, around ten o'clock, he told me he had grave reservations about the entire process.

"Warren," he said, in obvious distress, "if I had known how vicious this process is, I wouldn't have let you propose my nomination."

I understood how he felt. The closest thing I had seen to this was the treatment former Senator John Tower received when George Bush nominated him for secretary of defense. Allegations of excessive drinking and womanizing, based on hearsay, defeated his nomination. David's case was worse, in that the innuendo he faced was based on nothing at all.

As we talked, it was obvious that if he could turn the clock back two months he wouldn't have accepted the nomination. Clearly the attacks had pained him personally, but I think he was even more disturbed by their impact on his mother and close friends.

I had seen this coming. The Supreme Court nomination had turned his life upside down. David is the most private person I know. He truly hated seeing his face on the cover of *Time*. He couldn't believe it when we went to the grocery store and he was mobbed by people who wanted his autograph on their shopping bags. This was not how he wanted to live his life. This "outing" threat was the last straw. He didn't think anyone should be put through the anguish the media were inflicting on him.

As he told me of his frustrations, I feared he might walk away from the nomination. Finally I grabbed his shoulders. "David, I know what you're going through," I declared. "It's outrageous what they're doing to you. But it's your destiny to serve on the Supreme Court. I've believed that for a long time. Don't let them get to you."

I was beside myself. I'd worked so hard, for so long, to bring him to this point, and now I really feared he might throw the nomination away.

As we talked I could look out my window and see the Potomac River, serene in the moonlight, and people strolling on the plaza below, oblivious to the drama in my third-floor apartment.

"I know it's tough, but you're tough. You're going to win this fight. The day you get to that hearing and let them see the real you, the David Souter your friends know, the rest of this will evaporate. This is your destiny. The Court needs you. Just be patient."

In time, as I had expected, his inner strength took over—for David, for all his mildness, is one of the toughest people I know. He had been angry and needed some time to work it through.

He had a scotch, I had a bourbon, and we talked. I insisted that whatever our frustrations with the media, he was going to blow the Judiciary Committee away. He just had to ride it out.

By three o'clock or so he'd agreed, and after that he never looked back.

We'd decided several weeks earlier, during the sessions at Tom Rath's lakefront condo, that David should begin his testimony with an opening statement. This wasn't customary, but David's image had been distorted by the media. He needed to present the real David, not wait and hope that his true self would appear piecemeal, under questioning by sometimes hostile senators. First impressions would be crucial.

The challenge was not to demonstrate his intellect, but to show that he understood and cared about the lives of others less fortunate than himself. In short, he had to replace the media's bizarre creation with the real David Souter. Just how this would be done was, of course, up to him.

On September 12, the day before the hearings began, Tom Rath and I were with David in the Executive Office Building. He was about to leave for a White House luncheon when he asked if Tom and I wanted to read a draft of his opening statement. We read it and were greatly moved. Maybe we were too prejudiced to judge, but we believed the statement would convince America that David was as fine a man as we knew him to be.

David arrived at the Hart Office Building shortly before ten on Thursday the thirteenth, somber in a dark suit and a black-and-white-striped tie. I escorted him to Room 215, a huge hearing room. I'd taken him by for a look the day before, but now it was crowded with politicians, reporters, photographers, activists and citizens with a taste for history.

The proceedings began at 10:05 with Chairman Biden's opening remarks, followed by ten-minute statements by each of the thirteen other committee members. The less said about these orations the better. Even the best senators, confronting a national television audience, tend to lose control.

As David's home-state senator, I had the honor of introducing him. I made no pretense of objectivity. I was an advocate, making the opening argument. I spoke of our twenty-year friendship, of his outstanding service in the attorney general's office, of the excellence of his mind and of his record as a judge. Turning personal, I added, "David Souter is my friend. I trust him, I respect him, and I like him. He has made me think, he has made me reflect, and he has made me laugh."

Striking a note that I thought was crucial, I added that great judges "must have certain human qualities, not fixed life résumés. I know that David Souter, shaped by his experiences, knows that judges must understand that their decisions are not merely academic or scholarly exercises but, rather, the best hope of resolving the human dilemma."

Finally, fighting to hold down my anger, I made the statement I quoted at the start of this chapter, that it was remarkable that someone so blessed with humility, graciousness, frugality and charity was viewed by some people as out of touch with modern life. I wanted to draw the line, because I was absolutely sure that most people viewing these hearings were going to agree with me that it was not David but his media critics who were out of touch with American values.

After a recess for lunch, it was David's turn.

David's opening statement was a virtuoso performance. He was modest and soft-spoken, intelligent and self-confident. He sat by himself at the witness table, with only a notepad and a glass of water before him. David wanted no aides passing him notes and whispering in his ear; Tom Rath and I were just behind him, but we were expected to keep our opinions to ourselves.

His message was that he was, indeed, a man who understood the realities of human life as well as the requirements of the law.

He spoke of his boyhood in a small town where "we were aware of lives that were easy and we were aware of lives that were very hard."

He spoke of his pro bono work with two indigent clients when he was a young lawyer. He described helping one woman who had lost custody of her children and another who had been evicted from her home. He told how, as a trial judge, he had dealt with criminals and victims and jurors and litigants of every type, including "children who were the unwitting victims of domestic disputes."

When his years as a trial judge were over, he said, he took two lessons with him:

> The first lesson, simple as it is, is that whatever court we are in, whatever we are doing, whether we are on a trial court or an appellate court, at the end of our task some human being is going to be affected. Some human life is going to be changed in some way by what we do, whether we do it as trial judges or whether we do it as appellate judges, as far removed from the trial arena as it is possible to be.
>
> The second lesson I learned in that time is that if, indeed, we are going to be trial judges, whose rulings will affect the lives of other people and who are going to change their lives by what we do, we had better use every power of our minds and our hearts and our beings to get those rulings right.

A moment later, he concluded,

> I am mindful of those two lessons when I tell you this: That if you believe and the Senate of the United States believes that it is right to confirm my nomination, then I will accept those responsibilities as obligations to all of the people in the United States whose lives will be affected by my stewardship of the Constitution.

When David finished this simple, eloquent, humane statement, Tom Rath and I exchanged a glance. Even though we'd
read a draft of the statement—and as well as we knew David—we
were stunned. David had just nailed down his seat on the
Supreme Court.

Two more days of questioning lay ahead, but his critics never
laid a glove on him. He made it clear during Joe Biden's opening
round of questions that any senator who chose to debate the law
with him was extremely unwise—which did not prevent several
from doing just that.

If senators tried to press him on *Roe* v. *Wade,* he said politely
but firmly that it would be improper for him to comment on
issues that might soon come before the Court. The committee
accepted that as reasonable, although there were differences
about where the line should be drawn.

The Democrats who were most skeptical of him, Ted Kennedy
and Howard Metzenbaum of Ohio, could only bring up cases
he'd argued as attorney general, or decisions he'd written on the
state supreme court, to try to show that he was insensitive to civil
rights or women's rights. It was true that as attorney general,
David had argued some cases that he wouldn't have argued if the
choice had been his. He was serving his client, the governor, and
most people understood that, but when Kennedy continued to
press him on a case with racial implications, David finally said:

With respect, Senator, let me address a couple of points that you
raise. Maybe the best place to start is with the fundamental one.
That is about me today, as opposed to me as an advocate in a voting rights case twenty years ago.

I hope one thing will be clear and this is maybe the time to
make it clear, and that is that with respect to the societal problems of the United States today there is none which, in my judgment, is more tragic or more demanding of the efforts of every

American in the Congress and out of the Congress than the removal of societal discrimination in matters of race and in the matters of invidious discrimination which we are unfortunately too familiar with.

That, I hope, when these hearings are over, will be taken as a given with respect to my set of values.

That is as close to anger as David will ever come in public and he made his point forcefully. Ted Kennedy made a mistake when he tried to impute racism to David.

After Kennedy's bumbling attempt to cross-examine the nominee, David and Tom went for a break in a nearby office and were joined by Alan Simpson, the tall, bald, acerbic Wyoming Republican.

"You know, when I was growing up we loved Western movies," Simpson drawled, "and most of all we loved Roy Rogers' movies. There'd always be a scene where Roy and the bad guy had a shootout in front of the saloon, and it always ended up with the bad guy biting the dust. And some old codger would say, 'You don't mess with Roy Rogers.' Judge, that's what I thought when you finished with Ted Kennedy: 'You don't mess with old Roy!' "

David gave two more memorable responses that afternoon.

Howard Metzenbaum asked David if he thought he understood, not as a lawyer but as a human being, how a woman felt when she had an unwanted pregnancy.

David hesitated a moment before he replied:

Senator, your question comes as a surprise to me. I was not expecting that kind of question, and you have made me think of something that I have not thought of for twenty-four years.

When I was in law school, I was on the board of freshman advisers at Harvard College. I was a proctor in a dormitory. One afternoon, one of the freshmen who was assigned to me, I was his adviser, came to me and he was in pretty rough emotional shape and we shut the door and sat down, and he told me that his girl-friend was pregnant and he said she is about to have a self-abortion and she does not know how to do it. He said she is afraid to tell her parents what has happened and she is afraid to go to the health services, and he said will you talk to her, and I did.

I know you will respect the privacy of the people involved, and I will not try to say what I told her. But I spent two hours in a small dormitory bedroom that afternoon listening to her and try-ing to counsel her to approach her problem in a way different from what she was doing, and your question has brought that back to me.

I think the only thing I can add to that is I know what you were trying to tell me, because I remember that afternoon.

The room was hushed. David hadn't said what he told the young woman—whether to have an abortion or to have the child—but no one could doubt his concern or his compassion.

A moment later, Alan Simpson, annoyed by some of the ques-tions he'd heard, asked bluntly, "David Souter, are you a racist?"

"The answer is no," David replied.

"A crazy question to ask, is it not?" Simpson added.

"Far be it from me to say that a question from you, Senator, is crazy."

That was one of several times that David's quiet wit had brought laughter, but when the laughter stopped, Simpson asked him to elaborate and David said he had two thoughts.

The first is something very personal and very personal to my fam-ily. In a way, it surprises me when I look back over the years when I was growing up that never once, ever in my house that I can remember did I ever hear my mother or my father refer to any human being in terms of racial or ethnic identity. I have heard all the slang terms and I never heard them in my house.

After speaking of his parents a moment longer, David said:

Another thing that occurred to me, and it is equally personal—and I think I will not offend the two people involved by saying this—two of my closest friends in this world are sitting in the row behind me. You have already heard from Warren Rudman. I heard Warren Rudman talk about what it was like to be discriminated against when he was a kid because he was Jewish. Somewhere out there, there is somebody who is discriminating against a friend of mine who is close enough to me to be a brother.

And there is another friend of mine in that category in the row behind me. You haven't heard from him today. His name is Thomas Rath. I can remember Tom Rath telling me years ago about his grandparents, and his grandparents remembered the days when there were help-wanted signs up around the city of Boston that said "No Irish need apply." And that meant them.

So if you want to know whether I have got the vision, if you will, behind the answer to your question, I will be content to have you look to my friends.

It was a moving response and not just to me and Tom. I could see how transfixed the members of the committee were. David said a lot that day that would impress legal scholars, but with spontaneous replies like that he won the respect of millions of ordinary people who cared about what kind of man he was.

At the end of the day, Joe Biden said to me, "Your friend should be in the theater." He meant that David's impact had been highly dramatic and highly effective. But it was dramatic because it was genuine. David and I had discussed anti-Semitism and he truly did not understand it. Blind, irrational prejudice was beyond his comprehension.

The hearings continued for four more days. David testified again on Friday and Monday, and others spoke for and against him on Tuesday and Wednesday.

Howard Phillips, chairman of the Conservative Caucus, opposed the nomination, citing the fact that David, as a board member of the Concord Hospital, had participated in unanimous decisions to permit abortions there.

Leaders of the National Organization for Women, the National Abortion Rights Action League, and the Planned Parenthood Federation of America also opposed the nomination because David had refused to endorse *Roe* v. *Wade*.

But the advocates, pro and con, had little impact. David had won on the first afternoon he testified.

Republican senators had little choice but to go along with the president's nominee, whatever their concerns. Most Democrats recognized that even if his views on *Roe* were uncertain, he was an intelligent, compassionate man, and almost certainly the best they were going to get from the Bush administration.

In the end, Ted Kennedy was the only member of the committee to vote against David. The full Senate confirmed David by a vote of 90 to 9. I was particularly glad that Joe Biden overcame his concerns to vote for confirmation.

A night or two after David was confirmed, he accompanied me to a dinner party at the home of Meg Greenfield, the chief editorial writer for *The Washington Post*. Knowing that this would probably be one of David's few ventures into Washington society, I joked to Jim Lehrer, as we were leaving, "Take a good look at this guy—you'll never see him again!" Jim reminded me of this several years later, and added, "You were right."

Not long after David joined the Court, he sent me a beautifully framed and matted photograph of him and the other justices, in street clothes, taken soon after his swearing-in ceremony. Mounted below the picture was a check for a hundred dollars, David's repayment of the money I'd loaned him at the airport the Sunday he flew to Washington to meet the president. The inscription said, "To Warren from David, thanks for staking me to the job interview."

There were other postscripts to David's joining the Court. At one time or another, after David began to cast votes, all of the senators who voted against him came to me and said they'd been wrong.

But perhaps the best ending to this story is a scene in a railroad station in Wilmington, Delaware, on Monday, June 29, 1992.

That was the day the Supreme Court announced its long-awaited decision in *Planned Parenthood of Southeastern Pennsylvania* v. *Casey,* the case in which the pro-life forces had hoped to muster five votes to overturn *Roe* v. *Wade.* Four votes were there, those of Chief Justice Rehnquist and Justices White, Scalia and the most recent addition to the court, Clarence Thomas. To form a majority, they needed only one vote from the centrist trio of Kennedy, O'Connor and Souter, and past votes by Kennedy and O'Connor had suggested that either might help overturn *Roe.*

Instead, Kennedy, O'Connor and Souter signed an unprecedented three-person opinion, joined by Justices Blackmun and Stevens, that dramatically reaffirmed *Roe.* In court that morning, each of the three read aloud a segment of the joint opinion.

There was little doubt that David had been the catalyst who had drawn O'Connor and Kennedy to the defense of *Roe,* or that he was the principal author of the eloquent statement on stare decisis that was the heart of the opinion.

The opinion was a masterpiece not only of law but of political realism and judicial candor. It said in part:

> For two decades of economic and social developments, people have organized intimate relationships and made choices that define their views of themselves and their places in society, in reliance on the availability of abortion in the event that contraception should fail. The ability of women to participate equally in the economic and social life of the Nation has been facilitated by their ability to control their reproductive lives.

Where, in the performance of its judicial duties, the Court decides a case in such a way as to resolve the sort of intensely divisive controversy reflected in *Roe* and those rare, comparable cases, its decision has a dimension that the resolution of the normal case does not carry. It is the dimension present whenever the Court's interpretation of the Constitution calls the contending sides of a national controversy to end their national division by accepting a common mandate rooted in the Constitution.

The Court is not asked to do this very often, having thus addressed the Nation only twice in our lifetime, in the decisions of *Brown* and *Roe*. But when the Court does act in this way, its decision requires an equally rare precedential force to counter the inevitable efforts to overthrow it and to thwart its implementation. Some of those efforts may be mere unprincipled emotional reactions; others may proceed from principles worthy of profound respect. But whatever the premises of opposition may be, only the most convincing justification under accepted standards of precedent could suffice to demonstrate that a later decision overruling the first was anything but a surrender to political pressure, and an unjustified repudiation of the principle on which the Court staked its authority in the first instance. So to overrule under fire in the absence of the most compelling reason to re-examine a watershed decision would subvert the Court's legitimacy beyond any serious question.

A decision to overrule *Roe*'s essential holding under the existing circumstances would address error, if error there was, at the cost of both profound and unnecessary damage to the Court's legitimacy, and to the Nation's commitment to the rule of law. It is therefore imperative to adhere to the essence of *Roe*'s original decision, and we do so today.

Harry Blackmun, the eighty-two-year-old author of *Roe,* added a concurrence that called the Souter-O'Connor-Kennedy opinion "an act of personal courage and constitutional principle."

I quote at length from the *Casey* decision because of its historical importance, because of the precision of its language and its logic, and because I am profoundly proud that the man who wrote those words is my friend.

I was in New York on the Monday that the *Casey* decision was announced. Tom Polgar, my legislative director, called in great excitement to tell me that *Roe* had been affirmed. He read me some of the decision and said that David clearly had been instrumental in persuading O'Connor and Kennedy to support *Roe*.

By coincidence, I was taking a train that afternoon to Wilmington, where I was to appear with Joe Biden at the Delaware Forum, a series of public meetings on national issues that Joe sponsors. On the train ride down, I stared out into the rain and grew more and more proud of what David had done. As David noted in his opinion, two Supreme Court decisions in our time addressed issues that could have torn the nation apart. The first was *Brown*, declaring separate but equal public schools unconstitutional. The second was *Roe*, which gives a woman the right to control her own body. Now *Roe* had been affirmed, as *Brown* had been affirmed, and there could be no turning back. The combined efforts of the Reagan and Bush administrations and the religious right to overthrow *Roe* had been defeated, probably for good.

I wasn't surprised at David's stand on *Roe*. I thought that, throughout his testimony, he had been giving clues to anyone who would listen that neither as a believer in stare decisis nor as a compassionate human being was he likely to vote against *Roe*. Still, it was good to have it in writing.

When I got off the train in Wilmington at six o'clock, the platform was packed with commuters. At first I didn't see Joe, then I spotted him waving at me from far down the platform. Joe had agonized over his vote for David and I knew how thrilled he must be. We started running through the crowd toward each other, and when we met we embraced, laughing and crying.

"You were right about him," he kept saying. "Did you read that opinion? You were right!"

People stared at us as if we were crazy, but we just kept laughing and yelling and hugging each other, because sometimes there are happy endings, even in politics.

CHAPTER FIVE

THE KEATING FIVE

Everybody *Doesn't* Do It!

Each House may determine the Rules of its Proceedings, punish its Members for disorderly Behavior, and, with the Concurrence of two thirds, expel a Member.

THE CONSTITUTION OF THE UNITED STATES

The Savings and Loan debacle of the 1980s was the greatest financial scandal in American history, one that will eventually cost the taxpayers at least $500 billion.

No one intended such a result. In 1980, when Jimmy Carter signed legislation that increased the ceiling on federal deposit insurance from $40,000 to $100,000, expanded the S&Ls' authority to make consumer loans and lifted the limit on interest rates they could pay, he called it a boon for consumers. In 1982, Congress made matters worse by allowing S&Ls to make unsecured business loans and large investments in commercial real estate. The new laws put S&L operators in the enviable position of being able to gamble with other people's money. If they won, they won; if they lost, the government would pay.

These laws, plus the Reagan administration's hostility to government regulation, led to disaster. Both David Stockman and Don Regan, devoted as they were to a "free market," repeatedly turned down requests for more money and staff to regulate the S&Ls. Later it struck me as a curious sort of free market that forces taxpayers to bail out an industry's incompetence and/or criminality.

The combination of government deposit insurance and government laissez-faire led to an orgy of high-risk investments and loans. Some S&L operators were crooked, others were inept. Many, even as they squandered hundreds of millions of dollars, indulged themselves with expensive cars, private jets, yachts, lavish vacation homes and princely tours of Europe. Their government, in its wisdom, had given them a license to steal.

I'm not going to explore the complexities of the S&L disaster, but its economic and political dimensions are basic to understanding the subject of this chapter, the Senate Ethics Committee's investigation of the so-called Keating Five.

By 1989, when our investigation began, the American people were waking up to the fact that they had been robbed of hundreds of billions of dollars. But who was to blame? The S&L crisis was a scandal without a villain. There was no Richard Nixon masterminding a Watergate cover-up, no Ollie North shredding documents.

The disaster had occurred on Ronald Reagan's watch, but he murmured "What elephant?" and ambled away unscathed. Charles Keating went to jail when it was shown that his Lincoln Savings and Loan had cheated depositors, many of them retirees, out of millions. But one businessman, however venal, could not be held responsible for such a cosmic disaster as the S&L mess.

Congress was a natural candidate, but who in Congress? As David Rosenbaum noted in *The New York Times,* "So many politicians are to blame that few are left to point fingers."

Then came charges that five United States senators had among them taken more than a million dollars from Keating and his friends and companies, and in return had tried to intimidate the federal regulators who were struggling to expose his crimes.

The crucial political fact about the Keating Five was that four of them were Democrats. If they were to become the scapegoats for the multibillion-dollar S&L disaster, the result might have been the destruction of a party that was already reeling from its third straight presidential loss. If the four Democrats accused of helping Keating could be defeated, and their party discredited along with them, the party might also lose its majority in both houses of Congress. For the Democrats the Keating Five investigation was potentially a one-way ticket to the political graveyard.

For all its political implications, the Keating affair remained a very human story that turned on money, politics and human weakness, and it was impossible not to feel some sympathy for the five senators, even as I regretted their poor judgment.

After thirty years as a lawyer and ten as a senator, I was not naive about human nature. I knew that my colleagues faced extraordinary temptations and sometimes succumbed to them. Other senators sometimes came to me with their troubles, treating me as a combination of legal adviser and father confessor. We talked about their problems with money, with women, with drug-abusing or alienated children, with wives who hated politics. One colleague tearfully told me that his girlfriend was pregnant, his marriage was a disaster, and there was no solution except to resign. I urged him to reconsider, and today he's one of the most powerful men in Washington.

Two senators who didn't come to me for advice—I wish they had—were my Republican colleagues David Durenberger of Minnesota and Bob Packwood of Oregon. Durenberger was a first-rate senator, but in the midst of a divorce, pressed for funds, he cheated the government out of some money. He deserved to be censured by the Senate, but I hated to see it happen, and when it was over I told him, "David, if this had been a criminal trial, and I'd been your lawyer, I would have had you plead innocent because of temporary insanity."

Insanity is rare in the Senate, but insecurity is a way of life. In an ever more venomous political atmosphere, incumbents are surrounded by enemies anxious to accuse them of real or imagined sins. They may wake up any morning and discover that the media are trumpeting the most outrageous charges against them. Decades of honorable service can be undermined by accusations from a former aide, spouse or friend, and the public and media are eager to believe the worst.

By the time Bob Packwood resigned from the Senate in disgrace he had become a figure of contempt and ridicule, but I will always see him as a tragic figure, a man of enormous talent brought down by a bizarre flaw in his character. He was without question one of the smartest and best senators with whom I served. In the struggle for tax reform and a balanced budget he was always a voice of reason, and, it should be remembered, he was one of the Senate's leading advocates of population control and abortion rights.

The Packwood affair was different from the Keating investigation, in that one turned on sex and the other on money, but the two cases were alike in that both became intensely partisan issues and revealed the Senate's great difficulty in carrying out its constitutional duty to police its own members.

Over the years, I had heard rumors that Packwood had a drinking problem, along with what was once called an eye for the

ladies, but nonetheless, when the first charges against him surfaced in *The Washington Post* on November 22, 1992, I was
astonished. Some fifteen women charged Packwood with crude
and entirely unwelcome sexual advances, most of them dating
back to the 1970s. Although I was soon to leave the Senate, I
was still vice chairman of the Ethics Committee, serving with
Chairman Terry Sanford of North Carolina, and by December 1
we had ordered a formal investigation.

The investigation dragged on for a long time, largely because
the committee deadlocked along party lines on whether or not to
hold public hearings. The Republicans feared that public hearings would hurt their party, just as the Democrats had feared
public hearings in the Keating case.

Packwood did not really deny the charges. He issued a semi-
apology, sought treatment for alcoholism and said he couldn't
remember many of the alleged events. He and his supporters
may have hoped that if he stalled long enough, the charges
would fade away. In an earlier era they might have. But it was
Packwood's misfortune to have become a symbol to millions of
women of the sexual abuse they had suffered for far too long.

In the summer of 1995 the Packwood case was finally
resolved. On July 31, the Ethics Committee, by a 3–3 party-line
vote, rejected public hearings. The Republicans argued that they
had interviewed the women, that Packwood had in effect admitted his guilt and waived his right to cross-examine his accusers,
and that the committee had all the information it needed to ren-
der a decision. Public hearings would only embarrass the Senate
and detract from the serious work then in progress. I agreed.
There was no need for hearings except to serve up Bob Packwood's head on a platter.

Politics was the unspoken issue. The Republicans were looking
ahead to a presidential campaign in which they would be the

party of "family values" running against a president whose baggage included not only rumors of infidelity but a lawsuit alleging the harassment of a young state employee while he was governor of Arkansas. The last thing the Republicans needed was weeks of televised hearings of tearful women describing how Bob Packwood stuck his tongue in their mouths. Moreover, such hearings would have been a disaster for Bob Dole, who was running for president as a leader who made the Senate run smoothly. I'm sure that Dole kept hands off the Ethics Committee, as Senate leaders traditionally had, but everyone knew that his best interests lay in disposing of the affair as quickly as possible.

At that point, with public hearings denied, I have no doubt that the Ethics Committee would have proposed that Packwood be censured and stripped of his chairmanship of the Finance Committee and the full Senate would have agreed. But that was not good enough for Barbara Boxer of California, one of the four women elected to the Senate in 1992, in the aftermath of the 1991 Clarence Thomas/Anita Hill hearings, who insisted that Packwood's accusers had a right to tell their stories in public.

On August 2, by a largely party-line 52–48 vote, the Senate rejected Boxer's call for public hearings. Only three Republicans voted with the Democrats: Olympia Snowe and Bill Cohen of Maine, and Arlen Specter of Pennsylvania, who had learned his lesson during the Thomas/Hill hearings, when he outraged millions of women with his hostile questioning of Anita Hill.

That seemed to have ended the Packwood affair. He would be censured and stripped of his chairmanship and the Senate could put this sordid episode behind it. Then, incredibly, on the next day, August 3, the committee announced that two more women had made charges against Packwood. One of them was a fifty-five-year-old teacher who said that the senator had given her an unwanted kiss on a 1971 camping trip. But the charge that mattered was from a woman who said that in 1983, when she was a seventeen-year-old intern in Packwood's office and had sought a college recommendation, he came to her home when her parents were away, kissed her and forced his tongue into her mouth.

Charges that Packwood had forced himself on a girl of seventeen were bad enough, but they were followed on August 25 by an extremely unwise decision on the senator's part. He announced that he had changed his mind and now wanted public hearings so he could cross-examine his accusers.

That was the end for Packwood. Republicans had taken a big political risk by voting against public hearings, and now he was saying he *wanted* public hearings, and on charges involving a girl of seventeen. Packwood said he had changed his mind because he wanted to challenge the woman's version of the encounter. Some people thought he was stalling, hoping he could at least complete the Finance Committee's extremely important agenda, which included deficit reduction, tax cuts and welfare reform, before he lost his chairmanship. If so, he badly misread the mood of the Senate.

Mitch McConnell of Kentucky, the Republican chairman of the Ethics Committee, is a tough and somewhat humorless man and not someone to cross. He and other Republicans felt betrayed by Packwood. They had offended a great many women by defending him, and now they believed he had double-crossed them. On September 6 the previously deadlocked Ethics Committee voted 6 to 0 for Packwood's expulsion from the Senate.

One day later, facing certain expulsion, a stunned Packwood resigned. He had been harshly judged. However offensive his behavior, he had not killed, raped or stolen money. The last senator to face expulsion had been Harrison Williams, in 1981, who had been filmed taking a bribe in the Abscam investigation, and who also resigned before actual expulsion took place. Most of the senators expelled before that had been Southerners convicted of treason during the Civil War. Packwood's real sin, one of his colleagues commented, wasn't kissing the women but trifling with his fellow senators. *That* was unforgivable.

The Founding Fathers, when they provided for congressional self-regulation, assumed that in ethical matters its members would place the good name of the institution ahead of politics. For a long time that was true. But it wasn't in the Packwood case, nor was it in the Keating Five investigation a few years earlier, which I believe was the first time the committee was seriously politicized. The trend reflects the increasingly vindictive tone of national politics.

The Ethics Committee by law has three members from each party, and thus is the only Senate committee in which the majority party cannot dominate the minority. Since a majority vote is required to take action, in theory only bipartisan actions can be taken. In fact another outcome is possible. The committee can deadlock along party lines, in which case it will eventually have to report back to the Senate its inability to reach a decision. The Ethics Committee would then be exposed as incapable of passing an honest, bipartisan judgment on its peers. The Senate would then either appoint a new committee or take the matter under consideration directly to the floor, where dozens of charges and punishments might be proposed. That kind of partisan free-for-all was my worst nightmare as I fought for an honorable outcome to the Keating investigation.

For nearly two years, from late 1989 until late 1991, as we and the Democrats deadlocked along party lines, we were playing a dangerous game. The Democrats wanted the least possible punishment for the Five and were stalling, hoping we would give in. We were stalling too. The difference, as I saw it, was our motivations. The Democrats were trying to save their party. We were trying to save the Senate, which would be disgraced if the actions of three of the Five went unpunished.

The story of the Keating Five has a large cast of characters, but it begins with the man who gave the scandal its name. Charles Keating eventually went to prison, but at the time the five senators were exchanging favors with him he was a highly successful and respected businessman with major interests in each of their states. Both because of his prominence and his lavish political donations, it would have been unusual for any senator to spurn Keating. As long as senators must raise millions of dollars to run for reelection, and the campaign finance laws stay as they are, there will be people like Keating seeking to buy political influence.

Keating was an odious figure, and one who symbolized the rotten way we finance political campaigns. There was nothing illegal about the money that Keating gave to senators and, except in one case, nothing unusual about the amounts involved. The easiest way to raise money is to get it from special-interest political action committees and from rich men like Keating who will give all they can and encourage their friends and employees to do the same.

The current system gives the public the impression that members of Congress can be bought by rich contributors. That isn't true in the vast majority of cases, but it is certainly true that money buys access and sometimes it also buys influence. Senators resist reform because the present system favors incumbents, whose power enables them to raise more money than their opponents, and for many of them reelection is more important than anything else. But to resist reform is shortsighted and terrible for the institution of the Senate. As long as the present system prevails, politicians are increasingly going to be held in contempt and our political system will suffer for it. Political campaigns should be about who is the better candidate, not who can raise the most money.

I was proud to run two successful campaigns without taking money from out-of-state political action committees. Not only did I owe nothing to special interests, but I avoided even the appearance of compromise. Many people in New Hampshire contributed to my campaigns, and they often told me how they felt on issues, but few ever asked me for any favor greater than lunch in the Senate dining room. That's true of many senators. Most are perfectly capable of taking money from a PAC and then voting against it if that's what their conscience demands. The PACs understand that, which is why they spread their money around, like fertilizer, hoping a few flowers will sprout.

One useful reform would be to increase the maximum individual donation from one thousand dollars to two or three times as much. Political parties should be permitted to raise more money—money that is reported—for their candidates, and limits should be put on donations by PACs. In presidential campaigns we should close the loopholes that permit the so-called soft money to reach candidates indirectly via state political parties.

The biggest problem isn't how much money politicians raise but how they spend it. Senators aren't raking in millions to buy themselves yachts and limousines. They've become middlemen, raising money from special interests only to pass it along to television stations for the political advertising they need for reelection.

But the airwaves belong to the American people, and broadcasters should be required by law to give candidates free airtime in the final weeks of a campaign. It would cost only a tiny percentage of the stations' income, and the benefit to our political system would be immense. The law should also provide that a candidate who accepts free time must accept limitations on how much additional time he or she can buy. I proposed such legislation in the 1980s, but the National Association of Broadcasters defeated it. Someday I think we'll have such a system. The result would be shorter and less expensive campaigns, candidates who don't appear to be selling their souls, and perhaps even restored public trust in our political system.

The existing system puts cruel pressures on members of Congress to raise massive amounts of money or face defeat by opponents who outspend them. Yet the system does not corrupt anyone. Politicians are responsible for their own ethical standards. If some of them are corrupt, it's because they let it happen. No matter what the pressures from without, ethics must come from within.

Charles Keating was a tall man with a mortician's grim countenance. He grew up in Ohio, served as a fighter pilot in the Second World War, earned a law degree, and went to work for the American Financial Corporation, which bought a Cincinnati-based S&L called Hunter Savings. In 1979, when Keating was executive vice president of American Financial, the SEC accused him and his boss of defrauding stockholders by approving $14 million in preferential loans to company insiders, including himself. Keating agreed to a consent order and a large fine, but later insisted he was innocent and simply wanted to avoid a court battle.

Keating became well known as a crusader against drugs and pornography. He served on a Nixon-appointed commission that upset the White House by concluding that pornography doesn't cause crime and that most anti-porn laws violate the First Amendment. Keating pleased the White House by issuing his own, one-man anti-porn minority report, one that agreed with the president's view. He also demonstrated his virtue by generous donations to charity and by making his private jet available to Mother Teresa when she visited the United States.

Keating moved to Phoenix around 1980 and started a holding company called American Continental Corporation, or ACC. In 1984, when he saw the possibilities that deregulation had opened up for S&Ls, he went to California and paid some $50 million in cash for Lincoln Savings and Loan in Irvine. There was a go-go atmosphere in California in those days: junk bonds, real estate speculation, luxury hotels. There seemed no limit to it. Keating could smell the money.

Under Keating's management, Lincoln began a pattern of questionable business practices that soon brought him into conflict with an unlikely and mostly unhappy federal regulator, Edwin J. (Ed) Gray.

Ed Gray had been a telephone-company public relations man who became Governor Reagan's press secretary in California and eventually President Reagan's choice to head the Federal Home Loan Bank Board, which supposedly regulated the S&L industry. Gray had no notable qualifications for the post, aside from loyalty to Reagan, but his superiors did not so much want him to regulate the industry as to hold its hand. I thought Gray was over his head as the bank board chairman, but I also believed he was an honest man, troubled by the S&L scandals and pained that the administration didn't give him the resources he needed to do a decent job.

S&Ls were originally supposed to specialize in home loans, but deregulation permitted Keating to pursue grander ambitions. When Keating bought Lincoln in 1984, residential home loans constituted 30 percent of its assets; by 1988 they were less than 2 percent. Lincoln's new interests included land development, junk bonds, a Las Vegas gambling casino and a huge luxury resort in Phoenix.

It was precisely to discourage such risky investing that Gray supported legislation to limit the amount of federally insured deposits that S&Ls could invest in high-risk ventures. This "direct investment" rule posed a threat to Lincoln's high-rolling and made Keating one of Gray's most vocal critics. Keating tried to get Gray fired, and when that didn't work he sent word that he wanted to hire him, but Gray said no.

By March of 1986 the Federal Home Loan Bank in San Francisco had begun an investigation of Lincoln's questionable investment policies and shoddy bookkeeping. Keating's holding company, American Continental, had by then begun selling $200 million worth of its own bonds through Lincoln's branches. By early 1987 the federal investigators had found evidence that Keating's employees were misrepresenting the bonds, telling potential buyers that they were federally insured when in fact they were not. Keating, for his part, had sued the Federal Home Loan Bank Board, trying to stop implementation of the direct investment rule, and was otherwise trying to stave off the collapse of his empire. Buying political influence was essential to his strategy for survival.

In April of 1987 two crucial meetings were held, first between Ed Gray and four members of the Keating Five, then between Gray's San Francisco investigators and all five of the senators. These meetings would become central to the Ethics Committee investigation of 1989–91.

The five senators were Democrats Alan Cranston of California, John Glenn of Ohio, Don Riegle of Michigan and Dennis DeConcini of Arizona, and Republican John McCain, also of Arizona. All of them hated the title "Keating Five," and each quite correctly asked for his case to be judged on its own merits. To lump them together as the Keating Five was, as one writer said, "shoddy journalistic shorthand." Nonetheless, it stuck.

Two of the Five were authentic American heroes. John Glenn's achievements, as a fighter pilot during the Second World War and

Korea, and as the first astronaut to circle the earth, had made him a national hero long before he entered politics, and he achieved renewed fame when his exploits were chronicled in Tom Wolfe's book *The Right Stuff* and the movie made from it.

Of the five, Glenn had known Keating the longest. The two Ohioans met in the early 1970s. They were not close, but both had flown during the Second World War and they sometimes talked about their war experiences. James Grogan, Keating's chief lobbyist, had worked in Glenn's office while in law school, and became an intermediary between the two. Keating's first major contribution to Glenn came in 1985, when his company donated $200,000 to the National Council on Public Policy, a political action committee for which Glenn was the spokesperson. The money was deposited in the PAC's nonfederal account, to be used on state campaigns, and there was no suggestion that Glenn received any personal benefit from it.

In addition, Keating raised $18,200 for Glenn's 1984 presidential bid and $24,000 for his 1986 reelection campaign.

In 1985, when some Ohio thrifts were faltering, Glenn had felt that Ed Gray's bank board didn't move fast enough to help out. So two years later, when Grogan and Keating sought his help during Lincoln's own troubles with the bank board, Glenn was sympathetic. At the first meeting with Gray, on April 2, 1987, he was angry when the regulator said he didn't know the specifics about Lincoln. But at the second meeting, when the San Francisco regulators who were actually conducting the investigation warned of possible criminal action against Lincoln, Glenn quickly cooled on the issue. A few months later, when Grogan offered to raise $100,000 to help with the huge debt from Glenn's 1984 presidential campaign, the senator declined.

John McCain's heroism was less well known than John Glenn's, but no less real. He was the son and grandson of admirals, and was himself a 1958 graduate of the Naval Academy, where he was known as fearless, as a leader and a hell-raiser. He became a pilot, one with a reputation as a carouser and ladies' man, and when the time came he was eager to fly in Vietnam.

On October 26, 1967, he was piloting an A-E4 Skyhawk over Hanoi when a SAM missile blew off his right wing. He managed to eject from the plane, but he landed with two broken arms and a broken leg, and was beaten by the Vietnamese who found him. For the next five and a half years, John McCain was a prisoner of war, one who defied his captors and in response was beaten, starved and tortured. When his captors learned that his father was the commander in chief of all U.S. forces in the Pacific, they offered to release him as a propaganda ploy. McCain's response was to curse them and say that he'd be released at the proper time—POWs captured before him rated earlier release—and not a moment sooner. During his years of captivity, McCain suffered more physical and mental torment than most human beings could endure and did so with superhuman courage and superlative patriotism.

McCain eventually left the navy, moved to Arizona, and was elected to the House of Representatives in 1982. He met Keating at a Navy League dinner in Phoenix, and they hit it off immediately. Among other things, Keating was a major real estate developer in Arizona, and McCain's second wife, Cindy, and her family had extensive real estate holdings there. In the mid-1980s, the two families began vacationing together at Keating's private resort in the Bahamas. Several times the McCains flew there on one of Keating's private planes.

Later the IRS questioned the fact that Keating's company claimed tax deductions for flying the McCains to the Bahamas. An embarrassed McCain, who thought his wife had repaid the expenses, sent American Continental $13,433, but the Democrats made much of those trips during the Senate investigation, even though the House Committee on Standards, which had jurisdiction, considered the matter closed.

Keating also raised a total of $56,000 for McCain's House races in 1982 and 1984, and $54,000 for his Senate race in 1986.

Soon after McCain entered the Senate in 1987, his fellow Arizona senator, Dennis DeConcini, sought his support in defending Lincoln from supposedly unfair treatment by the bank board regulators. McCain was sympathetic but said he wasn't going to negotiate for Keating or do anything improper, and he rejected DeConcini's suggestion that they fly to San Francisco to confront the regulators. A few days later, on March 24, DeConcini reported McCain's position to Keating, who declared angrily that McCain was a "wimp."

John McCain may be many things, but he is not a wimp. When the remark made its way back to him, he confronted Keating and heatedly told him their friendship was over. Nonetheless, McCain attended the April 2 meeting with Ed Gray in DeConcini's office, along with Cranston and Glenn. He went, he said, because he felt an obligation to American Continental's employees in Arizona to see if the company was being mistreated.

McCain apparently said little at that meeting, which ended when Gray suggested that the senators talk to the San Francisco–based regulators. McCain attended the next week's meeting with the regulators, who flew to Washington for it, but after they warned of criminal action against Lincoln, McCain ended his dealings with Keating once and for all.

The three other senators were not heroes—they were more typical of the institution.

Don Riegle grew up in Flint, Michigan, where his father was a Republican officeholder. In 1966, when he was twenty-eight and a graduate student at Harvard, Republicans from his hometown persuaded him to run against an incumbent Democratic congressman. Riegle campaigned hard and won.

In the House he was seen as brash, a young man in a hurry. He let it be known that he intended to be president one day. He wrote a book that was indiscreet about both his love life and his opinion of more senior colleagues. He became one of the antiwar Republicans who opposed President Nixon on Vietnam. In 1973 he switched to the Democratic Party, and in 1976 he was elected to the Senate.

Unlike many of my Republican colleagues, I liked Riegle. He was a highly partisan liberal, but I respected his intelligence, and when he gave me his word he always kept it.

Of the Five, Riegle had the briefest and in some ways the most puzzling relationship with Keating. They met in March 1986 at the grand opening of Detroit's Pontchartrain Hotel, which Keating had bought and restored. By early 1987 Keating had set out to cultivate Riegle, who was about to become chairman of the Senate Banking Committee. Keating's man Grogan arranged a meeting, and Keating offered to host a fund-raiser for Riegle at the Pontchartrain.

On March 6, before the fund-raiser was held, Ed Gray stopped by Riegle's office to discuss legislation. Riegle had been friendly with Gray, and he offered the regulator some advice: Why not talk to some of the senators who were concerned about the bank board's treatment of Lincoln? As their meeting ended, Riegle told Gray, rather mysteriously, that he should "expect a call" from some "Western senators" about Lincoln.

The next day Riegle flew to Arizona, where he toured American Continental, met with its employees, talked with Keating and raised the possibility of a meeting at which he and Gray might air their differences. Soon after returning to Washington, Riegle spoke with both Grogan and DeConcini about the idea of a meeting to include Gray and several senators. On March 23 Keating sponsored the fund-raiser for Riegle at the Pontchartrain, at which his friends and employees donated $78,250 to the senator.

Riegle did not attend the April 2 meeting with Gray in DeConcini's office. But after a complaint from Keating's man Grogan, he did attend the April 9 meeting with the regulators, but only after asking for and receiving a written invitation from DeConcini. At the meeting, when the regulators warned that Keating was likely to go bankrupt and/or be indicted, Riegle abruptly lost interest in his new friend's cause.

Dennis DeConcini came from Tucson, where his family had made a fortune in real estate. He attended law school, served in the army and became the Pima County prosecutor, with a reputation as a law-and-order Democrat. He was elected to the Senate in 1976 at the age of thirty-nine, Arizona's first Democratic senator in thirty years.

As DeConcini was a conservative Democrat, his support was often sought by both sides, and he sometimes gave the impression that his vote went to the highest bidder, politically speaking. I didn't know him well, but he had a combative personality and we clashed on several issues. I regarded him as difficult to deal with and didn't trust him.

In 1981 Keating and DeConcini met at a Tucson country club and soon thereafter the senator lobbied the Reagan administration to name Keating ambassador to the Bahamas. The White House rejected the idea, perhaps because of Keating's earlier troubles with the SEC. In 1982 Keating raised $33,000 for DeConcini's reelection campaign, and raised another $48,000 for his 1988 race.

In March of 1987 Keating called on DeConcini to help him in his battle with the bank board. DeConcini, after seeking support from Riegle and McCain, hosted the April 2 meeting with Gray that included all of the Five except Riegle. Gray said it was someone in DeConcini's office who ordered him to bring no aides to the meeting. The implication was that if the regulator met alone with the four senators, and a dispute arose about what was said, it would be his word against theirs.

According to Gray, DeConcini opened the meeting by saying, "Mr. Chairman, we're here to talk about our friend from Lincoln Savings."

Then, according to Gray, DeConcini offered a deal: if Gray would stop enforcing the direct investment rule against Lincoln, their "friend" would start making more home loans. DeConcini later denied having offered such a deal. Gray, who felt the senators were trying to intimidate him, said he was carrying out the mandate of Congress and could not make an exception for Lincoln.

There was no doubt about what was said a week later, at the April 9 meeting, because one of the regulators, who flew in from San Francisco to meet the senators in DeConcini's office, took detailed notes. DeConcini opened the meeting by saying, "We wanted to meet with you because we have determined that potential actions of yours could injure a constituent." He then suggested that the direct investment rule not be enforced against Lincoln.

The regulators felt that the senators were not so much seeking information as trying to intimidate them. However, they found an effective way to fight back. One of them, after listing Lincoln's dubious business practices, added: "We're sending a criminal referral to the Department of Justice. Not maybe, we're sending one. This is an extraordinarily serious matter. It involves a whole range of imprudent actions. I can't tell you strongly enough how serious this is. This is not a profitable institution."

Despite the warning, DeConcini continued to make calls in behalf of Lincoln to M. Danny Wall, Gray's successor at the board. It was not until September of 1989, when the government brought criminal charges against Keating, that DeConcini decided to return the $48,000 Keating had contributed to his campaign the previous year.

Alan Cranston was seventy-five when the Keating Five investigation began and had been in public office for thirty years. He was elected California's state controller in 1958, advanced to the Senate as a liberal, antiwar Democrat ten years later, and soon entered a leadership position as party whip.

Cranston was a battle-scarred survivor of politics in a big and expensive state. His 1984 quest for the Democratic presidential nomination had collapsed for lack of funds, and two years later he spent $11 million to win reelection by 105,000 votes out of 7 million cast. I saw him as a politician of the old school, one who viewed money as the mother's milk of politics and didn't worry much about where it came from.

Charlie Keating became, for Cranston, one of the most productive cows in the national pasture. The two men met through James Grogan, Keating's lobbyist, who first encountered Cranston at a Democratic fund-raiser in 1984. As Grogan later testified:

> I remember this meeting very clearly. It was the first time I ever met Senator Cranston, and I was struck by the fact that he immediately reached into his pocket and took out a 3×5 card. He said, I've been very good to the savings and loans. I've worked hard for the California savings and loans. You all should really support me. What is your name? He wrote down my name and phone number. He said, You know, it's nice to meet you. I look forward to meeting you in the future. And he was off.

Grogan soon received a call from Joy Jacobson, Cranston's campaign fund-raiser, and subsequently Keating raised $10,000 for Cranston's 1984 presidential campaign, and $39,000 for his 1986 reelection campaign. He also made available a $300,000 line of credit that Cranston never drew upon. In 1987 and 1988, in a series of donations closely related to Cranston's interventions in behalf of Lincoln, Keating produced $850,000 in corporate contributions for voter-registration projects that Cranston and his son controlled and $85,000 for a California Democratic Party voter-registration project. These projects were in theory nonpartisan, but Cranston clearly thought they would help his cause if he ran again. Keating, for his part, had no urgent reason to spend nearly a million dollars to register Mexican American voters in California, but excellent reasons for wanting another senator in his debt.

Grogan later testified that Cranston once greeted Keating at dinner by patting him on the back and saying, "Ah, the mutual aid society."

They were indeed. The liberal Democrat and the conservative Republican were soul mates: Cranston wanted money and Keating wanted help. Cranston once candidly declared of political donations, "A person who makes a contribution has a better chance to get access than someone who does not." Keating, for his part, when reporters asked if his donations had bought political favors, replied, "I certainly hope so."

Early in January of 1987, as the Democrats returned to the Senate majority, Joy Jacobson wrote Cranston a memo that said: "Now that we are back in the majority there are a number of individuals who have been very helpful to you who have cases or legislative matters pending with our office who will rightfully expect some kind of resolution."

Jacobson listed Keating as one of those friends in need, and added that Keating's man Grogan would drop by soon to discuss Lincoln's needs. In fact, Keating and Grogan met with Cranston on January 28, and on March 3 Lincoln contributed $100,000 to one of Cranston's voter-registration projects. A month later, Cranston attended the April 2 meeting with Gray, but he stopped by the April 9 meeting only briefly, to say he shared his colleagues' concerns about fair play for Lincoln.

Cranston's efforts in behalf of Lincoln and Keating's donations to him continued until the S&L was seized by the government in the spring of 1989.

The two meetings in April of 1987 would become central to the Keating Five scandal two years later. On April 13, 1989, American Continental filed for bankruptcy protection, which rendered worthless the $200 million in bonds it had sold through Lincoln, mostly to small investors. The next day the government took control of Lincoln, at an eventual cost of $2.6 billion, making it the biggest of all the thrift bailouts.

About that time an Ohio reporter called Ed Gray, who had returned to private life, to ask about the two 1987 meetings. His account of them, coming on top of Lincoln's failure, made national news. Radio talk shows helped fan the story into a raging scandal. The S&L disaster finally had a focal point: five senators who had taken millions (actually, a total of about $1.3 million, most of it going to Cranston) to protect one of the biggest and most crooked of the thrifts. The impact of the scandal was enormous. A poll taken just before the story broke showed Cranston with a 64 percent favorable rating in California; two months later it was half that.

In October of 1989, as the controversy intensified, Common Cause, the public-interest lobby, asked the Ethics Committee to investigate whether Keating's efforts to influence senators violated federal election laws or Senate rules of conduct.

On November 17 the committee named Robert S. Bennett, a former prosecutor and a very tough, talented, respected Washington lawyer, as its special counsel. Bennett had previously served the committee in the Harrison Williams and David Durenberger investigations. His selection suggested that the committee was serious about the Keating case, but it soon led to major conflicts when the Democrats decided that Bennett was too aggressive—too "prosecutorial"—to suit them.

During his boyhood in Brooklyn, Bob Bennett was known as a brawler, unlike his younger brother Bill, who was more the intellectual. Bill became a well-known Republican luminary during the Reagan and Bush administrations, but Bob always kept his political views to himself. His nonpartisan status enabled him to serve our bipartisan committee, and also to serve clients as diverse as Bill Clinton and Cap Weinberger. Whatever his politics, Bennett remained a brawler, which was just as well, because the Keating Five would become the fight of his life.

In addition to myself, the Ethics Committee was made up of five highly diverse senators. My fellow Republicans were Jesse Helms, who was straight as an arrow on ethical matters, and Trent Lott of Mississippi, newly arrived from the House, who was intelligent, politically shrewd, highly partisan, but always fair.

Howell Heflin, the Democratic chairman, was a bear of a man who'd won a Silver Star with the marines in the Second World War, then returned to Alabama, where he practiced law and eventually became chief justice of the state supreme court. We often disagreed during the investigation, and he could be maddeningly slow in making up his mind, but I respected his intelligence and trusted his word.

Terry Sanford, the former governor of North Carolina and former president of Duke University, was another senator I held in the highest regard. The third Democrat, David Pryor of Arkansas, was one of the most likable, most decent men I've ever known. My only concern was that he was too nice to punish any-

217

one. In previous investigations, he seemed never to have heard a defense that he didn't like. I once told him, "David, if you were a judge, you'd give all the murderers thirty days, with fifteen off for good behavior."

Bob Bennett later said, exaggerating a little, that the Keating Five matter should have been resolved in two weeks. I would say three or four months might have sufficed. In fact it was a year before we held public hearings and another year before we announced our conclusions. In my view, this was because the Democrats wanted the least possible punishment for the Five, and it was only because of steady pressure from the public, the media, the three Republicans and Bob Bennett that they finally moved as far as they did.

In March and April of 1990 we took depositions from the five senators and other witnesses in closed sessions. Keating was called but invoked his Fifth Amendment right not to testify. I'll never forget John McCain, the onetime Naval Academy hell-raiser, saying with tears in his eyes that he would never have done anything to dishonor the Senate or his family's long tradition of public service.

For many months our committee was deadlocked on a series of related questions: how many of the five senators who had, in effect, been indicted by the media should we officially investigate; should the hearings be public; what charges should be brought against them; and what punishments should be imposed on those who were found to have misbehaved? Once the facts of the case became clear, I fought to have McCain and Glenn dropped from the proceedings.

There never should have been a Keating Five. Perhaps there should have been a Keating Five Hundred, since most of us in Congress supported the S&L deregulation and did little while the disaster unfolded. But as for the relationships between Keating and these five senators, there should have been at most a Keating Three. Glenn and McCain were unwise to attend the two meetings, but their offenses simply did not merit a full Senate investigation.

That was where politics came in. McCain was the only Republican among the Five, and the Democrats would never agree to drop him and have the remaining senators—the possible scapegoats for the S&L disaster—be all Democrats. As long as the Democrats would not exclude McCain, the Republicans would not release Glenn. Both men were political hostages throughout the entire two-year ordeal. For John Glenn, who is as close to a Boy Scout as one will find in public office, the experience was excruciating. McCain, for his part, said that our investigation caused him more pain than he'd known during his worst days as a prisoner in Vietnam.

Bob Bennett agreed that Glenn and McCain should be dropped and made that recommendation to the committee, only to have it rejected by the Democrats. It's the only case I know of in which the Ethics Committee rejected its counsel's recommendation to end an investigation. Usually the committee was happy to drop charges against a colleague. But this was a special case.

Howell Heflin and I usually got along very well, even when we disagreed. As lawyers we spoke the same language. But our civility broke down once, at a closed committee meeting when I argued heatedly that it was an outrage to keep Glenn and McCain in the case. Suddenly, Chairman Heflin, sitting next to me, banged his gavel, wheeled in his chair and thrust his face inches from mine. Purple-faced, he bellowed that I was going too far. When he finished, rather than respond in kind I laughed and said, "Mr. Chairman, I'm sorry you feel that way." Some of the Democrats told me later they were sorry for what he'd done, and Heflin himself offered a semi-apology a few days later. The incident reflected the anger and frustration that simmered just beneath the surface of our very formal, and usually courteous, proceedings.

Another source of irritation between Heflin and me was that he repeatedly argued that one reason for keeping McCain in the case was the fact that he had accepted free plane rides from Keating several years earlier. In fact, as soon as McCain learned that no one had reimbursed Keating for the rides, he sent the money to Keating's company, informed both the House and the Senate ethics committees, and asked if they wanted other information or action. The House committee replied that he had taken all necessary action. A letter co-signed by Heflin and me, on behalf of the Senate Ethics Committee, dated July 18, 1989, stated: "Since you were not a member of the United States Senate at the time you filed your 1984 and 1985 financial disclosure reports, this Committee has no jurisdiction in the matter."

But that letter did not stop Heflin from later using the plane trips against McCain, despite my protests that this amounted to double jeopardy. It was one more example of what I saw as hypocrisy by our Democratic colleagues. McCain was going to remain their Republican hostage, no matter what.

I thought the Democrats were torn between their consciences and strong pressures from their fellow Democrats to protect their party. I was told that DeConcini and Riegle were lobbying other senators hard to avoid public hearings, and, failing that, to have no formal charges placed against them. Bennett heard so many stories of DeConcini's buttonholing committee Democrats to argue his case that, at his request, Heflin and I sent a letter to the five senators admonishing them not to contact committee members about the case.

By contrast, McCain and Glenn, both of whom I considered close friends, never asked me for a thing. The most they would say was, "Warren, whatever you're going to do, get it over with!" In an ethics investigation it is necessary to put aside not only partisanship but, what is much harder, friendship.

We also had a problem with leaks. As long as information was limited to the six committee members and Bennett there was no problem. However, Heflin, disregarding my concerns and Bennett's, decided that all documents, no matter how sensitive, should be given to all five senators and their lawyers. At that point the leaks became a flood. There was particular hostility between DeConcini and McCain, same-state rivals who disliked each other intensely. They and their staffs were leaking damaging stories about each other whenever an opportunity presented itself.

At the outset I think the Democrats were looking for a way to end the investigation without public hearings. If they could have issued a report based on our closed hearings, I think they would have. But the Keating Five case wasn't going to fade away. The Democrats were feeling intense pressure not only from the media and the public but also from Bennett and from many senators to hold hearings that would resolve this mess in an honorable way.

Heflin was facing reelection back in Alabama, and perhaps felt some pressure for action from his constituents. At some point, he told me that the Democrats wanted to hold what he called "adjudicatory" hearings on the five senators. I had two problems with that. First, I was still fighting for a decision to drop McCain and Glenn. Second, his idea of "adjudicatory," or fact-finding, hearings seemed pointless.

We'd already found the facts ad nauseam via a long investigation and closed hearings. The next step was to bring a bill of particulars, in effect an indictment, against those senators who merited one, and then to hold hearings in which they could defend themselves. Most Senate hearings have fact-finding as their goal, but Ethics Committee hearings are different: they are supposed to determine innocence or guilt.

I told Heflin that the concept made no sense to me, and we should proceed to determine whether there was credible evidence that any of the five had brought discredit on the Senate. No, Heflin said, we can't agree on that—and he was right, we couldn't agree if the three Democrats refused to. They wanted toothless hearings that would rehash the facts and give the Five a chance to defend themselves against charges that had never been specified.

Then one day, as we continued to be deadlocked, Jesse Helms stunned me by saying he was prepared to vote with the Democrats for hearings that would include Glenn and McCain. Jesse said there had been so much publicity that the public was going to demand a public hearing on all five senators. If Glenn and McCain were innocent, as we both thought they were, it would emerge in the hearings. Out of respect for my leadership, he said, he would not yet announce his position, but the honor of the Senate must be our overriding consideration.

Jesse's remarks helped me clarify my own position, for I was pulled in several directions. I felt it was terribly wrong for Glenn and McCain to be put through this ordeal. Yet I knew that public hearings were imperative. I also believed it was important that whatever action the committee took should be unanimous. The strength of the Ethics Committee traditionally had been that it acted unanimously and thereby gave the impression of bipartisanship. The Democrats showed no sign of compromise, and the choice seemed to boil down to public hearings on all five men or continued deadlock and possibly no hearings at all. If we announced ourselves permanently deadlocked, it was possible that the Senate would disband us and appoint a new committee. Then individual senators would take the Keating Five cases directly to the floor in what would become an extremely messy and partisan affair, one that would reinforce the public impression of a Senate that could not police its members' most outrageous behavior.

At that point, with Jesse and me prepared to compromise in order to achieve public hearings, the problem became Trent Lott. He had recently arrived after several terms in the House, where as a Republican he was part of what often seemed like an oppressed minority. Now, as a member of the supposedly more enlightened Senate, he found himself again the victim of a Democratic power play, because he believed passionately that McCain and Glenn should be dropped. He was absolutely intransigent on the issue.

I had told Heflin that I would not support hearings for all five senators unless both my Republican colleagues agreed with me. I was determined to have unanimity. The irony was that I fully agreed with Lott that hearings for Glenn and McCain would be wrong, but ultimately I had to think that the good of the institution was more important than any individuals. I had many conversations with Lott, trying to bring him around. I did everything but get down on my knees and beg him. Finally, to his great credit and my vast relief, he told me that against his better judgment he would make the vote unanimous.

It was not until October 23 that we announced that public hearings would finally begin on November 15, a year after we hired Bob Bennett. And even then they were compromised, because we had agreed to Heflin's unprecedented adjudicatory hearings. That was simply the best we could do.

Another problem was that Bennett asked the committee to define the standards he should apply to the five senators, but we could not agree among ourselves what such standards were. Senate Resolution 388 authorizes the committee to "receive complaints and investigate allegations of improper conduct which may reflect on the Senate. . . ."

But what is "improper conduct" that "may reflect on the Senate"?

To define those terms as they related to the specific actions of five senators in behalf of Keating was the point of the investigation, but never before had the Senate tried to define the circumstances wherein a senator might abuse his power while intervening with regulators in behalf of a contributor. Clearly there was a line to be drawn, one that had to do with not only impropriety but the appearance of impropriety, but where to draw it?

Bennett did extensive research on the question of standards. One of his major sources was former Senator Paul Douglas of Illinois, whose writings on ethics were highly regarded. Among other things, Douglas had argued that a "decent interval" should pass between the acceptance of a contribution and any favor done in behalf of the donor, lest there be an appearance of impropriety. But when Bennett suggested an "appearance standard," the Democrats protested that he was trying to create new rules and apply them retroactively.

In his search for standards, Bennett also spoke, under conditions of complete confidentiality, with former senior members of Congress who had unimpeachable reputations for integrity. He discussed with them not the specifics of the case but only general ethical questions, and he has never revealed the identity of those with whom he spoke, but their ideas helped guide his search for fair and honest standards.

Bennett was told by the Democrats that his role was not that of prosecutor but neutral fact-finder. That sounded high-minded, but the five senators were certainly going to deny that they'd done wrong, and they had hired some of the best lawyers in Washington to argue for them. If Bennett didn't state the case against them, who would? Not the Democrats on the committee. We Republicans were willing, but we had limited time to devote to the case—Bennett was the only one who knew all the facts—and if we took the lead we would look blatantly partisan.

The Democrats wanted Bennett to operate with one hand tied behind his back, and that's not his style. Bennett and I soon became allies. His disagreements with the Democrats were such that he feared he might either have to quit or be fired. He didn't want that to happen, but neither was he willing to compromise his role. One day he told me he might be finished on Capitol Hill but he had to look in the mirror when he shaved every morning and he wouldn't compromise. He felt, as I did, that he was fighting to protect the honor of the Senate, but sometimes, frustrated, he wondered why he should bother if many of the senators themselves didn't seem to care.

What we Republicans did was give Bennett our full support and encourage him to play a stronger role than the Democrats wanted. I told him, "Bob, you're the lawyer, lay out your case. Heflin may not like it, but you have no choice. What he's asking you to do is impossible."

It would have been hard for the Democrats to fire as respected a lawyer as Bennett without creating the impression of a cover-up, so they had to grit their teeth as our special counsel played a more aggressive role than they wanted—and, in the process, reinforced his reputation as one of the most independent and formidable lawyers in town.

The hearings began at 9:36 A.M. on November 15, 1990, in a crowded Room 216 of the Hart Senate Office Building. As a national audience watched on C-SPAN, we began with opening statements by the six committee members and Bennett.

Chairman Heflin noted that the hearings were adjudicatory and fact-finding in nature, that no charges had been filed against

the five senators, and that the special counsel was not a prosecutor, although he might appear prosecutorial from time to time.

I pointed out that we were not there to seek scapegoats for the
S&L mess, but for the much narrower purpose of finding out if
any senator took actions in behalf of Lincoln because of campaign contributions from Charles Keating. Ethical standards do
exist, I said, and we must determine if they had been broken.

David Pryor noted pointedly that the special counsel was not a
prosecutor, not a judge, and not a jury—the committee itself
made the final judgments.

Jesse Helms commented that serving on the Ethics Committee was a thankless job and suggested that future investigations
be carried out by retired senators and federal judges.

Terry Sanford declared that if an appearance of wrongdoing
exists where, in fact, there is no wrongdoing, the problem is not
that of the individual but of the institution, and the solution
might lie in public financing of campaigns.

Trent Lott said that if there was a real connection between
campaign contributions and senatorial actions in behalf of a
donor, then the rules of the Senate would have been violated, and
he quoted former senator Paul Douglas's opinion that there must
be "a decent interval of time" between a contribution and an
action.

The senators spoke briefly; Bob Bennett's opening statement
lasted several hours and made it clear that he intended to play a
major role in the proceedings. He set out the ethical standards
that he said existed in the traditions of the Senate:

> One, a Senator should not take contributions from an individual
> who he knows or should know is attempting to procure his ser-
> vices to intervene in a specific matter pending before a federal
> agency. . . .

Two, a Senator should not take unusual or aggressive action with regard to a specific matter before a federal agency on behalf of a contributor when he knows or has reason to know the contributor has sought to procure his services.

Three, a Senator should not conduct his fundraising efforts or engage in office practices which lead contributors to conclude that they can buy access to him.

Four . . . A Senator should not engage in conduct which would appear to be improper to a reasonable, nonpartisan, fully-informed person. Such conduct undermines the public's confidence in the integrity of government and is an abuse of one's official position. Such conduct is wrong in addition to appearing to be wrong.

These suggested standards were bitterly rejected by some Democrats, who said Bennett was trying to apply retroactively a new standard that would punish them on the basis of appearances rather than reality.

The hearings continued until January 16. There were twenty-six days of testimony and scores of witnesses. The senators' dealings with Keating, Lincoln, the bank board and one another were laid out in numbing detail; by the time we finished no one could say the Senate had covered up the Keating affair.

Cranston stayed away from the hearings because he was being treated for prostate cancer. But his lawyer, along with DeConcini, Riegle and their lawyers tried to put Bennett on trial, a tactic that was encouraged by the Democrats on the committee. In his opening statement, DeConcini delivered a highly personal attack on Bennett, accusing him, among other things, of "trophy hunting," with DeConcini and his colleagues as the trophies in question.

He accused Bennett of improperly serving as a prosecutor, and his lawyer later produced affidavits from two former U.S. attorneys accusing Bennett of being unfair. Bennett responded: "Senator DeConcini and his counsel would like me to be a flower girl distributing the flowers at a wedding in equal shares to each Senator without regard to the evidence. I will not do that."

In the public sessions, the committee members mostly praised Bennett, but there were tense confrontations behind the scenes. In one meeting, Heflin accused Bennett of being too prosecutorial, and Bennett shot back that it was not his job to be the sixth defense lawyer.

The hearings will not be remembered for their light moments, but Bennett did draw laughter one day when he was reading a list of the next day's witnesses and at the end added "Mother Teresa"—a reference to Keating's well-known cultivation of her.

Ed Gray was the star witness against the Keating Five, since he was the one who was being pressured on Keating's behalf. Soon after the public hearings were announced, Heflin, in a meeting with me and Bennett, seemed to suggest that Bennett should discredit Gray with a tough examination. Bennett had already questioned Gray closely, when he took his deposition, but now Heflin seemed to say that he should undermine Gray's credibility.

Bennett, in a tense exchange, told Heflin that he wouldn't play that sort of game and he would be our counsel only if he had the freedom to be perfectly evenhanded. I calmed the situation by saying that Bennett had misunderstood Heflin, although I knew he had not. The truth is that Bennett went to great lengths to be fair to all parties in the case.

One of the highlights of the hearings was Ed Gray's charge that Senator DeConcini had offered him a deal: If the bank board would stop enforcing the direct investment regulation against Lincoln, Lincoln would start making more home loans. Asked if he felt that was proper or improper, Gray replied, "Improper, of course. . . . Because we had adopted that regulation pursuant to the law that the Congress of the United States set up for the bank board. That was our job, to adopt regulations to protect the FSLIC, the safety and soundness of the thrift system."

Asked if he felt pressured by the four senators at the April 2 meeting, he replied:

> Yes. I felt awkward and pressured. The whole setting was an intimidating one under these circumstances because I had never had a meeting like this before. . . . Because there were only five principals there—myself and four United States Senators. No one else to hear. No one else to know what was said. It was just us. I recognized that immediately.

Asked why he didn't get up and leave, Gray said it was because the bank board had legislation pending to provide it with an additional $15 billion to deal with the S&L crisis and "I needed their votes desperately . . . I was living and dying by my hopes to get that legislation. The last thing I wanted was to make a bunch of Senators angry at me when our Thrift Insurance Fund was bankrupt and we needed it desperately."

Another key witness was James Grogan, Keating's chief lobbyist, who was given limited immunity from prosecution and whose testimony provided intimate details of his and Keating's dealings with senators and their staffs.

He testified of Riegle: "He had done favors for Ed Gray. He thought that he could set up a meeting." He added that Riegle wanted DeConcini and McCain to arrange the meeting and then invite him, so he would not seem the instigator. "It was apparent to me that Senator Riegle knew, as a shrewd politician, that this was a potentially politically explosive situation."

Grogan also testified that in late 1986 he asked Joy Jacobson, Cranston's fund-raiser, to use her influence with Cranston to kill a Senate proposal that would have harmed Lincoln. He said she called back to report that she had done so. Then, according to

Grogan, she added, "I want to switch gears and I want you to know this is totally unrelated" and proceeded to ask Grogan's help in securing a personal loan for Cranston's reelection campaign. Lincoln soon gave Cranston a $300,000 line of credit.

When the hearings finally ended, the facts of the Keating affair were clear but hard questions remained: what standards should apply and what punishments, if any, would be meted out to the five senators?

No one argued that the senators had violated any law in accepting Keating's money, and no one questioned their right to meet with regulators. Except in Cranston's case, the amounts of money the senators accepted were not unusual by Senate standards, however shocking they might seem to the average American. It was the proximity of Keating's money and the actions of some of the senators in Keating's behalf that were disturbing. This "linkage," Bennett argued, raised a serious appearance of impropriety.

Charles Keating had refused to testify, for fear of self-incrimination, but there was no doubt about his motives. He had been struggling to stave off federal regulators who were trying, with good reason, to put him out of business. He had hundreds of millions of dollars riding on what Ed Gray and his regulators decided. From his point of view, if he and his lobbyists could invest a few hundred thousand dollars, or even a few million dollars, in politicians who would then protect him from the regulators, it was money well spent.

After the hearings ended on January 16, the committee held meetings for more than a month, a total of thirty-three hours of deliberations, before issuing initial findings on February 27.

In the case of John McCain, we took note of the fact that at the time of the two meetings more than a year had passed since he had received a campaign contribution from Keating—the "decent interval" that Senator Douglas required. Moreover, the evidence showed that he had gone to the meetings reluctantly and, once he learned of the possible criminal charges, had taken no further action in Keating's behalf.

We concluded that McCain had exercised poor judgment in meeting with the regulators, but that his actions did not call for disciplinary action. In other words, case dismissed.

The finding with regard to John Glenn was almost identical. Glenn had been unwise to attend the meetings, but there was no "linkage" between Keating's earlier contributions and his participation in the meetings. We noted that some eight months later, after he knew of the criminal referral, Glenn nonetheless arranged a meeting between Keating and House Speaker Jim Wright. In most cases, we felt it was a strike against the senator if he continued to do favors for Keating after learning of the possible criminal charges. However, most of us felt that for Glenn to have arranged the meeting simply reflected the fact that he didn't walk away from an old friend—or that he was still somewhat politically naive, depending on how you chose to look at it.

Glenn and McCain had finally been cleared by our committee, but not without a long, painful and unnecessary ordeal.

In Don Riegle's case, there was no "decent interval" between money taken and favors granted. Keating began his courtship of Riegle in January of 1987, at a time when the senator was about to become chairman of the Banking Committee. In a meeting on January 28, Keating offered to raise $125,000 or more for Riegle's reelection campaign. In February, Keating's lobbyist, Grogan, discussed Lincoln's bank board problems with Riegle, and on March 6 Riegle suggested to Ed Gray that he talk to the senators who were concerned about Lincoln.

The next day Riegle flew to Phoenix to meet with Keating and discuss the idea of a meeting between Gray and several senators, and upon his return to Washington he talked about the meeting with DeConcini. On March 23, Keating hosted the Detroit fund-raiser that collected $78,250 for the senator.

Riegle was expected at the April 2 meeting but didn't appear. He went to the April 9 meeting only after requesting and receiving a written invitation from DeConcini. In both instances, it seemed that he was aware of the impropriety of doing Keating's bidding so soon after the fund-raiser. A year later, when the *Detroit News* published a story about the fund-raiser and the April 9 meeting, Riegle returned the $78,250.

In short, there seemed to be a direct link between Riegle's accepting Keating's money and his doing Keating's bidding, and Riegle's own actions suggested his concern about it. A decent interval did not exist; an appearance of impropriety did.

The committee's other concern was Riegle's behavior when he testified. He repeatedly said he did not remember things that numerous other people remembered clearly. He seemed, for such an intelligent man, to have a remarkably poor memory. Repeatedly, when he might have said, "Yes, I did that, and it was a mistake and I regret it," he said instead, "I don't remember."

Some of us felt that Riegle was being less than candid with the committee, and that impression hurt him. Had he been more forthcoming, the committee's judgment on him might have been more lenient. As it was, we concluded that "Senator Riegle's conduct gave the appearance of being improper and was certainly attended with insensitivity and poor judgment. However, the Committee finds that his conduct did not reach a level requiring institutional action."

I thought he should have been reprimanded by the full Senate, but the Democrats blocked that.

Senator DeConcini's dealings with Keating were far more complex than Riegle's. In 1981, soon after meeting Keating, he wrote the White House urging Keating's appointment as U.S. ambassador to the Bahamas. At that time, DeConcini learned about Keating's previous problems with the SEC, but he nonetheless asked Keating to serve on his 1982 campaign finance committee.

In July of 1985 Keating told DeConcini that he would raise $100,000 for his 1988 reelection campaign. That same month, DeConcini wrote letters opposing the direct investment rule and called White House officials asking that Ed Gray be fired. In the summer of 1986, DeConcini called White House chief of staff Don Regan six times to urge the appointment of Keating's friend and business partner Lee Henkel to the bank board. During that same period, Keating raised another $16,000 for DeConcini.

DeConcini was the chief organizer of the April 2 meeting, which was held in his office. Someone on his staff told Gray not to bring aides to the meeting. The evidence also indicated, although DeConcini denied it, that he asked Gray to suspend the direct investment rule pending the outcome of Lincoln's lawsuit against the bank board. Notes taken at the April 9 meeting show—and DeConcini did not dispute it—that he made that request to the agency regulators.

After the regulators warned of criminal charges against Lincoln, DeConcini didn't contact the bank board in Lincoln's behalf for twenty months. Then, at Keating's request, he contacted federal and state regulators seven times between December of 1988 and April of 1989, urging that a proposed sale of Lincoln be considered promptly. Instead, Keating's company folded and the government took over Lincoln.

I thought that DeConcini should have been reprimanded by the Senate, along with Riegle, but the Democrats would not agree to that. We had to settle for a rebuke, one somewhat tougher than what we had addressed to Riegle:

While aggressive conduct by Senators in dealing with regulatory agencies is sometimes appropriate and necessary, the Committee concludes that Senator DeConcini's aggressive conduct with the regulators was inappropriate. . . . The Committee has concluded that the totality of the evidence shows that Senator DeConcini's conduct gave the appearance of being improper and was certainly attended with insensitivity and poor judgment.

Those statements ended the case against four of the Keating Five. We had officially disapproved of Riegle's and DeConcini's actions, but the fact remains that both got less punishment than they deserved and that no serious effort was made to distinguish their misdeeds from the lesser ones of Glenn and McCain. The most you could say was that the charges against them had been aired in public, and it was up to their constituents to decide if they deserved more punishment.

The Cranston case was different. He was in a class by himself, in the amounts of money involved and the linkage between Keating's donations and Cranston's actions in his behalf. Four instances stood out.

At Cranston's urging, Keating contributed $100,000 to a voter-registration program on March 3, 1987, only weeks before the senator's participation in the April 2 and 9 meetings.

That fall, Cranston solicited a $250,000 donation from Keating, which was delivered by Grogan on November 6. At the time of delivery, Grogan and Cranston called Keating, who asked if the senator would call Danny Wall, Ed Gray's successor as bank board chairman. Cranston made the call six days later and argued that Lincoln should be taken out of the jurisdiction of the San Francisco regulators because of "personality" conflicts.

In January of 1988 Keating offered another contribution and asked Cranston to arrange a meeting for him with Wall. Cranston did so on January 20 and the meeting took place eight days later. On February 10 Cranston personally collected checks from Keating-controlled companies totaling $500,000 for voter registration.

In early 1989, while Cranston was contacting bank board officials about the sale of Lincoln, Joy Jacobson, his chief fund-raiser, solicited another contribution from Keating, one that wasn't made because his company declared bankruptcy on April 13.

The facts added up not only to an appearance of wrongdoing but to the reality of it. Cranston's actions came very close to violating the bribery laws. If they had involved a state senator while I was attorney general of New Hampshire, I wouldn't have hesitated to bring bribery charges.

On March 5 we informed Cranston that we were going to conduct an official investigation into his actions. Cranston declined to appear, but we had the facts, and all that remained was for the committee to decide what punishment to recommend to the Senate.

Cranston's supporters urged us to go easy on him. He was by then seventy-seven, was being treated for cancer and had announced that he would not seek reelection. In effect, they said, Why beat up on the poor guy? I thought we weren't beating up on him, just doing our job. He'd brought discredit on the Senate and he deserved to be censured.

I couldn't believe that the Democrats—having heard the evidence we had heard—could be so shameless as to insist that Cranston deserved no punishment. Time after time, as we debated possible actions against Riegle, DeConcini and Cranston, I would ask, "Can't we at least agree on Cranston?"

We couldn't. We remained deadlocked. The Democrats had to admit that Cranston had badly misbehaved, that something had to be done, but they wouldn't agree to censure him or even to reprimand him. The votes for censure didn't exist in the committee and may not have existed on the Senate floor.

As the deadlock dragged on, the pressures of the case were telling on all of us. More than anyone else on the committee, David Pryor tried to be a peacemaker. After a particularly nasty session, he would call me or come to my office and say, "Warren, this is terrible, we've got to settle it, it's not good for the Senate or for anyone."

David worried, he internalized all the frustration and anger, and on April 16 he suffered a heart attack. I'm convinced that the pressures of the investigation caused it. David left the committee, but returned later when his health improved.

Bob Bennett had produced a report urging that DeConcini and Riegle be reprimanded by the Senate and Cranston be censured. The Democrats rejected his recommendations, and in early August an angry Jesse Helms took Bennett's report, made a few changes, put his name on it and issued it as his own minority report. As vice chairman of the committee, I officially deplored this highly irregular action, but privately I admired him.

As the summer ended we continued to be deadlocked because the Republicans wanted the Senate to censure Cranston, while the Democrats wanted only a written rebuke such as we'd given the other four. After five frustrating meetings in September, Trent Lott first proposed that we declare ourselves hopelessly stalemated, then he proposed a compromise: a committee rebuke that the Senate could vote to accept.

A defiant Cranston sent word that he would not accept any solution that included a Senate vote. Pushed too far, he would fight us on the Senate floor, and given the Democratic majority he might have won.

In retrospect, I wish we'd taken the issue to the floor. I would have laid out the case against Cranston and called for his censure, and enough Democrats might have put the honor of the institution above politics to give us a majority. At the least, each senator would have been forced to take a stand.

Instead, the committee reached a compromise: there would be no floor vote, but the committee's reprimand would be filed with the clerk of the Senate and the case against Cranston would be presented on the Senate floor, although it would not be debated or voted upon.

The committee lacked the authority to censure Cranston, so we wrote the strongest reprimand we could, although the Democrats insisted on softening it by reminders that he had violated no laws and had not personally profited by the donations.

Congressional Quarterly aptly called this compromise a "murky plea bargain," and Jesse Helms was so disgusted that he refused to vote for it. He abstained, and the compromise solution was approved by a 5–0 vote, on November 19. I supported it because it was the best we could do and better than nothing. We had pushed the three Democrats as far as we could.

We had two hours to state our case on the Senate floor on November 20. The event had been carefully scripted. Heflin would read our resolution, I would summarize the case against Cranston, and Cranston would accept the judgment of the committee.

Heflin read the committee's findings: that Cranston had engaged in an impermissible pattern of conduct in which fundraising and official activities were substantially linked, that Cranston's conduct violated established norms of behavior in the Senate and was improper conduct that reflected on the Senate, that his conduct was improper and repugnant, and that the committee therefore, in the name of the Senate, strongly and severely reprimanded the senator.

I began by saying that the issue before us was not the S&L scandal, not the campaign-finance system, and not whether senators could take action in behalf of political supporters. The question, I said, was whether there was impermissible linkage between Cranston's official actions and contributions in violation of federal law, Senate rules or standards of conduct that govern all senators.

I reviewed the case against Cranston, with particular emphasis on the four instances when his actions and Keating's donations were closely linked in time. I concluded by noting that some of us on the committee, myself included, felt that Cranston's deeds merited action by the full Senate.

"The resolution we bring before the Senate today is not a perfect result," I said. "It is, however, for this institution an acceptable result, and it is certainly better than no resolution at all."

Next Cranston rose, supposedly to accept the committee's verdict.

Instead he double-crossed us.

"Mr. Chairman," he began, "I rise with deep remorse in my heart to accept the reprimand of the committee. I deeply regret the pain all this has caused my family, my friends, and my supporters, my constituents. . . . I am not proud of this moment."

He might decently have stopped there. Instead, he proceeded with a long and bitter defense of himself, combined with an attack on the committee.

He had done nothing wrong, he said, except fail to anticipate that by accepting money for "charity"—the voter-registration projects—he might be accused of the appearance of impropriety.

He insisted that ". . . my actions were not fundamentally different from the actions of many other Senators. . . . I am far from being the only Senator to do what I have done." He argued that he could not have violated established norms of Senate behavior because the Senate had no established norms of behavior.

He compared the committee to a "tyrant king" and complained that we had denied him due process. "What happened to me and the other Keating Five Senators can happen to any one of you," he warned.

It was an "everybody does it" defense, and by the time he finished I was trembling with rage. I thought of all the honorable men I had served with, in both parties, people of unquestioned integrity such as Bill Cohen and George Mitchell of Maine, John Chafee of Rhode Island, Sam Nunn of Georgia, Bill Bradley of New Jersey, Bob Dole of Kansas, Pete Domenici of New Mexico, Jack Danforth of Missouri, Slade Gorton of Washington, Carl Levin of Michigan, Joe Lieberman of Connecticut, and Nancy Kassebaum of Kansas, to name a few. I thought that Cranston's "everybody does it" defense was an insult to them all. I asked permission to speak, and in the few minutes remaining this is what I said:

> Mr. President, I must say regretfully that, after accepting this committee's recommendations, what I have heard is a statement I can only describe as arrogant, unrepentant, and a smear on this institution. Everybody does not do it.
>
> Members of this body attempt, by word and deed, publicly and privately, to take great care with their personal conduct as it might be perceived by the American people. That is equally true for Democrats and Republicans, liberals and conservatives. I have found that to be the one unifying thread in this body.
>
> For the Senator from California to rise and give a speech on this floor, after accepting this admonition, this serious reprimand, a reprimand because of circumstances he knows full well, rather than a vote, which I would have preferred, and to blame it on campaign finance and everybody does it, and you should all be in fear of your lives from the Ethics Committee, is poppycock. I

repeat, regretfully, that the statement is arrogant, it is unrepen-
tant; it is unworthy of the senior Senator from California.

Democrats were embarrassed by Cranston's arrogant and self-
pitying comments; Republicans were furious. "The committee
whitewashed him and he tarred us," one senator said, and
another added, "I heard the same speech twenty years ago when
Spiro Agnew resigned."

Cranston's final defiance had added an appropriately nasty,
partisan ending to a nasty, partisan affair. Some Republicans
spoke of belatedly seeking censure, but most people simply
wanted to put the whole sordid affair behind them.

That is what happened. After two years, the case of the Keating Five had finally been put to rest.

Keating himself was found guilty in December 1992 of seventeen counts of securities fraud by a California jury and sentenced
to ten years in prison. Throughout his trial, groups of people
who had lost their savings in his schemes, many of them retirees,
booed and jeered him whenever he entered the courthouse.

Bob Bennett made his peace with the committee Democrats;
at least one of them said he wanted Bennett to defend him if his
own sins ever came to light. John Glenn and John McCain were
cleared, but they never forgave those who had put them through
that long and unnecessary ordeal for political reasons.

For my part, I regretted that politics had dominated an ethics
investigation, but I wrote it off to experience and went back to
the business of trying to build majorities. You have to do that, or
the Senate would wind up like one of those third-world legisla-
tures where debates turn into free-for-alls.

Was justice done in the Keating Five affair? My view is that, in
failing to censure Cranston and reprimand DeConcini and Riegle,
the Senate showed its willingness to tolerate official misbehavior.

Still, perhaps there was a rough justice. We put the truth before the American people. As a result, the two senators who deserved no punishment continued to serve, and the three who deserved punishment chose not to seek reelection. To that extent, the system worked.

CHAPTER SIX

LOOKING AHEAD

By the time the Keating Five investigation finally played itself out, I had begun to wonder whether I wanted to seek a third term the next year. I wasn't enjoying the Senate much. I still worried about our failure to reduce the deficit, and I wasn't sure the glory of being a senator meant much if we were bankrupting America. I was also concerned about how the Senate was changing. More and more Republicans were arriving who had previously served in the House, such as Trent Lott of Mississippi, Dan Coats of Indiana and Bob Smith of New Hampshire. In the House they had been part of a bitter, frustrated minority, fighting a guerrilla war against the Democrats. The confrontational, take-no-prisoners attitude they brought to the Senate was not one with which I was completely comfortable.

The Republican Party I grew up with was starting to vanish: the party of Eisenhower, Taft, Dirksen and Baker, men who believed in a strong defense and less government, and who didn't think you could solve every problem by passing a law. If someone had told me in the 1960s that one day I would serve in a Republican Party that opposed abortion rights—which the Supreme Court had endorsed—advocated prayer in the schools, and talked about government-inspired "family values," I would have thought he was crazy.

To me the essence of conservatism is just the opposite: government should not intrude in anything as personal as the decision to have a child, it should not be championing prayer or religion, and family values should come from families and religious institutions, not from politically inspired, Washington-based moralists. Yet I could see the Republican Party gradually being taken over by "movement" conservatives and self-commissioned Christian soldiers whose social agenda I found repugnant.

As a senator, I had enjoyed sitting down with colleagues like George Mitchell, Sam Nunn, Bill Bradley, Joe Biden and Ted Kennedy and saying, "We have a problem here—let's find a way to solve it." They were Democrats, to the left of me politically, but just because we saw things differently I didn't question their morality or their patriotism. I didn't come to Washington to cram things down people's throats or to have people cram anything down my throat. I thought the essence of good government was reconciling divergent views with compromises that served the country's interests. But that's not how "movement" conservatives or far-left liberals operate. The spirit of civility and compromise was drying up. By the 1990s many nights I would go home and shake my head and think, We're not getting a hell of a lot done here. And then I would think, This isn't much fun.

The increasingly nasty partisanship in the Senate magnified my frustration over our continuing failure to do anything about the deficit.

Most people in Congress understood what the problem was. We had to stop runaway entitlements. Some entitlements were going to have to be means-tested—or, as I prefer, affluence-tested—we were going to have to sell that to America, even at great political risk. Politicians had lied to the American people for too long, pretending we could have everything we wanted. But too many members were still unwilling to speak the truth because it might cost them the life of power and privilege that meant more to them than saving America from economic disaster.

Some senators were willing to take risks; I think, for example, of centrists like Sam Nunn, Bill Bradley, Pete Domenici and Bill Cohen. But many movement conservatives, like many old-line liberals, had narrow constituencies and were afraid of doing anything that might upset them.

The Bush administration was another disappointment. In 1988 I supported Bob Dole for the Republican nomination and managed his primary campaign in New Hampshire. He was ahead until Bush hit him hard in the closing days with a negative ad that showed a two-faced Dole, flip-flopping on every issue, and concluded: "Bob Dole straddles, and he just won't promise not to raise taxes." Bush used the ad reluctantly, knowing that it distorted Dole's record, but he had been urged on by Lee Atwater and others who knew it would draw blood. They were right: the "straddle" ad won the primary for Bush and probably the nomination.

After the New Hampshire results came in, I was alone with Dole in his hotel suite when Tom Brokaw, interviewing Bush and

Dole from separate locations, asked Dole if he had anything to say to the vice president.

"Yeah," Bob snapped. "Stop lying about my record."

Dole took a lot of heat for that remark, which supposedly showed he was mean-spirited and was a poor loser. I thought his anger was justified, because Bush's ads really did cross the line. Dole was proud of his legislative record—and well aware that Bush had no legislative record—and he was furious to see it distorted.

Dirty politics is nothing new in America, but it may have reached a new intensity with the liberal campaign that defeated the nomination of Robert Bork to the Supreme Court in 1987. After Bork's defeat, a lot of conservatives decided that anything was justified. Bush got tough again in the general election, with the infamous Willie Horton ads, which portrayed Michael Dukakis as soft on black rapists. Dukakis was an intelligent man and a good governor, but he lacked the killer instinct. He never knew what hit him.

The brass-knuckles trend continued after Bush became president, when the far-right activist Paul Weyrich used unconfirmed charges of drunkenness and womanizing to defeat former senator John Tower's nomination to be secretary of defense. The ugliness of the Clarence Thomas nomination—and the 1992 campaign—were still to come. All this was part of the new mood in Washington, and it was no fun for those of us who were more concerned with national defense and the deficit than with the demonizing of those who disagreed with us.

The Gulf war was Bush's finest hour. If he had shown the kind of leadership on the domestic scene that he showed then, he would have been reelected. But he waffled on taxes and refused to confront the deficit, and he lost the people. I had seen a lot of Bush over the years and there were times during his presidency when he no longer had the zest that had been so basic to his personality. When I went to see him in the Oval Office in the spring of 1992 to express my concerns about his campaign, I was alarmed at the change that had come over him. He had always been highly focused and well informed, someone you could have exciting discussions with, but now he seemed listless. His mood and behavior baffled me on several occasions. People close to him later suggested this was caused by medication he was taking for a thyroid condition.

Bush was weakened politically by his flirtation with the religious right. On abortion and other issues he became their captive. The climax came when far-right spokesmen all but dominated the Republican convention in Houston in 1992. I was a delegate to the convention, but when I saw the agenda—Pat Robertson, Pat Buchanan and all the rest—I changed my plans and joined some other senators on a fact-finding mission to Croatia. I thought that with my views I might be safer in Zagreb than in Houston.

By the time the fall campaign began it was clear that the nation wanted change, and Bill Clinton skillfully presented himself as an agent of change. Still, the outcome might have been different if Ross Perot hadn't run.

I had met Perot a number of times. I thought he was both a patriot and an extraordinarily single-minded, stubborn man. I doubted that he was temperamentally suited to be president, but his televised lectures on the economy made a major contribution to public understanding of the deficit. Perhaps the key point about Perot was that he hated Bush: the unheralded victory in 1992 was that of the scrappy, self-made Texas billionaire over the well-born gentleman from Yale and Kennebunkport.

As far as my own political future was concerned, as 1992 began, the polls said I was still the most popular politician in

New Hampshire, and I expected only token opposition if I ran again. The question was what I wanted to do with my life. I had turned sixty, and I had to decide if I wanted to continue in the Senate or seek other challenges.

You don't casually walk away from a safe seat in the United States Senate. There are many powerful people in this country who would gladly spend millions of dollars for one of those one hundred seats. I think the power is probably exaggerated, but the fact remains that the Senate offers a great opportunity to do good—or ill.

If I didn't run, I would have time to embark on another career, but I would surrender that option if I served another six-year term. One of my concerns was financial. My savings were gone after a decade of college expenses and maintaining two homes and paying for travel that wasn't covered by my expense accounts. I was broke, and I didn't relish the idea of someday retiring with only my government pension, unable to do the things for my children and grandchildren that most parents hope to do. But money was not the major consideration. It would never have been a factor if the Senate had been doing things that were important and exciting.

I had not been an advocate of term limits, but my general feeling was that two or three terms were enough. The longer you stay in public office, the more distant the outside world becomes.

I talked to my family and friends. My children said I'd had a great twelve years but I should leave at the top of my game. I tended to agree. My friends were divided. Those who stood to gain from my incumbency urged me to seek reelection, while my true friends said, in so many words, "Warren, you've served in the army, you've served your state and your country, and you don't owe anybody anything. Do what's right for you."

That was where I came down. Life is an adventure, and two terms in the Senate had been a privilege. But it was no longer the joy it once had been.

Before I made my decision, I admitted in interviews that I was having a hard time making up my mind, and some cartoonists for New Hampshire papers had fun with me. One portrayed me as Hamlet, asking, "To run or not to run," and another paired me and Mario Cuomo as Tweedledum and Tweedledee.

I made up my mind in January, although I held off my announcement. Perhaps I tipped my hand on March 12, when my frustrations exploded during Senate debate on a tax bill:

> I've had many of my Democratic friends, as well as most of my Republican colleagues, ask me what are you going to do this year, are you going to run for reelection, and people tie it to all sorts of things, making a lot of money and having more free time. But that's all really unimportant. The thing that has really been troubling me for the last three or four months, as I have been trying to determine whether to spend another six years of my life in this place, is: Is it worth it? Can you do anything? Can you accomplish anything? Can you make the country better? Are you part of the solution, rather than part of the problem?

I hated the fact that I was answering those questions in the negative.

I kept my decision a secret from everyone except my family and a few close friends until March 24, when I announced it at the New Hampshire state capital at 9:30 A.M. I didn't even tell my staff until nine that morning. Because of the uncertainty, a big crowd of local and national media attended my news conference in the capital's Hall of Flags.

Not wanting to waste the opportunity, I not only announced that I wouldn't seek reelection but gave the media a twenty-minute lecture on the disasters this nation faced if Congress, the president and concerned citizens didn't take action to balance the budget. Given a captive audience, I thought I would use my announcement to serve a larger purpose.

The next day Jim Lehrer interviewed me on the *MacNeil/ Lehrer NewsHour.* In his introduction, Jim compared me to the character in the movie *Network* who declared he was mad as hell and wasn't going to take it anymore. Then he asked whom I was angry with, and I replied:

> To be perfectly frank about it, I'm angry at the entire government and to some extent I am unhappy with the American people for accepting the simplistic answers politicians are giving them and not recognizing that the entitlement programs that are the gene- sis of the deficit mess just have to be adjusted. They're going to have to take their fair share of reduction in those benefits if we're going to save America. Both political parties are absolutely petri- fied of doing it, because if one does it, the other is surely going to take political advantage. I'm disappointed with the Congress, and with both administrations I've served under, for not telling the American people we're headed toward third-class status at the end of this decade unless we do something about the problem of the deficit. But you can't get consensus, because people are concerned about their own political future. Frankly, Jim, I'm tired of it.

Many of my Senate colleagues greeted my retirement with shock and disbelief, but others said they understood. One Democrat told me, "I wish I had the guts to do what you've done, but I'm afraid to leave. I don't know what I'd do with my life." That was the fear that haunted many of my colleagues: Was there life after the Senate? Could they endure being mere mor- tals again?

One of my achievements during my final months in the Senate was winning the nomination and confirmation of three outstanding candidates for federal judgeships, and my success was due in part to my vote, the previous year, to confirm Clarence Thomas's appointment to the Supreme Court. It isn't a vote I'm proud of, but it's a textbook example of how our system works.

People often ask me about political compromise. Aren't politicians always selling their souls—or at least their votes—for some political or financial reward?

I rarely felt compromised by any vote I cast. I later regretted my 1981 vote for the Reagan economic package, but I cast it out of excessive optimism, not because I expected a payoff. Most senators, on the big issues, vote their consciences. The compromises are more subtle. Mostly they occur out of the public eye, when you're negotiating bills and balancing conflicting interests. A senator may favor the environmentalist position, but surrender to home-state pressure to protect the industries that provide much needed jobs, even if they also pollute the state's air and water. The system thrives on compromise. Liberals want $20 billion for a social program, conservatives think $10 billion is enough, so you split the difference and no one thinks he's sold his soul.

When Phil and I were writing the Gramm-Rudman bill, we both wanted to see the entitlement programs included in the automatic cuts, but we soon realized that such legislation would never pass the Senate, so we excluded entitlements. To me, that's not compromise, that's accepting reality, not a bad thing for politicians to do.

People ask me if there's a lot of logrolling, along the lines of "You vote for my project and I'll vote for yours." Frankly, there was less than I had expected. For example, I never supported farm subsidies, because I thought they were contrary to a free-market system. Many times, I could have told a farm-belt senator, "I'll support your subsidy if you'll support low-income heating subsidies for New England." But I didn't do that, and nobody made me any such offers. That was simply a matter of personal pride: I didn't think it was how a senator should behave.

The logrolling was more often between the White House and senators than between senators themselves. The White House political staff controls a great deal of patronage and becomes expert at wielding it. Typically, senators traded their votes on foreign policy issues—AWACs, say, or aid to the Contras—for a new highway for their state or a new science center for their state university. A lot of federal judges are appointed after senators cast votes they'd rather not have cast.

That was the case with my support for Clarence Thomas in the fall of 1991. I don't know what inspired George Bush to nominate Thomas. Perhaps his political staff convinced him it would be clever to challenge liberals to vote against a black conservative. Bush had the audacity to call Thomas the best-qualified candidate for the job, but he wasn't even close to being that.

Yet I voted for him. Why? Essentially, because he was going to be confirmed regardless of what I did. The final tally was 52–48 but that was misleading, because the White House had several votes held in reserve, mainly Democrats who would have supported Thomas if their vote was needed. If my vote had been the deciding one, I would have voted against Thomas, no matter what the consequences, but once it was clear that he would be confirmed I made a political decision.

The struggle to confirm Thomas had been exceedingly bitter, one of those legislative conflicts that damage everyone involved. I had no doubt that if I voted against Thomas, my ability to go to the White House and obtain federal funds and projects for New Hampshire would be at least temporarily crippled, along with my hopes of gaining the president's support for several lawyers who I believed would make outstanding federal judges.

That would have been all the more true if I chose not to run again and was a lame-duck senator the next year. So, considering all those factors, I took a deep breath and, one hour before the roll call, announced my support for Thomas.

That was the background to the events late in 1992 when I was pushing three outstanding candidates for the federal bench: Joseph DiClerico, who had served under me as an assistant attorney general and gone on to be an outstanding judge on the New Hampshire Superior Court; Paul Barbadoro, who had worked on my Senate staff, been my chief aide during the Iran-Contra hearings and become a brilliant trial lawyer; and Steve McAuliffe, also a former assistant attorney general in New Hampshire and another excellent lawyer. Steve was the husband of Christa McAuliffe, who died in the space shuttle *Challenger* tragedy in 1986. He was also a Democrat who had managed Joe Biden's New Hampshire campaign when Joe sought the presidential nomination in 1988.

Normally it would have been difficult to persuade a Republican White House to nominate a Democrat to the federal bench, but as the senior senator from New Hampshire I had a good deal of leverage. The next challenge was to get my nominees through the Senate, and to that end I had made Joe Biden, the chairman of the Judiciary Committee, an offer he couldn't refuse: I would make his friend and ally McAuliffe part of my Republican package if he would help me get my entire three-man package through the Democratic-controlled Senate. George Mitchell, the majority leader, endorsed the deal, in part because he knew Paul Barbadoro from the Iran-Contra hearings. Thus, the last act of the 102nd Congress was to approve my three nominees in the middle of the night, leaving several dozen others hanging.

That is how, thanks to a combination of a vote I'm not proud of and my friendship with two leading Democrats, three outstanding federal judges were nominated and confirmed.

On December 28, 1992, while most of my staff were on vacation, I went to my Senate office for the last time, to pack up all my photographs and personal belongings and have them shipped back to New Hampshire. It was a bittersweet moment. I thought I'd made the right decision, but it was hard to walk away from a life I'd loved. As I looked around my empty offices I didn't see the bare walls and packing crates. I saw the faces of all the wonderful young people who'd worked with me over the past twelve years. That was one of the joys of the Senate, to be able to hire tremendously talented people, still in their twenties and thirties, and watch them learn and grow.

Finally I turned to Marion Phelan, my longtime aide, and said, "I never carved my name in the Daniel Webster desk," and we headed for the Senate floor.

Each senator has a desk, the old-fashioned kind with tops that lift up like those that once were used in schoolrooms. By tradition each senator carves his name inside his desk, and the senior New Hampshire senator has the special privilege of carving his name in Daniel Webster's desk because, although Webster represented Massachusetts, he was a New Hampshireman.

The Senate wasn't in session, so Marion could go onto the floor with me. We took a chisel and other tools I'd need to do the job right. Several of the capital police came over to watch as I lifted the top of the desk and started to work. A lot of senators ignored the police, but having been an attorney general, I knew and liked law-enforcement officers and was always friendly with them. When I finished carving my name in the desk, I shook hands with everyone and made my exit. As I was leaving, the Senate chamber was dark and gloomy, the way it had been when I was sworn in twelve years before. I remembered how optimistic we'd been, with our new president and our new majority and our dreams of changing America. America hadn't changed a lot, but

I thought we'd done some good. I'd made a lot of mistakes but I'd done the best I could. I had no regrets.

I went back to my office and said good-bye to Henry Wrona, who'd been my office manager for twelve years, and to Allan Walker, my administrative assistant. Henry was nearing seventy and was a forty-year veteran of the Senate; he'd been a father figure to dozens of young people who'd worked for me. Saying good-bye to Henry, Allan and Marion wasn't easy. I embraced them all. They were in tears and I wasn't far from breaking down. Finally, I walked down the five flights of stairs to my car. Once I started I never looked back.

I helped start the trend of senators retiring who were relatively young, at the peak of their powers and not facing political defeat. In the next few years those ranks came to include George Mitchell and Bill Cohen of Maine, Sam Nunn of Georgia, Bill Bradley of New Jersey, Alan Simpson of Wyoming, David Pryor of Arkansas, Nancy Kassebaum of Kansas and Bennett Johnston of Louisiana. To lose people of that caliber, in just a few years, is a terrible blow to the Senate and to the country. It would matter less if they were going to be replaced by people of equal excellence, but recent elections suggest that won't happen. Their successors are more likely to be people whose very expensive campaigns have been financed by special interests and whose vision is far more narrow and partisan than that of Nunn or Bradley or Kassebaum.

Why are outstanding people leaving who could serve in the Senate another decade or two? The ones I've talked to are leaving for reasons much like my own. Some may have been more influenced by personal or financial reasons, but most are leaving because the Senate has become so partisan, so frustrating and so little fun.

Senators are burned out by endless partisan wrangling. The number of votes that senators cast each year doubled between the 1960s and 1980s, and many of the extra votes are politically inspired and meaningless. Members serve on more committees, too, and cast more votes there. And it's not that more work means more results. More often it leads to posturing and partisan gridlock. Senators spend far too much time dealing with colleagues who imagine the republic imperiled by flag-burners and gay activists, and whose idea of enlightened debate is to wave pictures of fetuses on the Senate floor. There's less time than ever for a social life or a family life, and the ever-increasing cost of running for election means that most senators must spend huge amounts of their time going with tin cup in hand to special interests for money.

Obviously there are still many outstanding people left in the Senate, men and women for whom I have the greatest affection and respect. But the trend today is not good, and it's not going to improve until several things happen. Congress must pass campaign-finance reform, so our legislators can be free of endless fund-raising and indebtedness to special interests. Both parties are going to have to try harder to recruit outstanding candidates. And voters are going to have to demand better, more responsible leadership.

As campaigns become more and more expensive, we increasingly see rich people buying television time to create electronic candidacies that are not only ridiculous but insulting to the men and women who have worked hard to create records of real political achievement. We need laws that limit how much of his own money a candidate can spend and, failing that, we need to teach voters to see how absurd most of these candidacies are.

Until we have more reforms, good people are going to keep leaving Congress—or won't go there in the first place—and they are likely to be replaced by zealots, ambitious multimillionaires and other dubious characters who are unlikely to advance the public interest.

I was particularly sorry to see Bill Cohen announce his retirement because we have been so close both personally and politically. Bill possesses courage, independence and high intelligence that are all too rare in the Senate now. On the night of his announcement, he told Jim Lehrer his reasons for leaving with his usual eloquence: "I think the long hours that we put into this job, with less progress, more wheel-spinning, more waiting around, less real debate, more diatribes—I think all of those have contributed to a lower quality of life, in terms of having time for one's family or being able to plan one's time. I think that's part of it but not all of it."

On January 3, 1993, I started my post-Senate career as a partner in the law firm of Paul, Weiss, Rifkind, Wharton & Garrison.

Nine months earlier, my announcement that I was leaving the Senate had prompted many calls from law firms, corporations and trade associations that wanted to hire me. I told them all that I couldn't talk to them until the Senate adjourned at the end of the year, lest there appear to be any conflict of interest between my votes and my future employment.

When I began to consider offers, most weren't what I wanted. I wasn't going to be a lobbyist. I didn't want to run a company because that would take all my time and I wanted some left for public service. I talked to several Washington law firms, but most of them wanted me for my political connections and I saw myself as more than just a "rainmaker" who brought in business. I'd practiced with a major firm in New Hampshire and been attorney general of my state, and I felt I had something to contribute.

Arthur Liman, our distinguished counsel during the Iran-Contra investigation, had contacted me on behalf of Paul, Weiss, and the fact that he was a partner there spoke volumes in the firm's favor. I talked with other partners and found them to be people I liked, people of great integrity who would give me a chance to do the kind of work I wanted to do. I've developed a practice that deals largely with corporate governance, corporate investigations and related matters. It's a rewarding and challenging practice, but I still have time for public service, and in particular for the labor of love we call the Concord Coalition.

I always intended to continue the fight in private life for a balanced budget, and I had it in the back of my mind that I could achieve things as a private citizen that I couldn't as a senator. I thought I might be more effective if I was freed from the constraints of party discipline. I would still be a Republican, but I would no longer have to worry about offending my president or my majority leader or anyone else. As outspoken as I was in the Senate, there were times I had to bite my tongue and be a team player.

One day in the summer of 1992 Paul Tsongas and I were separately being interviewed on *Face the Nation*. I had known and admired Paul when he was a senator from Massachusetts. He left the Senate because of a battle with cancer, but he recovered and sought the Democratic presidential nomination that year as a champion of fiscal sanity. He lost the nomination to Bill Clinton (Pander Bear, he called the future president), but he'd made countless friends around the country.

Bob Schieffer was going to interview us both from Washington, and when the producer said Paul was in Concord, Massachusetts, only about twenty miles from my home in New Hampshire, I offered to drive there to simplify the logistics. We were interviewed at the lovely old Concord Inn, and afterward Paul and I stayed for a cup of coffee.

My interview was mostly about the deficit, which of course was what Paul's presidential campaign had been all about. We shared a common passion, and as we talked we hit on the idea of starting a grassroots organization to fight for a balanced budget.

We were both tremendously excited by the idea, and we were extremely lucky that a few days later I received a call from a remarkable businessman and public servant, Pete Peterson. Pete had been president of Bell and Howell at age thirty-four, president of Lehman Brothers in his forties, and had served as President Nixon's secretary of commerce. He had also written and spoken forcefully on the need for deficit reduction.

I didn't know Pete well at that time, but he said he'd seen me on *Face the Nation* and previously during my interview with Jim Lehrer, and he wondered if I'd like to work with him on deficit reduction. I told him that Paul Tsongas and I had been discussing the same thing. Pete was already an admirer of Tsongas, and he was fascinated by the idea of two former senators, one Republican and one Democrat, leading a national movement for a balanced budget.

Pete flew to Washington for breakfast with Paul and me in the Senate Dining Room, then Paul and I flew to New York for a brainstorming session with Pete and some of his friends. His guests included Alex Kroll, the extraordinarily creative chairman of the Young and Rubicam advertising agency, and Daniel Yankelovich, who is without peer as an analyst of American public opinion. We received invaluable ideas from Pete and his friends on what the goals and methods of our organization should be, and how it could be financed and structured. We also got our name, the Concord Coalition, which denoted not only that Paul and I had first discussed our plan at the Concord Inn, but that on April 19, 1775, ordinary people, mostly farmers called Minutemen, answered a call to arms and defeated the British redcoats in the tiny town of Concord, Massachusetts. More than two hundred years later, we believed, our nation was again imperiled and needed citizens to fight to save it.

The Concord Coalition would never have happened without Pete Peterson's advice, contacts, commitment to the cause and financial support in the early months. Today Pete serves as the coalition's president, and Paul and I are co-chairs of its board of directors.

The coalition works for a balanced budget by organizing informed citizens to bring grassroots pressure on political leaders. We have more than 150,000 members and chapters in every state and virtually every congressional district.

Affluence-testing of entitlements is central to the coalition's Zero Deficit Plan, which proposes to end the deficit by the year 2002. Our proposal is adapted from one introduced by Pete Peterson in his 1993 book, *Facing Up: How to Rescue the Economy from Crushing Debt and Restore the American Dream.*

Entitlement payments, including the two "megaprograms," Social Security and Medicare, would be subject to a sliding-scale, across-the-board means test, starting at a family income level of $40,000. This would reduce entitlement payments by a net of $50 billion by 2002, the largest single policy change in the Zero Deficit Plan.

The estimated 58 percent of Americans with incomes of less than $40,000 in 1997, when we would like to see the means test begin, would lose nothing. But payments to the 42 percent of Americans with incomes above $40,000 would be scaled back. For each additional $10,000 of income above $40,000, the individual would lose 10 percent of his or her entitlement payments, up to a maximum 85 percent loss for people making $120,000 or more.

The Zero Deficit Plan combines affluence-testing with other reforms, such as setting a higher deductible for Medicare, accelerating the rise in Social Security retirement age, cutting back on

COLAs in the already generous federal retirement benefits, increasing the federal gasoline tax over several years and limiting the home-mortgage interest deduction to $12,000 for an individual or $20,000 for a couple. Couples paying for a home worth up to $300,000 or so would not be affected, but those with million-dollar homes would get less of a tax break.*

Working with Pete Peterson and Paul Tsongas on the Concord Coalition has been one of the highlights of my life. In them, and in the men and women we've worked with across America, I've found the seriousness and concern and dedication to fiscal responsibility that I too often failed to find in my colleagues in Congress.

Paul is a hero to thousands, perhaps millions of people. I've traveled with him on speaking tours all over the country, to college campuses and civic meetings and senior citizen centers. Sometimes he was undergoing radiation therapy, but that only inspired him more as he spoke out for courage in confronting the deficit. As he has faced his own mortality he has become ever more dedicated to building a better, saner world for our children and their children. Fiscal sanity is a crusade with Paul, and it has been a privilege and an inspiration to work with him.

The elections of 1992, 1994 and 1996 are linked in what may be a great transformation of American politics.

I had met Bill Clinton a few times in the 1980s. He was obviously intelligent and personable, and in 1992 he proved to be a brilliant national campaigner. I wasn't sure I knew what he stood for, but I thought he ranked with Presidents Kennedy and Reagan in his ability to communicate with the American people.

---

*Anyone wishing more information on the coalition's program and activities should write The Concord Coalition, Suite 810, 1019 19th Street, Washington DC 20036.

Soon after entering the White House, Clinton asked me to serve as vice chairman of the President's Foreign Intelligence Advisory Board. The PFIAB had originated with President Eisenhower and consists of about fifteen private citizens who are asked to evaluate the quality of intelligence reports the president is receiving. Its work is both top secret and time-consuming, but I had previously served on the Senate Intelligence Committee and this new assignment proved fascinating. During a period of turmoil at the CIA it has also been extremely important.

It was clear by the end of 1993 that President Clinton was off to a rocky start. He had campaigned as a "new" Democrat—supposedly more conservative and pragmatic than the "old" Democrats—but he seemed to be governing as an old-style liberal. His appointments—both those that succeeded and those that were derailed—did not always reassure the country, and his ill-conceived health-care plan was a disaster. He changed his mind too often and seemed to be guided more by polls than by principles. These and other factors led to the political earthquake of the 1994 congressional elections.

I campaigned for a number of Republican candidates in 1994, but I have to admit that I didn't sense the anger that people felt toward Clinton for what they saw as a betrayal of what he'd promised two years before. There's no other way you can explain the amazing results: not one Republican governor or member of Congress who sought reelection was defeated. It was a historic political victory, one that turned both houses of Congress over to Republican control and seemed to guarantee political oblivion for Bill Clinton.

As the new Congress convened early in 1995, well-organized House Republicans, led by Newt Gingrich, were poised to carry out a political revolution. Yet, by the end of the year, Gingrich and his forces had lost momentum, and Bill Clinton was looking stronger than anyone would have thought possible just a few months before.

Gingrich and his followers, including seventy-odd zealous freshmen, had read the election as an endorsement of their Contract with America rather than as a rejection of an unpopular president. They refused to concede that only a tiny fraction of the voters had ever heard of the Contract before Election Day. Moreover, in their euphoria—in being suddenly the majority after a generation in the political wilderness—they thought they could interpret the election as a mandate to do whatever they pleased. They seemed hell-bent on replacing the excesses of the left with the excesses of the right, ignoring the fact that mainstream America wants neither. Republican political analyst Kevin Phillips got it right when he wrote in an op-ed piece: "The United States can't afford another reckless economic and social experiment in which the failed liberalism of the 1960s gets replaced by the rightward overreaction of the 1990s."

Gingrich is a visionary and a brilliant political leader, but once in power he hurt his own cause by revealing a large ego and a shoot-from-the-hip style that distracted from the serious work at hand. By the end of the year, as Gingrich's negative rating plunged to record depths, Clinton's popularity rose again.

The Republicans were right in seeking a balanced budget and right in seeking $270 billion in Medicare reductions, but they were wrong when they tried to combine entitlement cutbacks with $245 billion in tax cuts. Either you want a balanced budget or you don't, and if you want one you don't get it by tax cuts, no matter how popular they might be. That's not leadership, that's pandering.

Nor did Gingrich and his fellow revolutionaries help their case by ducking such issues as term limits and serious campaign-finance reform while seeking regulatory reform and environmental rollbacks that were unwise and unpopular.

The truth is that, since 1776, this country hasn't had much taste for revolution. We move slowly on social change. In politics you have only so much ammunition, and it is always wise to focus carefully on your real priorities. Gingrich and his followers tried to do too much too soon, and they paid a price for their zeal.

Bill Clinton was both politically adroit and shameless in the debate over a balanced budget. Having in June agreed, under pressure from Congress and the public, that a balanced budget was necessary, he should have met the Republicans halfway in a positive, nonpartisan attempt to achieve that goal. Instead he exploited the issue for partisan advantage. His differences with the Republicans on Medicare were minimal, but he resorted to "Mediscare" tactics to convince millions of older Americans that he was their champion against heartless Republicans who were out to destroy the program. Clinton knows as well as anyone that entitlements must be reduced before the budget can be balanced, but he chose to practice the politics of fear. His performance was both effective and irresponsible, and I believe that in the long run he will hurt both himself and the country with his partisan distortions.

As this book goes to press early in 1996, negotiations toward a balanced budget have broken down, with each side accusing the other of bad faith. Whether because of politics, principles or both, President Clinton and the Republican majorities in Congress have gone as far as they can or will toward compromise and failed to reach agreement. It appears that the question of whether or not we are to balance the budget—and, if so, how—will have to be resolved by the November elections.

The Republicans made two serious tactical blunders in the negotiations. First, shutting down the government was one of those ideas that sound better over cocktails than they prove to be in reality; the main effect of the two shutdowns was to remind Americans that their government does in fact perform many essential services. The other blunder was proposing a tax cut of some $250 billion—along with proposals for slower growth in Medicare and Medicaid—so that Clinton could accuse Republicans of wanting to cut services for the elderly and the poor so as to pay for a tax cut for the rich. In fact the Republican tax cut would have helped the middle class primarily, but Clinton convinced millions of Americans otherwise. In any case, a huge tax cut, as part of a deficit-reduction package, was wrong logically, politically and morally.

(It should go without saying that I consider millionaire publisher Steve Forbes's "flat tax" proposal to be complete madness. It is supply-side all over again, and if we embrace that fantasy a second time we shall deserve the awful punishment that will surely follow. Even Forbes admits that his flat tax would cost the government hundreds of billions of dollars in revenues, but when he is asked how we would then avoid huge new deficits, he offers the discredited supply-side mantra that lower taxes will produce such prosperity that tax revenues will inevitably rise. This is Reaganomics without Reagan, the trickle-down theory, and supply-side economics is reborn like those horror-movie monsters who refuse to die. Forbes is either ignorant of economic events in this country between 1981 and 1985 or he thinks Americans are fools.)

As I watched the historic, profoundly important budget negotiations in the final months of 1995 and early 1996, I recalled our efforts, ten years earlier, to achieve a balanced budget through Gramm-Rudman. I thought about the similarities between 1995 and 1985, and the lessons our successes and failures might hold for those who are carrying on the fight.

Politically speaking, Gramm-Rudman came at a good time. By the summer of 1985, the public was increasingly concerned about our fast-rising deficits. In theory President Reagan was opposed to deficit spending and had just been overwhelmingly reelected. The next presidential election was three years away. Both parties were under pressure to reduce the deficit—and hoped to gain partisan advantage thereby—so we were able to rally a bipartisan consensus in the Senate and win reluctant support from the White House.

The genius of Gramm-Rudman was the automatic cuts, the forcing mechanism that would produce budget cuts if Congress refused to meet the agreed-upon goals. For a time Gramm-Rudman worked. Then, in 1990, politics as usual counterattacked. President Bush and the Democratic Congress were unwilling either to raise taxes or to lower spending sufficiently to meet the requirements of the law, and neither were they prepared to accept the automatic cuts, so they simply scuttled the law and put us back on the path to a $5 trillion national debt.

In 1995 the situation was in many ways different. For one thing, the financial dangers of the deficit were far greater and even more obvious. By then, financially speaking, we were playing Russian roulette with five cartridges in the chamber. Moreover, the political landscape had shifted. We had a Democratic president who wanted neither to raise taxes nor to cut spending, and paid only lip service to a balanced budget until the election in 1994 of Republican majorities in both houses of Congress forced his hand.

Thus, the 1995 debate was far more politicized than it had been ten years earlier. Now we had a Democratic president, facing reelection and in deep political trouble. We also had a Republican Senate majority leader who was running for president. In the House we had seventy-odd Republican freshmen, most of them zealously committed to a balanced budget and unwilling to be bound by the old rules of political compromise.

By the time the negotiations broke down in January it was clear that the president didn't really want a balanced budget deal at all. Instead he used his political skills to define the issue his way and run on it in the fall.

The president and most Democrats believe that they are fighting to preserve the social safety net that was largely put in place by Franklin Roosevelt in the 1930s and expanded by Lyndon Johnson in the 1960s. If you allow for rhetorical excess, there is some truth in the Democrats' claim, although it begs the question of whether we can afford that safety net.

The Republicans see themselves as the tough-minded saviors of our economic future, and there's some truth in that too. Although they weakened their case with the tax-cut proposal, Bob Dole and his Senate colleagues deserve great credit for admitting that the time has come for at least a limited cutback in entitlements and that some entitlements should be means-tested. This took political courage. As a result, even Bill Clinton and most Democrats are now prepared to agree that the growth of entitlements must be slowed. The debate has shifted at last from whether or not to cut to how big the cuts should be.

The fact is that we are only a few years away from a crisis in which either older Americans must accept major cutbacks in entitlements or younger, working people, whose standard of living is already declining, must accept major tax increases. At that point, we can expect generational political warfare as younger taxpayers revolt. Given their traditional support of Social Security and its recipients, the Democrats would almost certainly be identified as the party of the old—a losing proposition—and once this happens they will probably think twice about their position on entitlements. This process may have already started. For years both parties could gloss over the hard choices simply by borrowing more money, but now the money is running out and hard decisions must be faced. If we move sensibly in the next year or two there may still be time to avoid the generational crisis.

If Bill Clinton wins the election, and increases his support in Congress, he will probably move toward a balanced budget on his own terms, and, safely reelected, they might be more realistic than those he has so far embraced as a candidate. Even if he wins and continues to face hostile Republican majorities, the fact that he won the electoral debate will probably force Congress to meet him halfway on an agreement.

If Bob Dole or another Republican wins, and Congress remains Republican, he will surely move toward a balanced budget. It is all but impossible to achieve balance in seven years, largely because so many economic factors are beyond any president's control. But Dole proved, during the negotiations with Clinton, that he and other key Republicans are committed to actions that will eventually balance the budget and clearly, in the short run, will make the deficit an ever-smaller percentage of gross domestic product.

The worst-case scenario is a divided and stalemated government. Bill Cohen, on the evening he announced his retirement from the Senate, summed it up in an interview with Jim Lehrer:

"I am reasonably convinced that this country has to decide whether or not we want to have one-party government, at least for a period of time. We had President Bush in office with a Democratic Congress and now we have President Clinton with a Republican Congress. As a result, we're seeing stalemate, stagnation, and paralysis. We have to decide as a country whether we want to give the reins of government to one party, to move either to the conservative side or the liberal side, and see where that takes us economically. If the country is going to continue to vote for divided government we're likely to have greater division in the future."

I agree entirely. As much as I would like to see a Republican elected with a Republican Congress, if the second choice is either Democratic rule or continued division, I would reluctantly choose the former. It would be better for the country.

The winter's negotiations broke down partly because the issue was not simply numbers but involved matters of principle. If the issue was simply money, the negotiators could have split the difference, one way or another as they usually do. But the Republicans wanted to return welfare and elements of Medicaid to the states, to return power to the local level, while the Democrats saw this as an invitation to social inequity and administrative chaos. On that issue alone, as well as the question of how much to lower taxes and how much to reduce entitlements, the two parties were too far apart for compromise, and it is probably not a bad idea to take the debate to the people in the fall's elections. We are at a turning point in American economic history. The two parties are arguing not generalities but specific economic policies. In a time of economic hardship, we are debating how the burden should be allocated and what policies to trust. Whichever way we choose, we need a clear mandate.

We don't need another Gramm-Rudman with its automatic cuts, which were both its strength and its weakness, for they allowed politicians to avoid the hard issues. It is time for our politicians—and the people—to face the budget issues directly and honestly, and the elections of 1996 may be the moment of truth.

Even though I've expressed optimism that Bill Clinton in a second term or a Republican in a first term will move toward a balanced budget, and even though I'm delighted that both parties have taken a new look at entitlements, my experience with Gramm-Rudman suggests a degree of skepticism. The same political pressures and human weaknesses that led the political establishment to scuttle Gramm-Rudman in 1990 could very easily reappear in the year 2000 and tempt our leaders to yield once again to the lure of deficit spending. We the people must be ever vigilant, through our votes, our voices and organizations like the Concord Coalition. Our leaders are good people, but they need help.

The excess of zeal shown by the House Republicans enabled Clinton to present them as radicals, and they were further weakened by their alliance with the so-called Christian right—which, it has been noted, is neither Christian nor right. I have in mind here Pat Robertson's Christian Coalition and related groups that try to advance social and cultural conservatism in the garb of Christianity. I don't even like the Christian Coalition's name. The millions of Christians in this country reflect just about every conceivable political point of view. For one highly conservative group to proclaim itself "the Christian Coalition" strikes me as decidedly un-Christian arrogance.

The New Testament speaks eloquently of love and compassion and forgiveness, but one looks in vain for those qualities in the political agenda of the Christian right, which allies itself with the rich and comfortable in our society, not with the needy and afflicted.

In my experience, religious zeal and politics don't mix. Look at Belfast, Beirut and Bosnia if you want proof. Does the comparison sound extreme? Not when doctors are being gunned down outside abortion clinics and innocent government workers are bombed in Oklahoma City. You can't indulge in hateful rhetoric about baby-killers and government plots against freedom and then walk away when some people take you seriously.

Politically speaking, the Republican Party is making a terrible mistake if it appears to ally itself with the Christian right. There are some fine, sincere people in its ranks, but there are also enough anti-abortion zealots, would-be censors, homophobes, bigots and latter-day Elmer Gantrys to discredit any party that is unwise enough to embrace such a group. In a sense the 1994 elections were misleading, because the country is more centrist today than ever—particularly the younger generation.

If you have the good fortune to travel widely in our country, you soon realize what an incredibly diverse people we are. We reflect countless races, religions and lifestyles, and we often differ on questions of morality and behavior. The only way so diverse a nation can survive is by all of us practicing a high degree of tolerance.

But tolerance is not the way of the Christian right. Its leaders want to impose their one-size-fits-all morality on everyone. It won't work. When any group tries to impose its values on everyone else, the result will inevitably be resentment, hatred and violence.

The Republican Party must not join forces with people whose views are so repugnant to mainstream America. There are millions of disaffected voters in America besides those of the religious right. There are the blue-collar workers who broke with their Democratic past to support Reagan, Ross Perot, Pat Buchanan and others who gave voice to their frustrations. Millions of middle-class voters have supported reformers like John Anderson and Paul Tsongas. The Republican Party, as it seeks to build a national majority, should be pursuing these people and addressing their concerns, not allying itself with radical rightists who will drive out the mainstream moderates who win elections.

There is much talk today of a third party. Perot, in 1992, won nearly 20 percent of the vote. Many disgruntled voters would like to see him or Bill Bradley or Colin Powell or someone else run as a third-party candidate in 1996. I hope it doesn't happen. Third parties reflect the universal hunger for a quick fix. Throw the bums out, we say—the bums being the two parties that have governed for more than a century—and make a fresh start.

History doesn't support this theory. Third parties have never worked here, and the experience elsewhere—in Italy, say—is that third parties lead to fourth and fifth parties and soon to chaos. Suppose Perot was elected president as an independent, while the Republicans controlled the Senate and the Democrats won back the House. What would the prospects for effective government be with that division of power?

We Republicans must shun the extremists and win over the disaffected voters who have been flirting with Perot and other independent, reform-minded, often populist candidates. To reach that goal we need proven leadership, and in 1996 we have it in Bob Dole. Having worked closely with him for more than fifteen years, I support him without hesitation. For me, the issues in a presidential campaign usually come down to this: Which candidate would you trust to make life-and-death decisions for yourself and your loved ones? By that standard, for me, no other candidate is even a close second to Dole. In the early primaries of 1996 Dole faced serious challenges from Steve Forbes, Pat Buchanan and Lamar Alexander. Forbes, refusing to accept public funds and thus not bound by campaign spending limits, spent millions of his own dollars trying to convince the voters that he is just one of the guys. Buchanan may be "one of the guys," but that is his only possible qualification for public office, aside from a talent for simplistic solutions.

Another friend of mine, Colin Powell, almost ran for president, then chose not to, and said he wasn't interested in the vice presidential nomination. I hope he reconsiders, because he would be the ideal running mate for Dole, if he is the nominee.

If Dole is nominated, and if Colin wants to be president, four years as Dole's vice president would be the best possible stepping-stone, assuming that Dole, because of his age, serves only one term. It would spare Powell the overwhelming effort of either challenging Dole for the Republican nomination or of running as a third-party candidate as well as the need to raise huge sums of money. And four years as vice president would be excellent preparation for a run on his own in the year 2000.

From Dole's point of view, Powell would be the strongest possible running mate in a tough race against Clinton. Besides bringing many African-American votes to the Republicans, Powell's candidacy would send a strong message that Dole's was a centrist party that was rejecting the extremists who have already made clear their loathing for—and fear of—Powell. Moreover, given the urgency of the racial problem in America, Powell's candidacy would be a great symbolic step toward unity. He is living proof that a man of color can make it to the top in our society on the basis of talent, courage, intelligence and strength of character.

In early November of 1995, in a remarkable display of political obtuseness, a group of far-right leaders called reporters in and denounced Powell and his possible candidacy. They included Paul Weyrich, head of the Free Congress Foundation; Gary Bauer, head of the Family Research Council; David Keene, president of the American Conservative Union; Grover Norquist, president of Americans for Tax Reform; Chris Ardizzone, legislative director of Phyllis Schlafly's Eagle Forum; and former Defense Department official Frank Gaffney. Ralph Reed, director of the Christian Coalition, sent a letter of support.

Not only did these political pipsqueaks question Powell's views on such issues as abortion and gun control, but they challenged his character and his military record. This from people who not only have never heard a shot fired in anger, but have never even dropped by a PX for an ice-cream cone. It was an amazing display not only of arrogance but of fear, because these people know that Colin Powell embodies the very opposite of the ignorance and bigotry that they represent.

In an earlier demonstration of arrogance, some of these same people had launched an attack on Bob Dole's top Senate aide, Sheila Burke. I worked closely with Sheila for a dozen years and consider her both a tremendously talented chief of staff and a wonderful human being, a view that is widely held in the Senate.

What did the right wing have against this forty-four-year-old ex-nurse, who is also a wife and mother of three? Well, she was raised as a Democrat, she is pro-choice, and in some regards she is more liberal than Dole. All of which has nothing to do with her skill at doing, day in and day out, exactly what Bob Dole wants her to do. But the right-wingers, wanting to get their hooks into Dole, decided to make an example of Burke.

Columnist Robert Novak called her the Queen of the Senate and a "militant feminist." A *Wall Street Journal* writer revealed her to be "a former liberal Democrat," and Phyllis Schlafly called her Hillary Lite. The attacks were ludicrous but also revealed the viciousness that these people display toward anyone they perceive as a threat.

Paul Weyrich implied that Dole was helpless before the scheming Burke because he came "from an era when you treated women with deference." The idea that Dole couldn't deal with strong women was laughable, when you consider that he's married to one of the most impressive women in America; the truth is that it's these uptight right-wingers who have a problem accepting women in positions of authority. Dole supported Burke and the controversy passed, but the episode was another example of why the far right will inevitably alienate reasonable people.

In my mind, the title I gave this book, *Combat,* has more than one meaning. As I wrote the book I saw an unexpected theme emerge: the importance of my Korean War experience on my life and the bond I felt with other senators, such as Bob Dole, Dan Inouye and Bob Kerrey, who had also known combat. If you have that experience, not much is left in life that will intimidate you. As Bob Kerrey and I once joked, while our colleagues exchanged bloodcurdling insults on the Senate floor, they were only shooting blanks. If, as a young man, you have seen your friends die for their country, you are left with a sense of what is important in life and what is not.

I don't mean to overstate the importance of combat. Many brave men never have the opportunity to be tested on the battlefield, and others, to paraphrase Shakespeare, have heroism thrust upon them. Still, if it happens to you, you will never be the same again.

Politics is the process whereby civilized societies resolve their differences short of war. If its consequences are not as final, its passions are often as unbridled. I came to respect those who proved themselves in political combat as much as I did heroes of the battlefield. A Bob Dole or a Howard Baker had to possess all the courage and resolve that a military commander needs. The same is true of leaders like Paul Tsongas and Pete Peterson, who have sought political reform as private citizens.

Politics is too important to be left to politicians. When Thomas Jefferson said that eternal vigilance is the price of liberty, he meant the vigilance of every citizen. We face a political crisis in this country today. It has to do with the economy, and it has to do with widespread disenchantment with a system that too often favors an elite and does nothing about how most people live their lives.

This crisis will not be resolved until millions of citizens are concerned enough, angry enough, to take action. It is not enough to vote and look away. We have to make demands upon our politicians. We have to organize and work with others to pursue political reforms. If our leaders are corrupt, we should throw them out. If our parties are ineffective, we should reform them. If extremists and incompetents are running for office, we should oppose them.

At the end of the twentieth century, the United States won the Cold War. In the new century our challenges will be economic and political. We can be great or we can have chaos. The choice is ours. Democracy starts with each one of us. This is the combat we all must join, for ourselves, our children, our country and generations yet unborn.

INDEX

ABOUT THE AUTHOR

As a young man, WARREN RUDMAN saw combat as a platoon leader and company commander during the Korean War. He later served six years as attorney general of New Hampshire. Rudman, a Republican, was elected to two terms in the United States Senate, where he fought for a balanced budget, campaign-finance reform, and an end to Pentagon waste, and was often called "the conscience of the Senate." He played a leading role in the Iran-Contra and Keating Five investigations and the nomination of his friend David Souter to the Supreme Court. Since retiring from the Senate in 1992, he co-founded the Concord Coalition, which works nationally for a balanced budget; practices law with the international law firm of Paul, Weiss, Rifkind, Wharton and Garrison; advises Senator Robert Dole's presidential campaign; and serves as vice chairman of President Clinton's Foreign Intelligence Advisory Board. He divides his time between New Hampshire and Washington, D.C.

ABOUT THE TYPE

This book was set in Galliard, a typeface designed by
Matthew Carter for the Merganthaler Linotype Company in 1978. Galliard is based on the sixteenth-century
typefaces of Robert Granjon.